THE CORPORATE DILEMMA

Traditional Values
versus
Contemporary Problems

THE CORPORATE DILEMMA

Traditional Values
versus
Contemporary Problems

Dow Votaw and S. Prakash Sethi

School of Business Administration
University of California, Berkeley

With contributions by
ROBERT CHATOV and PHILLIP BLUMBERG

Prentice-Hall, Inc., *Englewood Cliffs, New Jersey*

Library of Congress Cataloging in Publication Data

VOTAW, DOW.
    The corporate dilemma.

    Includes bibliographical references.
    1. Industry—Social aspects—United States—
Addresses, essays, lectures.   I. Sethi, S. Prakash.
II. Title.
HD60.5.U5V68   301.24'8   73-403
ISBN   0-13-174193-4

© 1973 by Prentice-Hall, Inc., Englewood Cliffs, N.J.

Printed in the United States of America

10   9   8   7   6   5   4   3   2   1

Prentice-Hall International, Inc., *London*
Prentice-Hall of Australia, Pty. Ltd., *Sydney*
Prentice-Hall of Canada, Ltd., *Toronto*
Prentice-Hall of India Private Limited, *New Delhi*
Prentice-Hall of Japan, Inc., *Tokyo*

Modern economic belief can be understood only as the servant, in substantial measure, of the society which nurtures it. And not the least of its services to that society is to render instruction to the young which, rather systematically, excludes speculation on the way the large economic organizations shape social attitudes to their end.

JOHN KENNETH GALBRAITH
The New Industrial State

To
Marian and Donna

Contents

Preface

We have brought together in this book a group of essays and comments revolving around the experiences that large corporations have had, are having, or are likely to have as a result of their having become involved more closely and intimately than ever before in a broad array of contemporary social problems. These experiences are summarized as a "dilemma" because one of the chief characteristics of the experiences has been a feeling of consternation, frustration, and dismay as cherished traditional values have run into trouble when brought to bear on social issues or used as a guide for responses to social challenge.

Some of the essays and all of the comments were written especially for this book. Most of the essays were first published elsewhere anl transplanted here because they seemed especially appropriate to the subject matter. Many thanks are owed to Robert Chatov and Phillip Blumberg for letting us use their work. Within the space and time constraints imposed on this project, we could not be exhaustive. Many important and interesting issues receive no mention at all or get only perfunctory recognition in passing. Our goal, however, has been to be selective and representative rather than detailed and comprehensive. The book shows the effects of that policy. All we can hope is that the reader who becomes interested in learning more will be stimulated to pursue his own course of action and will profit therein from the highly selective material he has seen here. But there is plenty to keep one busy even if there is no temptation to venture outside.

We wish to express our thanks to the Institute of Business and Economic Research, University of California, Berkeley, for supporting the research that went into some of the essays in this book. Particular thanks

are due to Mrs. Ellen McGibbon and Mrs. Betty Kendall for their typing
and clerical assistance in the preparation of the manuscript. We are also
grateful to the publishers of *California Management Review, Business
and Society Review,* and *Oklahoma Law Review* for their permission to
reprint material earlier published in those journals. Finally we would
like to thank Professor Edwin M. Epstein, Schools of Business Administration, University of California, Berkeley, for his helpful comments.

Dow Votaw
S. Prakash Sethi

Berkeley, California

PART ONE

Introduction

"The present mood in Western society, especially in the United States," writes Walter Weisskopf, "is pessimistic, eschatological, apocalyptic." [1] The causes of this mood are numerous, intricate, and interrelated in complex ways; some are easy to identify, others are hidden in the depths of the human psyche; many are the product of historical events, others of frustration, dashed hopes, and disappointed expectations. Among the causes is the dissonance resulting from the collision between accepted traditional values and contemporary reality. Human beings cannot help but be affected when their cherished ideals and basic assumptions manifest an inconsistency with the existential world. Present social changes have given rise to aspirations and expectations of a different order and magnitude, and these have arrayed themselves in apposition with certain traditional values of society—especially of the corporate system. Some of these values have proved themselves to be inappropriate to the solution of social problems and, in some cases, barriers to even the perception and understanding of contemporary issues. One of the results of this dissonance is the "corporate dilemma."

To a much greater extent than ever before in the United States, the corporation finds itself in the arena of social conflict, partly against its will, partly with its consent, and partly of its own volition. Regardless of how it got there, it is now deeply involved and appears incapable of extracting itself. Were the phenomenon confined to abstract or philosophical speculation, without showing up in actual events, it prob-

---

[1] Walter A. Weisskopf, *Alienation and Economics* (New York: E. P. Dutton & Co., Inc., 1971), p. 13.

1

ably could be shrugged off as unimportant or passed off as the proper domain of the academic or the cleric.

Unfortunately for corporate peace of mind, inconsistencies between beliefs and values are having their effects upon the real world. What is more, the podium and the pulpit appear, as often as not, to be parties to the conflict or suffering from a similar dilemma. Even more dismaying for the corporation, many observers see in the dilemma evidence that, as a social instrument, the corporation has outlived its usefulness.

The clash between traditional beliefs—and the power structure and distributive systems based on them—and contemporary issues, to which the corporation is both a party and a witness, is a phenomenon as old as human society, but it is still not very well understood. The process is a continuous one and is often invisible. Even when visible, it does not always attract much attention or hold it for a very long time.[2] Like social conflict itself, the clash between belief and reality must be regarded as a constructive force and not a largely dysfunctional phenomenon.[3] If traditional attitudes and ideologies are to change at all, they must come into contact with the existential world and its constantly changing components. To maximize the appropriateness of the adjustment, it would seem that at least three crucial elements should be present: some understanding by affected institutions and individuals of the social phenomenon, a reasonably accurate perception of reality, and a tolerance for change. We hope that this book will help to improve understanding, make a modest contribution toward tolerance and accuracy of perception, and suggest some ideas through which changes may be effected.

In addition to emphasizing the presence of constructive elements in social conflict and in the clash between traditional belief and reality, it is also important to note that tradition and traditional belief also play positive as well as negative roles in society. During the transition from the medieval (i.e., "tradition-bound") period to the modern (i.e., "dynamic" or "innovative") period, enhanced by the French Revolution and by currents in sociological thought since the beginning of this century, it became almost customary to assign negative and polemical values to the word "tradition" and to set it apart from the positive values associated with "modern." Among other things, "traditional society was conceived as society bound by cultural horizons set by its tradition, while modern society was seen as culturally dynamic, oriented to change and

---

2 See Anthony Downs, "Up and Down with Ecology—the Issue-Attention Cycle," *The Public Interest,* 28 (Summer 1972), 38-50.

3 For an excellent treatment of this subject and a summary of other writings, see Lewis Coser, *The Functions of Social Conflict* (New York: The Free Press, 1964).

innovation." [4] When it became obvious that this view was based upon an assumed equivalence between "tradition" and "traditionality," the tide began to turn, and tradition is now more often seen as "an essential framework for creativity," [5] and not simply as an obstacle to change. In other words, tradition need not be restrictive. It is part of the process of ordering experience.

Eisenstadt prefers to look at tradition as the "reservoir of the most central social and cultural experiences prevalent in a society, as the most enduring element in the collective social and cultural construction of reality." [6] It is not our purpose to portray the "bad, old, traditional" values of the corporation as having come into conflict with the "good, new, modern" progress, but rather to observe and evaluate the structure of such social phenomena. Certain prevalent social and cultural experiences are being confronted by a group of contemporary social problems, some of which do not appear to be amenable to understanding or solution within the constraints of traditional views.

The unprecedented economic growth of American society, in particular, and most of the industrialized world, in general, has created certain socioeconomic problems and side effects in the industrialized nations and the underdeveloped ones as well. At present, these problems do not appear to be amenable to understanding or solution within the constraints of the traditional views. Notwithstanding, one should not assume that if there were no limiting traditional values, the social problems would be resolved any more quickly or satisfactorily. Traditional values are already in the process of change, but they still serve as a sort of template against which the eventual solutions will find their shape. Where tradition is seen as totally static and unbending, confrontations with reality can produce serious harmful effects. But where it is viewed—at least in part—as a framework without which cultural creativity is impossible, the confrontation is a factor in a normal social process. Better understanding produces better adaptation and better solutions, however, even where the process is "normal."

It has also been suggested that every tradition has both symbolic and organizational dimensions.[7] Each dimension develops its own dynamic, a fact which helps to explain the conflicts and tensions that appear *within* a tradition. These events can be detected in certain traditions

---

[4] S. N. Eisenstadt, "Intellectuals and Tradition," *Daedalus* (Spring 1972), 2.

[5] Edward Shils, "Tradition and Liberty: Antinomy and Independence," *Ethics*, 68 (April 1958), 153-65.

[6] Eisenstadt, "Intellectuals and Tradition," p. 3.

[7] *Ibid.*, p. 4.

and in traditional values associated with the corporation, raising even higher the potential for consternation when traditional values are confronted by contemporary problems. The tradition of private property, for example, has had its symbolic dimension in the "shareholder-owner" and its organizational dimension in the structure of the corporation as contemplated by the incorporation laws. As each has developed its own dynamic, tensions have risen. The manager's attempt to use the symbolic dimension as a source of legitimation for his own exercise of power has come into conflict with the organizational dimension, where the shareholder-owners cannot—and in many cases, do not—behave in a manner consistent with the tradition of private property. When the traditional value comes into contact with contemporary social problems, the clash is accentuated by the tension already existing within the traditional value itself. The alacrity with which the new doctrine of social responsibility has been embraced by wide sectors of the corporate system may be partly attributed to the intensity of that conflict.

The adoption of new terminology is considered by some as the first step toward changes in attitudes that lead to changes in actions. Some others believe the reverse is true. The adoption of terms like social responsibility by the existing power structure, it is sometimes argued, is designed to divert attention from the discussion of such basic issues as the role, form, or even the raison d'être of current social institutions. Internalization of the symbols makes the institution as given and limits discussion to the external questions of how and whether the institution can *really* be expected to devote its resources to the solution of problems outside its traditional areas.

No organization or institution in any society can escape the impact of social conflict. Some organizations will be directly involved, others peripherally, but all will feel the effects. Some will become involved early or will themselves be protagonists from the start; others will sense the social upheaval only indirectly through their members or employees or from the milieu in which they function. All will be forced to respond, sooner or later and to a greater or lesser extent. How they respond will depend largely upon the nature and intensity of the conflict, the traditional values and ideologies of the organization or institution, and its accustomed role in society. The perceived reasons for the response and the form it takes will be major determinants in the success with which the challenge is met and with which the character and integrity of the institution are maintained.

American society today is being swept by conflict and confronted by a wide variety of problems. Its institutions and organizations are being drawn into the fray. Some of them helped to cause the disputes and to bring about the problems; others are innocent bystanders. Some are protagonists, some are targets, and still others are just incidentally affected by the social pressures. Although no organization or institution has been entirely immune, some have been more involved than others. Among those more deeply affected is the large corporation, an institution that has often played an important contributory role in social problems, but which has considered itself, until the recent past, above the fray and with very limited responsibility in social matters except indirectly or in a way incidental to the performance of its primary function—the production and distribution of goods and services.

Today, however, the corporation is finding itself immersed in the conflict, frequently on its own initiative. Perhaps more important than any other factor in this change in corporate involvement is the widespread belief that there is a close and systematic interrelationship between the great business corporation and society as a whole and that the good health of one depends upon the vigor of the other.

The lines between socially responsible behavior and the profit motive have always been arbitrary, shifting, and uncertain. As Henry Ford II has said,

> There is no longer anything to reconcile, if there ever was, between the social conscience and the profit motive. Improving the quality of society—investing in better employees and customers for tomorrow— is nothing more than another step in the evolutionary process of taking a more farsighted view of return on investment.[8]

The new and wider involvement has produced a dilemma. Traditional corporate values and ideologies often appear to aggravate rather than to alleviate contemporary social conflicts and problems. Time-tested responses to social challenge appear to make conditions worse rather than better—or not to have any measurable effect at all. Old friends and supporters have turned hostile; the old formulas do not produce the same results that were once routinely expected of them. Not only is the corporation being drawn into the arena of contemporary social problems, it is viewed by many to be one of those problems itself, or a major causal factor in creating social problems, or a barrier to their solution.

In the process of working their way out of the dilemma, those who manage the great corporations have discovered that the lines of communication with the society they inhabit are overloaded with messages, blurred by overlapping and conflicting signals, and often completely smothered by static. Frequently, the language is foreign, the signs and symbols undecipherable, and the identities of the messages' originators

---

8 "The War That Business Must Win," *Business Week* (November 1, 1969), 64.

unclear. Even the conflicts and problems themselves have a chimerical quality about them, sometimes appearing to be sharply outlined and easily distinguished and, at other times, veiled and rapidly changing in image or conformation. The welfare problem in the morning materializes in the afternoon as a crisis of power or privilege. The pollution problem on Thursday has become the unemployment problem on Friday. It is no surprise, then, that the corporate dilemma is accompanied by a generous supply of frustration and confusion.

This book is not going to do much about mitigating social conflict, solving social problems, clearing up the garbled communication, or offering surcease from frustration. The most it can hope to do is to shed some light on the corporate dilemma and its causes. If the book can examine a few of the traditional values and responses that seem to be out of phase with the problems on which they are being brought to bear, if it can provide a little more understanding of the phenomenon of corporate social responsibility, and if it can say something useful about some of the critical or representative areas of interaction between the corporation and society, it will have accomplished all that can be reasonably expected of it.

The format of the book takes the corporate dilemma and the underlying conflict between traditional values and contemporary problems in a step-by-step progression. Parts I and II set forth a broad framework and some introductory comments by the principal authors about the origin and implications of the new corporate social responsibility. Professor Robert Chatov then provides a theoretical, as well as practical, assessment of the role of ideology in corporate behavior, especially with regard to corporate reaction and response to social pressures. In the next section, Professor Phillip I. Blumberg introduces us to one of the areas where the relationship between the corporation and other groups in society is undergoing rapid change—the employee's duty of loyalty and obedience. Here we get another glimpse of how deeply and profoundly traditional values and ideologies are being affected by contemporary social problems and by social change.

Understanding the role of the corporation in society requires more than an examination of the impact of the corporation on the individual. Part V of the book makes some observations on the relationship between the corporation and two other social institutions—the church and the state. Institutional conflict between church and corporation is relatively new, but from its history and characteristics we may be able to gain some knowledge of other institutional relationships involving the corporation and, perhaps, some perspective with regard to the clash between traditional values and beliefs and a rapidly changing social environment.

Corporation and state have long had a dramatic, active relationship, ranging in character from open warfare to peaceful cooperation. Frequent change is probably one of the most notable attributes of this particular confrontation between social institutions. The essay on the corporation and the state in Part V, however, treats of one of the constants in the relationship—the role of the state in the gap between business values and concepts—on one hand, and reality on the other.

The final section looks at some of the causes that have led to the failure of the traditional corporate responses to changing social needs and how different corporate responses might be developed to fulfill new and rising social expectations. This section also deals with an approach to the definition and measurement of social responsibility through the process of corporate social audit.

We believe that the reader will conclude, as we have, that although clashes between traditional values and contemporary problems are a ubiquitous, normal, human phenomenon, they should not be ignored nor their impacts underestimated. Better understanding of their components may lead to quicker resolution and fewer harmful effects.

PART TWO

Reflections on Corporate Social Responsibility

COMMENT

A major manifestation of both the new involvement by corporations in social problems and the dilemma in which that involvement has placed them is the widespread adoption of the new doctrine of corporate social responsibility by the great corporations and their spokesmen. The wholesale endorsement by the corporate community of at least some of the elements of social responsibility is, in part, a response to contemporary social problems and should, quite properly, be viewed in that light. It is our thesis, however, that this new social responsibility is much less a product of the well-known contemporary issues to which it seems a response than it is of certain basic forces and changes at work in our society. If it were merely what it appears to be on the surface, an expedient response to temporary social pressures, those who have embraced it would be subject to much less frustration and confusion than they are now, and the discrepancies between traditional values and contemporary problems would be less pronounced.

Social responsibility has not become an almost universal topic of conversation and concern only because of racial unrest, urban decay, and a variety of threatening ecological issues—to mention just a few of the seemingly causal forces. Although it may not have dawned on many of us yet, the kind of social responsibility with which we are now concerned may itself be a new phenomenon and not just a charitable contribution in new clothing or an old way to quiet the restless natives.

There is enough evidence to compel us to consider the possibility that the phenomenon is not a superficial change, an expedient response to transitory social pressures, a temporary surface disturbance that can be tranquilized by cosmetic public relations or speeches by the chairman of the board, or that will go away as Ralph Nader mellows with old age and men and women of minority racial groups obtain and hold better jobs and a fairer share of the American opulence. It makes a difference, in our conduct as well as in our understanding, whether social responsibility is the product of a minor social adjustment or a sign of deep, far-reaching social change. The phenomenon of social responsibility may be the result of mutations more akin to the Reformation or Industrial Revolution than to consumerism or the push for racial equality. The case does not have to be proved conclusively to justify the purpose for which we are writing: to urge the inclusion in our calculations about social responsibility and its implications the likelihood that appearances may be deceiving and that our thinking about it may involve a *post hoc* fallacy.

The first article, by Dow Votaw, explores in two parts these deeper origins, together with their implications and the implications of the acceptance by a large portion of the corporate community of the principle, in some form, of the new social responsibility. Because social responsibility can be viewed as a response, as a state of mind or an attitude, as a condition in fact, or as a combination of these and other social theories, it is little wonder that some of those who adhere to it have discovered that their perceptions of what they have embraced differ somewhat from the perceptions of their fellows. This article aims at clarifying some of the resulting confusion and examining the problem of defining and fixing the parameters of social responsibility. Our objective is to lay a foundation for the discussion which follows in the subsequent sections concerning the many facets of the new demands being made upon the corporations, the bases and sources of these demands, and, if we succeed, the likely changes these demands may make in the organizational structure and decision-making within the corporation and in the existing relationship of the corporations to other societal institutions—economic, social, legal, and political.

GENIUS BECOMES RARE

Dow Votaw *

Fashion in social comment has borrowed heavily in recent years from Madison Avenue, particularly from that portion of the thoroughfare that specializes in laundry detergents: the contents and their efficacy are usually underanalyzed and oversold and promise too much. Like the brand names of the best-selling detergents (as "Blast" or "Surge"), the labels affixed to social issues and to commentaries upon them are often chosen more to titillate than to inform.

There is nothing unethical, and certainly nothing illegal, about titillation, or about tacking the suffixes "ism" or "ist" to such neutral words as race, sex, and consumer in order to provide emotional or ideological content. In many instances, the effect is to dramatize or to attract attention to important questions that might not otherwise obtain the audience or the respect they have earned. But the Madison Avenue phase in social comment passes very quickly and if not promptly supplemented with substance and analysis, the comments fade rapidly from public view or linger on as empty slogans which are still capable of giving the impression that they are the products of careful thought and analytical investigation. Obviously, not all social comment is subject to these charges, with respect to either the advertising phase or the lack of analytical follow-up. In too many instances, however, not unlike Madison Avenue, after real genius has gone into the dramatizing, titillating, and labeling of a social issue, genius becomes rare.

One such social issue bears the label "corporate social responsibility" or, because most people now seem to know what is intended, just "social responsibility." The term is a brilliant one; it means something, but not always the same thing, to everybody. To some it conveys the idea of legal responsibility or liability; to others it means socially responsible *behavior* in an ethical sense; to still others the meaning transmitted is that of "responsible for," in a causal mode; many simply equate it with "charitable contributions"; some take it to mean socially "conscious" or "aware"; many of those who embrace it most fervently see it as a mere synonym for "legitimacy," in the context of "belonging" or being proper or valid; a few see it as a sort of fiduciary duty imposing higher standards of behavior on businessmen

---

* Professor of Business Administration, University of California, Berkeley. Reprinted, with permission, from *California Management Review*, 15 (Winter 1972).

than on citizens at large. Even the antonyms, socially "irresponsible" and "nonresponsible," are subject to multiple interpretations.

Whatever the interpretation—and this brief list by no means exhausts the possibilities—the term has received a great deal of attention during the last few years. Corporation presidents and chairmen of the board rarely make public statements without giving it prominence. The editors of *Fortune* and other business periodicals devote whole issues to it. Politicians are enchanted by its broad appeal. Every oil spill and smog alert brings it to the front page of the daily newspaper. It has become the title of college courses and purports to be a proper subject for scholarly research. The pages written about social responsibility would fill a small library. With few exceptions, however, these pages contain little that might truly be described as "analysis" of this now-ubiquitous social phenomenon or of its implications. Not many of the commentaries carry us beyond the Madison Avenue phase of development. Peter Drucker wrote recently in this connection: "The time for sensations and manifestos is about over; now we need rigorous analysis, united effort, and very hard work." [1]

It is easy enough to say that the time has come to get down to work; it is not at all easy to say where one ought to begin. However, there should be no major disagreement over the desirability of removing obstructions from the field of observation, of improving the focus on the matter to be analyzed, and of obtaining a clearer idea of what it is we intend to observe. The primary goals are to determine, with as much accuracy as possible, the real nature of the forces with which we are concerned and to consider a few of the often-overlooked implications of the phenomenon of social responsibility. Only time will reveal all the implications of what is now being so enthusiastically embraced, but it would be unwise to wait for time and experience to do our thinking for us. While many are embracing social responsibility without thought of consequence, others are resisting it on grounds that might have been valid in the nineteenth century but which are subject to question today. None of us fails to see the signs of change in all aspects of our public, private, and professional lives, but we are not all interpreting the signs in the same way. Consumerism, racial unrest, a degraded environment, conflict between the generations, new life styles, violent protests, and revolutionary rhetoric are all signs and symptoms of change, yet we do not agree on what they mean and many of us mistake the symptom for the change itself.

It is possible to respond to these signs by blaming them on an in-

---

[1] Peter F. Drucker, "Saving the Crusade," *Harper's Magazine* (January 1972), 71.

vasion of foreign ideologies and by seeking their cure in such wistful activities as strict adherence to the tenets of "free enterprise," individual liberty or "the American way," or by minding one's economic knitting and letting the government or the church take care of social problems, or by increasing corporate budgets for public relations, or by being a bit more generous in donations to favorite colleges and the United Crusade. One may also respond, as some are doing, by sprinkling ashes on the head, murmuring *mea culpa,* we are to blame, and rushing head-long into the unfamiliar social arena with money, manpower, the best of intentions, and no understanding of what is really going on. These reactions do not help very much and may actually make the situation worse. Such responses, I believe, are based on a misreading of the signs and symptoms and on an unawareness of the real forces at work—failings, it should be noted, not confined to the business community, but found also in government, in academia, and elsewhere in society.

Even if one's primary concern is with the implications, not the origins, of social responsibility, it is soon discovered that not much can be learned about implications without first taking a careful look at the *underlying* social forces which number among their consequences the phenomenon of social responsibility itself, as well as the other signs and symptoms to which reference has already been made. The implications of social responsibility are not going to be visible or even accurately forecast until we have some idea of the nature of the forces with which we are dealing. History helps, but more important than history is understanding. I would like to make a rather tentative beginning at analysis in two areas that have not yet been thoroughly explored. The first starts from the premise that social responsibility is more than a mere response to momentary social pressures and pursues the question of just what it is and from whence it comes. The second line examines some of the implications of new or increased social responsibility in the light of this better understanding of the nature of the forces that are giving it impetus.

ORIGINS OF "SOCIAL RESPONSIBILITY"

Introduction

There are several approaches to be considered in support of the view that the phenomenon of social responsibility is more than a super-ficial reaction to temporary social pressure. First, social responsibility is a condition in fact, not just a policy or a response. Even if no corpora-tion president had ever heard or used the term, there would still be a condition of social responsibility. In the very nature of human society is the long-range requirement that each portion of it be responsible to that society in an acceptable way. What has happened recently is that successful performance of the economic role has ceased to be the only kind of socially responsible behavior that society requires from the private sector in discharge of its obligations. Thus, when a leader of business embraces social responsibility, he is not just embracing a preexisting obligation, he is also acknowledging a new standard by which the discharge of that obligation is to be carried out. He may believe that the renewed commitment to social responsibility is merely his response to pressures resulting from unjust racial conditions in society or to widespread concern over a degraded environment, but, in fact, it is now a recognition and adoption of changing standards by which he conducts himself in a socially responsible fashion. He cannot escape it; his only choice is to satisfy its standards or not, at his risk. The response, and there plainly is one, is not to the identified social issues directly, but to the vaguely articulated, but profound, changes in how society expects the businessman to behave.

Second, many of the important social problems to which the doctrine of social responsibility seems to be a response are not themselves isolated or transitory issues. They appear to be connected in substantive ways and many of them to rise from the same deep, basic social or historical currents. A sailor may respond expediently to a sudden gale by heading into it, reefing his sails or by other defensive conduct, but if he is wise, he does not respond expediently to the fact that he is afloat in a liquid medium. In other words, corporations may respond expediently to pressures perceived to be temporary or unusual but not to long-run forces or to those seen to be characteristic of the medium in which the corporations operate. Expedient reactions to long-run forces or to inherent characteristics of the environment are usually self-defeating, because the pressures are unremitting, and the expedient responses to them are ineffective and may interfere with or prevent the development of long-range alternatives. Thus, it becomes important that corporate reactions to social change be based on accurate perceptions of the changes taking place.

The third approach consists of evidence that a few businessmen are seeing the long-range character of some of the pressures to which they respond. Some examples from a speech made by Louis B. Lundborg, Chairman of the Board, Bank of America, before the Rotary Club of Seattle shortly after a "rampaging mob of demonstrators" had totally destroyed the Bank of America branch at Isla Vista, provide us with some interesting information about how some leaders of business now regard social responsibility.

There is a new value system emerging in America, starting with the youth but becoming one of the new facts of life for the rest of us to deal with. . . . Our dealing with it will jar us out of most of the comfortable assumptions that we have grown up with all of our lives.

In part, of course, this is the rebellion of youth against parental authority. . . . But I am convinced that it goes far, far beyond that . . . this activist movement is not something fleeting that will go away if we can just keep it cool for a while . . . I am not afraid that the left-wing radicals will win. I am only afraid of how they will be defeated.

For generations we have been mouthing the cliche, 'You can't stand in the way of progress.' Now there is a new generation that is saying, 'The hell you can't.' That generation—and an increasing number of its elders—are saying, 'Prove to us that it really is progress.' In a sense, that is the essence of everything that is stirring and boiling and seething: thoughtful people in increasing numbers are asking about one thing after another, 'Is it really progress—progress for the human condition?'

Take Zero Population Growth for example—it is a growing movement and one which we must consider in our plans—is there any part of our economy that isn't dedicated to the Great God Growth? Has anyone calculated what would happen if growth suddenly stopped? We had better do some calculating, because it just *could* happen. And in my judgment, it won't necessarily be fatal if it does.[2]

How many Lundborgs there are we have no way of knowing, but there are some, and their numbers are growing.

Historical Currents

It is said that history repeats itself. Exact replication is, of course, impossible. Differences of time, place, and casts of characters are alone enough to eliminate the chance that history might actually record for a second or third time precisely the same event or sequence of events. Obviously, the ancient proverb was never intended to say any more than that historical patterns appear to be repeated from time to time and that similar events can usually be expected to bring about similar consequences. Were it not true that history "repeats itself" in this sense, there would be little incentive to record or study history, as nobody could reasonably believe that something worthwhile might be learned from it, and the recounting of past events would still be the exclusive property of troubadours and epic poets. On the other hand, men often behave as though there were no patterns in history and nothing to be learned from previous events or generations; some overtly deny the

---

[2] Louis B. Lundborg, "The Lessons of Isla Vista," *The Business Lawyer* (January 1971), 951.

relevance of anything that has gone before or assert an intolerable bias in the recording and interpretation of past events. Evidence of an anti-historical trend in contemporary culture and of a turning away from history, historical study and historical explanation have been pointed to with alarm by many modern historians.[3] As some historians wryly observe, however, this is not the first time that charges of irrelevance or bias have been leveled at the profession, and most men still view with some respect the role which the past plays, even in our limited ability to understand the present and to prepare for the future.

I am willing to take the risk, then, of going against the grain of only a relative few, when I suggest that an event which appears on the surface to be essentially a contemporary issue, the phenomenon of business social responsibility, is in part a manifestation of certain basic social and attitudinal changes the pattern for which can be found in medieval England and at various other times in the history of Western society. If this endeavor is successful, perhaps we can take it as a *laissez-passer* to examine social responsibility in the light of some of its other possible antecedents and, thus, to establish a background against which the implications of the new social responsibility may be more accurately appraised.

Quietly and slowly for decades, the view with which leaders of business have regarded their relationship to society and their role in it has been undergoing profound change. An historical parallel of this change is to be found in England during the early years of the thirteenth century, when the great lords finally came to see themselves as something more than just a group of self-seeking individuals and acquired a new sense of "community of the realm." [4] They realized that, while they were the *leaders* of the medieval corporate society, that society was not "theirs." It did not "belong" to them! They owed it certain responsibilities. Magna Carta was as much a product of this change of attitude as it was of the struggle between the great lords and the crown, and the change in outlook was one of the necessary ingredients for the development of constitutional government.

One of the anvils against which our whole political system was shaped must, then, have been this new sense of community and responsibility. It clearly was not a mere surface response to transient stimuli. In the reign of Henry II, the first tentative signs of the evolving community appear, both in the King, who begins to distinguish himself from the office he holds, and in the great lords. By the latter part of the twelfth century, people actually begin to talk about it, and

---

[3] *Daedalus* (Winter 1971) is devoted largely to this question.

[4] Norman F. Cantor, *The English* (New York: Simon and Schuster, 1967), Chapter 5.

in the thirteenth century the sense of community is firmly impressed upon the magnates of England. English history, and our own, would have been very different had these changes of attitude not occurred or not occurred when they did.

One does not have to look very far for evidence that most of the great lords of American business, during the late nineteenth and early twentieth centuries, looked upon the economy as though it were "theirs," as though it belonged to them, and rarely regarded themselves as more than a group of self-seeking individuals. They were encouraged in their view by the alleged teachings of *laissez-faire* capitalism, economic individualism and social Darwinism. But this once prevailing view appears to be changing. While we are constantly reminded that some of the great lords of business still regard the economy as "theirs," more and more the dominant attitude is coming to be that of "community of the realm." The leaders of business recognize that, although they *do* operate the economy, it is not "theirs."

This historic parallel suggests that there may be more to the doctrine of social responsibility than we at first had thought. It may be one of the building blocks for new social, political and economic structures in our society. The late A. A. Berle raised and emphasized similar, but not identical, points in constructing his case for an evolving constitution in the corporate system.[5] A new, built-in receptiveness, a hospitality for increased social responsibility on the part of business, may be one of the manifestations of a more profound change of attitude. It took five hundred years for the thirteenth century "community of the realm" to have its full effect, but it is beginning to look as though it will not take that long for the twentieth century change of attitude to make its mark. And there are other deep-lying and far-reaching forces pushing in the same direction.

Biological Phenomena

Writing not long ago in the *Bulletin of the Atomic Scientists,* John Platt reminded us of certain sudden, profound and parallel transformations in the arrangement of the components in living systems, ranging from the molecular level, through single organisms and individuals, to large, complex social organizations such as corporations, industries, and even whole societies and civilizations.[6] Others have made the same sort of observation and provided some empirical support for the view that

---

[5] A. A. Berle, Jr., *The 20th Century Capitalist Revolution* (New York: Harcourt, Brace and Company, 1954).

[6] John Platt, "Hierarchical Growth," *Bulletin of the Atomic Scientists* (November 1970), 2.

we are embarking upon a scientific revolution of such scope and intricacy that parallels and even causal connections between molecular and societal levels of organization are likely to seem commonplace someday.[7] Platt refers to the sudden transformations as "hierarchical jumps" and compares them with the "quantum jump" of an electron.

The most dramatic jumps and those of the largest scale have been witnessed in the area of social evolution; the Reformation and the Industrial Revolution are the most prominent examples. These great changes go deeper than ordinary political revolutions and are much more than a simple exchange of power between one small group and another. They are fundamental alterations of value, personal attitudes, ways of work and social organization. The democratic revolution, beginning in the United States two centuries ago, and the communist revolutions of the present century are comparable but less profound. Tom Kuhn in his wonderful little book, *The Structure of Scientific Revolutions*,[8] documents a whole series of these jumps in the field of scientific ideas. The Copernican model in astronomy replaced the Ptolemaic in a very few years, even under the slow-moving conditions of the Middle Ages, and, at a later time, quantum mechanics completely vanquished the classical paradigm with a jump that was even more rapid.

Among the most interesting aspects of these observations, and most applicable to our discussion here, is the pattern of common characteristics that the hierarchical jumps seem to possess. One of them is a "cognitive dissonance" which precedes the jumps and accompanies them. By this is meant that a sort of static pervades society; existing ideologies, values and goals appear to lose their meaning, to be inconsistent with events, and no longer to fit the old predictions; a dissonance is felt between long-cherished ideals and actual practice. Our consecrated policy of unremitting growth, for example, instead of providing only satisfactions, seems now to be aggravating our problems, by widening the gap between us and the underdeveloped third world and by providing much of the pollution, crowding, and other environmental degradation we see around us; our time-tested economic assumptions, as one author put it, "are being overwhelmed by ecology," [9] and even a few leaders of busi-

---

7 C. D. Darlington, *The Evolution of Man and Society* (New York: Simon and Schuster, 1969); Arthur Koestler and J. R. Smythies, eds., *Beyond Reductionism* (New York: The Macmillan Company, 1969); Jacques Monod, *Chance and Necessity* (New York: Alfred A. Knopf, Inc., 1971).

8 Thomas S. Kuhn, *The Structure of Scientific Revolutions* (Chicago: The University of Chicago Press, 1962).

9 Garret Hardin, "To Trouble a Star: The Cost of Intervention in Nature," *Bulletin of the Atomic Scientists* (January 1970), pp. 17 and 20.

ness are beginning to think the unthinkable thought of "no-growth." [10]

A second characteristic of the jumps is the universal, comprehensive nature of the dissonance. Most of us are aware of a widespread change in life style, among our colleagues—not all of them young—and among our children, and of a noisy dissonance developing between our goals and values and those of this new style. There is hardly a phase of our lives that is not affected in some way by the growing incongruity between our values and assumptions, on one hand, and actual events on the other. Our sanctification of work and our respected virtues of frugality, self-discipline, and competitive spirit are being replaced by "a voluptuary system." [11] Even madness is conceived to be a superior form of truth.[12]

We must consider the possibility that the new model of socially responsible behavior, at least in part, is a product of our being well into another of these hierarchical jumps and that the new model may be the result of attempts to penetrate the dissonance or to establish a new pattern of social organization. This is not to say that we should throw up our hands in resignation and horror or that we should expect a sharp rise in the suicide rate, but it is to say that we should know more about what may be going on before we embrace it or try to change it.

Louis J. Halle makes a very similar argument [13] when he describes our present condition as one of the by-products of a major crisis in the evolution of human life, brought on by a new and cosmic adjustment taking place in the relation between the conceptual world created by man himself and the real, existential world around him. Every reflective person is aware of the tendency of human beings to see patterns where there are none, to inject orderly concepts into situations where chaos prevails, and to find cause and effect in random events. The human mind cannot tolerate chaos and one of its basic functions is to order the chaos of reality, to build a rational conceptual world on which the mind can obtain a hold. The mind cannot deal with accidents until it multiplies them infinitely. Yet the existential world is chaotic, never holds still long enough for men effectively to close the gap between it and their concepts of it. When the gap widens, when certain concepts no longer even give the illusion of bringing order to chaotic reality, a dissonance is created,

---

10 Lundborg, "The Lessons of Isla Vista," pp. 948 and 951; *Final Report of the 1970 San Bernardino County (California) Grand Jury,* excerpted in *Cry California* (Spring 1971), 4.

11 Daniel Bell, "The Cultural Contradictions of Capitalism," *The Public Interest* (Fall 1970), 16 and 43.

12 R. D. Laing, *The Politics of Experience* (New York: Pantheon Books, 1967); Doris Lessing, *Briefing for a Descent into Hell* (New York: Alfred A. Knopf, Inc., 1971).

13 Louis J. Halle, *The Society of Man* (New York: Harper & Row, 1966).

and men are confronted with a conceptual crisis. Halle apparently believes that we are now in the midst of such a crisis and that major changes
are beginning to take place in Western man's view of reality. Once more,
social responsibility is provided with a potential source far more extensive and longer lasting than the transient social factors to which it is
usually attributed.

Changing Role of the Economy

Certainly related to the first two deep-flowing currents we have
examined, but worthy of separate comment, is the observation that the
economy appears no longer to be the center of society. This is just another way of describing what others have called a "post-industrial society," a mature industrial society, or the "engulfing of the economy by
the whole system." In such a society, production is no longer the primary
goal because it has already been achieved. In a land of scarcity, economics
is king; in a land of plenty, economics is just another member of the
court. Much of the dissonance the economy is experiencing today is the
result of its not now knowing where it stands in relation to the whole.
As Alfred North Whitehead wisely observed many years ago, when one
is lost, he should ask, not "where am I?" but "where are the others?" The
economy appears to be trying to find out where the others are and to
adjust to its own changing role in society. It seems likely that the "new
social responsibility" is part of this search for the whole and of the necessary adjustment to no longer being its center. Marxists have always believed that the economy was not only the center of society but also the
origin of all social phenomena, including culture, and, given their ways,
probably always will believe it. But what is the evidence that they are
wrong, at least as far as the mature industrial society is concerned, and
that our economy is no longer the focus of society?

For one thing, few readers would have read this far if they really
believed that successful performance of the strictly economic aspects of
business was enough to permit them peacefully to go to sleep at night
believing that they had done all they possibly could to promote the well-
being of the society in which they live, or even the well-being of their
own interests. Accusations of fouling the environment, of contributing
to racial unrest, of promoting war, of degrading the quality of life, and
of perpetuating systems of privilege and injustice are too common these
days to permit the luxury of believing that the charges are solely the
work of a few New Left dissidents. It is all too plain that a successful
business system does not by itself create a beautiful, peaceful, refined,
gracious, and tranquil civilization. What this really means is that it is
no longer necessary for society as a whole to shape *itself* to the economy

in order to produce the necessaries of life, but it is becoming increasingly necessary for the economy to adjust to the rest of society. We once believed that certain concessions had to be made to environmental degradation, to a particular distribution of privilege, even to discrimination and injustice, in order for the economic system to produce what was needed. We may have been correct at the time, or correct for the wrong reasons, but the belief that we still are correct is becoming impossible to sustain. Businessmen will view this change as both a curse and a blessing.

Further evidence of the shift of the economy from center stage is found in a decline in the importance of the occupational base and a growth in the importance of cultural tastes and life styles as the ways in which individuals wish to be identified. We need only look to ourselves, and among our friends, colleagues and children, for corroborating evidence. Art and culture, instead of the economy, are beginning to shape the social structure. Daniel Bell has observed: "Anything permitted in art is (now) permitted in life as well." [14]

Henry Wallich said several years ago that the purpose of a free economy is not production but freedom.[15] A similar statement might have been made forty, fifty or even one hundred years ago, but it would have been wholly without meaning or content; production was the overriding social, as well as economic, goal, and paying lip service to freedom would have been tolerated and ignored, or misinterpreted as meaning the freedom of those engaged in commerce, or simply found irrelevant. Now, the statement is readily perceived as a way of saying that the economy is no longer the focal point of society and the goal of production need no longer be the paramount one. Social responsibility must be looked at as, among other things, a growing recognition of these facts by the leaders of business and as a search for a new set of relationships between the economy and the society.

One would be led naturally to predict that, in order to have any reasonable chance of success in this search, the leaders of business must also change their view of themselves and of their role in the whole society. This view does indeed seem to be developing as part of the new sense of community, but the impetus for a change in this concept may be found also in another place. Many businessmen and academicians have recently employed an analytical tool known as "systems theory" or "systems analysis," a technique which is beginning to give them insight into certain types of vexing and persistent problems. One of the foundations on which systems theory is constructed has to do with the relation-

---

[14] Bell, "The Cultural Contradictions of Capitalism," p. 35.

[15] Henry C. Wallich, *The Cost of Freedom* (New York: Harper & Bros., 1960), p. x.

ships among different systems and between subsystems and the whole system. As this idea has become accepted in the firm and its subsystems, and even in the private economic sector and its subsystems, leaders of business have become increasingly amenable to the idea that the private economic sector and the economy as a whole are simply subsystems and, perhaps, not even the most important ones of a very complex whole system.[16] This tractability is beginning to offset a strong tradition in Western thought which has led us to believe that we can subdivide our society into functional elements, study each more or less in isolation from the rest, and establish criteria for the improvement of each with little, if any, reference to the remainder of the system. In Garret Hardin's words, "we can never do just one thing," [17] and the growing impact of this simple principle on the leaders of business, the responsibility for one's acts, is being seen to extend far beyond the firm and the stockholders, suggesting that the new social responsibility has deeper roots than expediency or convenience.

Constraints of the forum in which this essay appears dictate a bringing to an end of the discussion of social forces which must be taken into account if we are to understand the phenomenon of social responsibility and its implications. The list has by no means been exhausted, but perhaps the patience of the reader has. Let us consider now some of the implications of the new social responsibility and of what has been said so far.

IMPLICATIONS OF "SOCIAL RESPONSIBILITY"

Were we to accept the no longer completely tenable view that the new social responsibility is little more than a passing fancy, a mere reaction to the social and economic problems of the moment, we would still be faced with the important task of evaluating its implications. Where the contrary is not only believable and possible, but also probable, the question of implications assumes a position of crucial concern, for the elemental social forces which appear to lie behind the phenomenon of social responsibility are, themselves, harbingers of basic social change. Some of the implications to be examined, like certain structural and organizational changes, are the direct offshoots of concepts of social responsibility; others, like changes in the system of privilege, while still related to social responsibility, are more immediately the product of the underlying forces.

---

16 See Koestler, *Beyond Reductionism,* and Monod, *Chance and Necessity,* for sharply different views of the relationship between the whole and its parts.

17 Hardin, "To Trouble a Star: The Cost of Intervention in Nature," p. 17.

Even at this stage, several preliminary and general conclusions are possible. *First,* social responsibility is not a matter of sanctionless free choice on the part of business leaders; it is not a charitable contribution which the failure to make punishes in no measurable way. The unspoken, but not unclear, question being asked of business is: *"How* will the private sector be socially responsible?" not "Will it be socially responsible?" And "by sticking to our economic knitting" is not an acceptable answer to the question. Many feel that the social message is contained, not in a question at all, but in an imperative: "You will be socially responsible, or else!!" *Second,* social responsibility looms rather large as a major connecting link and channel of communication between the economy and the society as a whole, a function that was performed in different ways when the economy played the dominant role. The needs, demands and pressures of society can be communicated to business in a nonmandatory fashion, at first, leaving room for response through the mechanisms of social responsibility. If the response is inadequate, inappropriate or not forthcoming, society may communicate its wishes in the form of mandates.

A *third* conclusion grows out of the question of whether, under the conditions we have been considering, there may be a substitute for liberal capitalism as the economic system we have chosen to employ. The answer is, I think, that there is no substitute visible at the moment which would perform as well as the system we now have. Most of the important problems we face are, or will be, found in all advanced industrial or mature industrial societies, without reference to the particular economic system. There is no evidence that other systems eliminate the concern for social responsibility, are better adapted or more successful at understanding and solving the problems of racial or religious minorities, of ecology and the environment, or of the unrest of the young—or of doing so without creating problems even more frustrating and profound. If this view is generally accepted, it should be noted that social responsibility again takes on enhanced importance, not as a mere reaction to the issues of the moment, but as a primary means of adapting the old system to the achievement of new goals. There is mounting evidence that some business leaders actually do regard social responsibility in just this way.

Much of what has been said so far has been somewhat abstract in character, though not without empirical support, and we have been led to adopt, at least temporarily, the view that there is more to social responsibility than a public relations campaign or a search for legitimacy. "A test of good theory," it is said, "is that it have practical implications." What, in other words, does this new social responsibility really mean to business?

Economic Implications

One group of implications deserves to be brought into the open at the outset; these are the strictly economic ones. Unfortunately, they are often disregarded by those who seek to impose social responsibility by fiat from outside the private sector and by many who rush to embrace social responsibility from within. It is neither naive nor callous to inquire what will happen to the price and market systems and the profit motive as the new socially responsible behavior becomes more widespread and increases in intensity. Nobody has the answer to the query. It is plain that there will be major changes, but, if our basic thesis is correct, most of these changes would eventually take place whether or not business responsibility continues to be an important social mechanism.

We hear Cassandra cries from some quarters. In a recently published article,[18] the author concluded that there can be no significant chance of social responsibility or other non-profit oriented activity in a competitive product market and that the market treats non-profit maximizing expenditures the same, whether they result from inefficiency, embezzlement or charity. If that conclusion is accurate, we *are* doomed, because, as we are only just now coming to realize, the market is rigged against the environment. But we have already seen that economics is too narrow a base from which to carry out decision analysis, even in the single firm. The doomsayers on one side are matched by equally extreme views in the opposite direction which hold that only the greed of the capitalist prevents us from achieving a state of economic and environmental bliss or that private business can easily absorb the costs of cleaning up the environment and solving our social problems. All these extreme positions, it seems to me, are based on a very narrow and largely inaccurate idea of what social responsibility (and economics) is all about.

The issue raised by the potential advantage to be obtained by the nonresponsible competitor is not to be shrugged off lightly, however, especially in the short run. At the same time, it must be noted that the issue, thus stated, is concerned with only one small aspect of social responsibility and is based on the assumption that society measures, and will always continue to measure, the performance of the private sector exclusively in terms of profit. Obviously, certain types of conduct can be required of business by society only when expectations are uniformly applied across a market or an industry, but social responsibility neither begins nor ends here. In the final analysis, does anyone really believe

---

[18] Henry G. Manne, "The Myth of Corporate Responsibility," *The Business Lawyer* (November 1970), 533-39.

that our present social system, or any conceivable system, would work if we had to depend exclusively upon the self-imposed socially responsible behavior of managers for the preservation of the environment and the achievement of other social goals? There is already ample evidence that society is both willing to impose uniform standards in some areas and unwilling now to accept profit as the sole measure of success. Sociologists and psychologists have finally begun to confirm what most of us suspected all along, that a much more basic and important source of motivation than profit, as far as individuals are concerned, is achievement.[19] One might safely predict that as society comes to recognize and to accept other factors than short-run profit as measures of achievement, economics will also.

Nor is socially responsible conduct necessarily inconsistent with profit as a standard of measurement, whether or not society specifically imposes such conduct as one of the many constraints within which private economic activity is carried on. Peter F. Drucker, Neil W. Chamberlain,[20] and others have suggested that the socially responsible firm is likely to be more socially conscious, more aware of change, more alert to social problems, and more successful.

> The individual organization that anticipates a problem has, therefore, the duty of doing the unpopular: to think the problem through, to formulate a solution, and to lobby for the right public policy despite open disapproval by other "members of the club." No one who has taken this responsibility has ever failed—or even suffered. But whenever an institution shrinks back, pleading "the public won't let us," or "the industry won't let us," it pays a heavy price in the end. The public will forgive blindness. It will not forgive failure to act on one's own best knowledge.[21]

Seeing social needs as business opportunities and business as a revolutionary force [22] appear to be more or less express theorems of modern business ideology, but one is often surprised at the vehemence with which some leaders of business resist the application of these theorems where matters of pollution or consumer safety are concerned. It is not clear what criteria are used for distinguishing one kind of social need

---

19 David C. McClelland, "Business Drive and National Achievement," in *Organization and Human Behavior,* ed. by Gerald D. Bell (Englewood Cliffs, N.J.: Prentice-Hall, Inc., 1967).

20 Neil W. Chamberlain, in a paper on managerial innovation.

21 Peter F. Drucker, *The Age of Discontinuity* (New York: Harper & Row, 1969), p. 204.

22 Andrew Hacker, *The End of the American Era* (New York: Atheneum, 1970), p. 65; and Walter Hamilton, *The Politics of Industry* (New York: Alfred A. Knopf, Inc., 1957).

from another, but there does seem to be a great reluctance on the part of many businessmen to recognize as opportunities those social needs which have been caused or substantially contributed to by private industry itself. Fortunately, not all react in this fashion, and the socially conscious and the revolutionary are still among the most successful.

Organizational and Structural Implications

Often overlooked or ignored in discussions of the new social responsibility are the organizational and structural alterations that must come about if the firm, the economy and the society are to adapt to the pressures of social change. The new pressures are powerful, fast-moving and implacable and must be accommodated if present basic institutions are to survive. Among the great talents of the corporate form of organization in America has always been its ready adaptability to changing needs and conditions, but little attention has been given, up to this point, to the structural and organizational modifications made necessary by social responsibility. Changes in corporate structures alone will not be sufficient, of course, but they are an important part of the total change that must be made if we are to meet and deal with our pressing problems. Most of our present social institutions evolved for the purpose of dealing with a set of problems wholly different from those we face today, and not all of them are well-suited to the altered circumstances.

Many commentators during the last few years have emphasized the inadequacy of our decision-making machinery, both public and private, to deal with our problems, particularly those of the environment, and have emphasized the dangers of continuing our present procedure of trying to cope with each "environmental atrocity" only after it has reached the point of "clear and present danger to life and health." [23] It will not be enough that the chairman of the board or the president expresses his concern before civic clubs and chambers of commerce. Knowledge *of* and concern *for* the potential impact of conduct on the rest of society must permeate all levels of organization, public and private, and must become as important in the decision process as labor costs, expected revenue or markets. Avoidance *of* and adjustment *to* perceived dangers must be fast and effective. The DDT's of the future (political, social and economic, as well as chemical) cannot be handled as they have been in the past and their dangers discovered only after the peregrine falcon and the brown pelican have vanished from the earth and man himself threatened in ways of which we have only recently begun to learn; we cannot continue to approach our oil spills simply by laying in large

---

[23] Editorial, *Fortune* (February 1970), p. 93.

supplies of straw. Neither new technology nor a new plant location can any longer be loosed upon society where the *only* tests that have been met are the economic ones.

Present organizational and structural forms in the firm probably cannot provide the ubiquitous concern, anticipation, fast reaction time, and other critical elements which are necessary. There is a tendency on the part of some academics and businessmen to say that organizations are "just people." If true, it would mean that prescriptions for organizational change would have to be aimed primarily at changing people and that the non-people aspects of organizations could be ignored. Unfortunately, for this simplified view, organizations are created by people and consist of people, but they are much more than "just people." [24] While the attitudes of people need to change also, what we are mostly concerned with here are the changes in the relationships among people and groups of people. Whether we are talking about a university or a corporation or a whole society, the way in which people are "organized" with respect to each other is important, apart from the people themselves, and plays a crucial role in the nature, scope and effectiveness of the activities in which people are engaged.[25]

For organizational changes in the corporation to be brought about as part of a larger need to change social institutions which have proved inadequate to deal with modern problems or as a response to new technology or new relationships between the firm and the rest of society is certainly not unique to issues of social responsibility. Cybernetics and the computer have already produced major changes in corporate structures and organization, as has the involvement of many large corporations with military hardware and military procurement, and the first signs of corporate organizational responses to minority group pressures, consumerism and pollution are beginning to appear. The appointment of the Reverend Sullivan to the General Motors Board and the new "consumer affairs vice presidents" established by some of the automobile companies are examples of these first, very preliminary changes in structure and organization. Unquestionably, at the moment, they are little more than gestures, but gestures have a way, under proper conditions, of taking on a life and vigor not originally expected or intended for them and of gaining respectability and acceptance far beyond what their creators had contemplated. The Sherman Act is an excellent model for the incarnation of social gestures. Characteristic of social organizations

---

[24] Charles Perrow, *Organizational Analysis: A Sociological View* (Belmont, Calif.: Wadsworth Publishing Company, Inc., 1970), Ch. 1.

[25] David C. McClelland, *The Achieving Society* (New York: The Free Press, 1967), Ch. 1.

at all levels appears to be a preliminary defensive response to social pressure or challenge, and it often takes the form of token behavior or mere gestures, which are followed by changes of attitude encouraged or supported or made legitimate by the gesture; the change in attitude then brings about substantive changes in organizational structures or behavior.

Two aspects distinguish the organizational implications of corporate social responsibility from other present pressures for organizational change. In the first place, few of those who are embracing social responsibility have given any thought to the structural and organizational implications; even the purely public relations type of gesture is not universal. The reason, I think, is plain. Most corporate executives are still viewing social responsibility as no more than an expedient response to current pressures and cannot seem to stop equating it with charitable contributions and aid to higher education. The second distinguishing aspect is that the stakes are higher, the urgency greater, and the issues involved much more pervasive. By the same token, the changes required are likely to be more profound and more at variance with traditional organizational forms, and the attitudes and value judgments needed in order to institute the changes would appear to involve sharper breaks with the past. The rapid changes in society itself and the decline in the leverage of the economic sector combine to impose greater penalties for delay or failure.

Having said all of this, is it not now incumbent upon me to say what these organizational changes must or will be? The veil of the future conceals the details, but there are a few predictions that might be made as to the shape which the changes must necessarily take. Fundamental to any discussion of organizational change is the acceptance of the idea that actions, not words, are the goal, and that public pronouncements by executive officers, while perhaps a desirable and necessary first step, are not enough. One need only have read the daily newspaper during the last few years to find numerous examples of the contrast between the words of chief executives of well-known American corporations and the actions of their subordinates in the actual conduct of the business. It is one thing for the bank president to announce the new policy of social responsibility, including more liberal loan standards for businessmen from the minority communities, and quite a different, and much more important, thing to continue to reward loan officers on the single basis of the security and profitability of their loans. Furthermore, what is the relationship between the president's profession of social responsibility and his bank's making "secure and profitable" loans to the industrial polluter or environmental degrader?

Even at this rather nonspecific level, it can properly be asked whether it is realistic to expect the leaders of business to possess attitudes in advance of the attitudes of society as a whole. The reason that the bank's loans to the polluter and the degrader are secure and profitable is that society does not penalize these people by withholding custom or imposing restrictions on their behavior. In the social responsibility area, the answer of the business leader to the query about his membership in the avant garde is usually in the negative, while at the same time extolling the virtues of business innovation and daring or seconding the suggestion that business is in essence a revolutionary force. Social responsibility is going to require the same sort of innovative, daring and revolutionary leadership which business has often been willing in the past to apply to products, technology, markets and such revolutionary organizational forms as the conglomerate.

Somehow, social awareness must be made an integral part of the decision process at every level of the business organization, and not just on a voluntary basis. The penalties for social non-awareness must be at least as severe as those imposed on the careless employee for cost non-awareness. The idea that social responsibility is "good" must be made to infiltrate all levels. The value system must come to include a social element acceptable to all. The lower echelon employees, in trying to please their superiors within the context of acceptable standards, must have as one of their standards the "goodness" of socially responsible behavior. Just what this means in terms of actual organizational structures and supporting principles is not easy to discern. Some have suggested that there must be shifts to less hierarchical and more horizontal types of organization and, perhaps, to more temporary forms and work groups. The computer and other technological innovations may actually reinforce or facilitate such horizontal shifts by providing large and easily accessible sources of data at all levels and the convenient use of simulation and model techniques. That outside pressures will shape and encourage these internal changes in structure and organization seems rather obvious, and such conceptions as Mechling's and Despard's "anti-corporation" may eventually play a role in bringing such pressures to bear.[26]

Already looming on the legal and political horizon is a rapid growth in the scope and protection of employee rights of free speech, a development which may well prove to be a necessary concomitant of effective corporate social responsibility. It is easy to see how the decline in the influence of the economy over society and a stepping up of the flow of influence in the opposite direction will enhance the pressure for an extension of certain civil rights, including free speech, to the corporation. There is already strong support for the view that "blowing the

---

[26] John Brooks, "The Marts of Trade: The Anti-corporation," *The New Yorker* (October 9, 1971), p. 138.

whistle" by employees is the only practical method of effectuating social responsibility.[27] Whether or not that proves to be the case, the role of the individual employee seems very likely to expand, emphasizing the interlock between shifts to horizontal structures and the extension of constitutional protection of personal rights to the private economic sector.[28]

In addition to the organizational changes which may be necessary in order to make sure that every engineer, copywriter, loan officer, designer, and manager is environment- and society-conscious and that the decisions made as a result of this consciousness are given a reasonable chance of implementation, some organizational changes must be made for the purpose of improving the flow of environmental and social information *to* the corporation. Present forms of organization are very poorly equipped to receive this kind of information, except through traditional economic pipelines and based on aggregations of market behavior. Market information has its important uses and most firms cannot help but be extremely sensitive to it, but we do not need a soothsayer to tell us that market information is not only inadequate, it can also be misleading and inaccurate and can produce corporate responses which aggravate rather than alleviate social and environmental problems. The flow of market information about DDT, "no-return" containers, and enzyme and phosphate detergents, for example, stimulated precisely the worst corporate responses, as far as the environment was concerned.

In some fashion, corporate antennae must be made sensitive to frequencies beyond the economic. Channels must be opened up whereby new voices can gain effective access to the corporation. Present structures are simply not tuned to pick up environmental and social information at an early stage. The only present means of changing institutional behavior, and not very efficient ones at that, are force of law and disruption. The capacity of even very small numbers of individuals for disruption is now so large and the sensitivity of our society to interruptions of its normal flow is now so great that society probably cannot in the future afford the luxury of disruptive means of attracting corporate attention or of conveying social information or of bringing about organizational change. Usually the problem must reach a critical stage before legislation, strikes, boycotts, sit-ins and demonstrations are stimulated, and, by that time, the remedy may be ineffective or so strong that it creates prob-

---

27 Ralph Nader's appeal in 1971 to employees of corporations and government to disclose a wide range of confidential information where responsibility to society is seen to transcend responsibility to the organization is an example. The *New York Times* carried detailed stories: January 15, p. 43; January 27, p. 32; and March 21, p. 16.

28 See the Blumberg article in Part IV.

lems of its own. General education is a solution to some types of communication problems, but for many it is too slow, too vague or does not work at all. Other techniques are necessary.

Corporations may have to install mechanisms by which economic criteria may be offset, countered or argued with. It is difficult at the moment to conceive of an adversary system whereby the economic champion can meet the social and environmental champion on the field of combat and still produce a socially desirable end. What is needed is not a winner-take-all procedure, but one that yields a balanced outcome after having taken into account both categories of criteria. Whether this can best be accomplished through balanced education of individuals or through what has been called an "antieconomic office," like the *Washington Post*'s "in-house critic," or a "countercommercial group," or through a combination of the two is something only experience can answer.[29] These comments are also relevant to the handling of technology, a matter discussed separately below.

Another possibility is to provide for *direct* representation of social and environmental voices in the corporate structure. There would undoubtedly be bad effects as well as good effects of so doing, but some of the specific suggestions for bringing about this representation appear to avoid the more serious negative effects, and experience abroad has shown that negative effects may turn out to be less bad than expected. At any rate, the present situation is so seriously defective that we are actually considering alternatives which do not have to be perfect in order to be much better than what we have.

A necessary prerequisite to our making any progress at all along these lines will be the abandonment, once and for all, of the received legal model of the corporation, where the only voice outside the management that is represented in the corporate structure is that of the shareholders, realizing that the question of whether even that voice is heeded or heard has been the subject of endless debate for the last forty years. Perhaps there should be some improvements in the machinery by which the shareholder's voice is represented; perhaps the institutional shareholder should be "encouraged" to play a more active role; but that is another subject. At any rate, the received model tells us that the shareholder's voice is the only one that should be heard and asserts that the reason for this rests on certain concepts of property and ownership, which, unfortunately, have not been tenable for three-quarters of a century.

---

[29] David M. Kiefer, "Assessing Technology Assessment," *Wall Street Journal* (January 7, 1972), editorial page.

Furthermore, there are many others whose stake in the corporation and in its decisions is comparable with and may even exceed that of the shareholders. Even as a supplier of capital, the shareholder is rarely what he used to be, if he ever was. Who are these others who have major stakes and may deserve to be represented in the corporate structure? The laborers, who work in the corporation's mills and offices and whose interest in their jobs may be closer to a rational property interest than that of the shareholders. The lenders, who may actually supply more of the money on which the corporation operates than do the shareholders. The suppliers, who provide the goods and services which the corporation requires for its activities and who may, through their credit terms, supply no small part of the firm's working capital. The consumers, who buy its products. Those who share the same air, water and space as the corporation. It has been seriously and, I think, correctly suggested that those who contribute to and draw from the same tax fund also have an important stake in corporate decisions and activities.[30]

The unreality of the received model becomes even more evident in the light of the fact that one-third of all shares purchased are held for less than six months. If we can, without undue trauma, extend the political franchise to high school students, perhaps we can find a way to give a voice in corporate affairs to some of the more easily delineated groups whose members are also profoundly affected by a decision process in which they have had no voice. Furthermore, many large corporations actually pay out more in local taxes, property and otherwise, than they do to shareholders and bondholders combined and, in doing so, have a much greater effect upon the local community than they do upon their "owners" and creditors.[31]

Meaningful representation for laborers, immediate customers, lenders, and suppliers is clearly within the realm of possibility, as common sense tells us. Not as easy, and probably not feasible at all, is representation for the ultimate consumer or for those who relate to the same air, water, space, and tax fund. The two-board system, long in use in Germany and now spreading to other European countries, may be a partial solution to the problem if it can be adapted to the American scene. A supervisory board or council, consisting entirely of those outside management, decides how well the managers are doing and is forbidden to interfere in the regular affairs of the company. A management board,

---

30 Alfred F. Conard, "The Corporate Machinery for Hearing and Heeding New Voices," *The Business Lawyer* (November 1971), 197-208.

31 Roger Starr, "Power and the People—The Case of Con Edison," *The Public Interest* (Winter 1972), pp. 75 and 86.

consisting of full-time officers, runs the company. Observers of the two-board system do not agree on the effects of its operation, but the examples of Germany and Japan alone are enough to support the conclusion that the system does not destroy free enterprise. Wider representation of outside groups with major stakes in the corporation might actually improve the effectiveness of a two-board system by disclosing far more areas of agreement than difference among the groups, including shareholders, and by better supervision of managers.[32]

It is worth speculating that another line of organizational change, not so much alternative as collateral, might be found in an extension of governmental prime contracting techniques to social needs. Perhaps our long experience with military contracting can be made to pay off in a more socially constructive fashion. Definition of specific problem areas and of priorities of attack by an appropriate agency of government might conceivably enhance the effectiveness of joint action by the public and private sectors. Social responsibility would be more likely to be viewed as a "good" by all levels of corporate structure if important aspects of it actually became the "business" of the firm.

Another speculative suggestion is that the recent trend toward conglomeration may prove to be an organizational innovation useful in facilitating adjustments in the private sector to the new social responsibility. Innovative ideas and adaptations in one industry or market may spread more rapidly to others, and the effect of the competitive deterrent to socially responsible behavior may be somewhat reduced.

As a supplement to and encouragement for organizational structures better calculated to take into account the social ingredient might be the periodic social audit recommended by Howard Bowen twenty years ago.[33] The standards by which social performance might be evaluated are not as easily determinable as the costs, profits and ratios which are now the primary parameters of economic audits, nor is the raw material for an audit in as readily available form, but they may be closer than many suppose. Furthermore, nobody can seriously argue that our evaluations of governmental performance are based exclusively or even largely on financial data.

---

[32] For a discussion of the two-board system, see Detlev F. Vagts, "Reforming the Modern Corporation: Perspectives from the German," *Harvard Law Review,* 80 (November 1966), 23; for a general approach to the representation issue, see Abram Chayes, "The Modern Corporation and the Rule of Law, in *The Corporation in Modern Society,* ed. by Edward S. Mason (Cambridge: Harvard University Press, 1960), Ch. 2. His point is that a decision is more likely to be responsible when those making it have to answer to those directly or indirectly affected by it.

[33] Howard R. Bowen, *Social Responsibilities of the Businessman* (New York: Harper & Row, 1953).

Managerial Implications

Closely related to the structural and organizational changes implicit in corporate social responsibility, and actually an inseparable issue, is the effect of social responsibility upon managerial characteristics and on the very kind of person who will be the manager in the years to come. Will he be the same manager who has functioned effectively under past assumptions of permanence, hierarchical organization, specialization, profit as the only measure of achievement, free air, water and space in which to dump one's waste, and organization loyalty as the major social adhesive? Many commentators have already given a negative answer to that question wholly apart from the pressures of social responsibility.[34]

It seems abundantly clear that the cost and efficiency-oriented manager will have to give way to men and women of broader outlook. One can sympathize with the manager who has been brought up in the traditions of cost and profit consciousness who is asked, on short notice, to accept a new and overriding value set which often pushes him in directions his instincts tell him are costly or dangerous, just as we have sympathized in recent years with the personnel vice president who is told rather abruptly to abandon his "best qualified for the job" training and instincts and substitute the entirely different standard required in order to hire the hard-core unemployed and the culturally deprived. Many individuals will not be able to make the transition and will, in the course of time, be replaced by those of more appropriate training and orientations. Cost and efficiency factors cannot be eliminated but will be joined by other elements in much more complicated models and decision processes.

A change in the hierarchy of loyalties in our pluralist society will alone be enough to produce and require a different breed of manager. After living for generations under a well-settled hierarchy of loyalties to corporation, country, family, society, profession and self, we have already moved into an era when some of the established priorities have been changed and others are up for grabs. In a very genuine sense, the new "social responsibility" means a reordering of the hierarchy.[35] It will

---

34 Mason Haire, "The Concept of Power and the Concept of Man," in *Social Science Approaches to Business Behavior,* ed. by George B. Strother (Homewood, Ill.: Richard D. Irwin, Inc., 1962); Rensis Likert, *The Human Organization* (New York: McGraw-Hill Book Company, 1967); and Alvin Toffler, *Future Shock* (New York: Random House, 1970).

35 Phillip I. Blumberg, "Corporate Responsibilty and the Employee's Duty of Loyalty and Obedience: A Preliminary Inquiry," *Oklahoma Law Review* (August 1971), 279, reprinted in Part IV of this book.

take a manager with characteristics very different from the present manager to operate effectively under a changing and much more complex set of ground rules.

Implications for Our Policy of Growth

It takes only a moment's sober reflection to make us realize that our national policy of rapid, unremitting, across-the-board growth is unacceptable as a long-range guide to action. "Accelerated growth cannot go on for long," wrote René Dubos in 1968, "let alone forever. In fact, it may be stopped earlier than anticipated by the growing awareness in the sophisticated public that uncontrolled technological growth damages the quality of life." [36] The dissonance between our commitment to growth and events which we observe around us has already been mentioned. Many of our most serious social and environmental problems are aggravated or even caused by our growth-oriented decisions. A "no-growth," or limited growth or selected growth idea may now have begun to replace growth as basic social policy. The stress caused by the unconscionable share of the world's resources which we in the United States (and Western Europe) consume is not alleviated by the policy of growth, nor is the widening economic gap between the developed and underdeveloped nations. Greater efforts to accelerate the industrialization of the underdeveloped nations, while maintaining our own commitment to growth, are doomed to ultimate failure, for at least two reasons: the earth's resources cannot sustain world-wide consumption at our rate, or the biosphere absorb the pollution involved, and the gap is now so wide that no conceivable effort, while we continue to grow, can be expected to have much effect upon it.

The liberal economists, a few decades ago, urged upon society a strong commitment to growth, and some will remember the accusations made by many of these people in the period immediately following World War II that American industry was unwilling to expand production and ally itself with the economic growth policy. (The Eisenhower administration, it should be noted, back in the 1950's intentionally chose a policy of price stability over one of growth.) Ideas of growth were deeply instilled in our society, and cries of "GNP" were heard in the land. Today, many of these same economists, together with some leaders of business, are evaluating no-growth or sharply restricted economic growth as a proper goal of public policy. "No-growth" is gaining respectability, and with it may come acceptance. While the ideology of growth still clearly

---

[36] René Dubos, *So Human an Animal* (New York: Charles Scribner's Sons, 1968), p. 192.

dominates the field, dissonance is being more and more widely recognized. Martin Bronfenbrenner believes that it is no coincidence that Japan has the world's highest measured growth rate and the world's most powerful and violent New Left protest movements and suggests that the *Zengakuren* and *gakusei* have become international symbols of protest against measured growth rates as indices of general progress or welfare.[37] The evidence is strong that no small part of the New Left and student movements in this country can be attributed to closely related protests.

There are alternatives to "no-growth" as a long-run policy, and each of them has its own problems. Sweden, for example, combines growth with generous social benefits and welfare services for all, but Sweden's small size and population limit its impact on world resources and on the biosphere and decrease its value as a model for the United States. Furthermore, cracks are beginning to appear in the Swedish facade and have not yet successfully been corrected. Restricted growth and selective growth appear to differ from no-growth only in degree. Whatever view is taken of the alternatives, one of the implications for the corporation of the new social responsibility is an obligation to face up to some of these issues rising out of our growth policy. They are directly involved in decisions, both public and private, being made today.

Implications for the Systems of Privilege

Social responsibility may also require the participation by businessmen in the unpleasant task of changing the system of privilege, of which they for generations have been the primary beneficiaries. Every society since the beginning of history can be characterized by its systems of privilege. Certain people and classes of people in every society enjoy advantages over their fellows in terms of power, wealth, prestige, influence, access to governmental procedures, and security against radical changes in public policy. Society tends to reward those persons and groups it considers most valuable, but changes are slow because one of the rewards of privilege is the ability to resist change and to preserve the status quo. The movement of the economy from center stage has stimulated pressures from several directions for changes in our system of privilege.

Although the privileged groups in our society are larger, more mobile, more open and more democratic than in almost any other society one might mention, they are, nonetheless, privileged groups, and pressures are building up for change. One of the most important of such

---

[37] Martin Bronfenbrenner, "Japan's Galbraithian Economy," *The Public Interest* (Fall 1970), 156-57.

groups or classes in our society can be described under one, rather loosely used, heading of "business," and it has enjoyed privileged status since the country was founded. Marked changes have taken place during the last forty years, and some aspects of privilege have been eroded or more widely shared, but the essential characteristics remain pretty much what they have been all along. Other groups, like consumers, the poor, racial minorities and environmentalists, are seeking better access to government and to the processes by which the important decisions of our society are made. Some labor groups have already attained many of the attributes of privilege but, as often as not, use them in concert with, and even identify with, the privileged groups of business, as in current attempts to obtain import quotas and higher tariff barriers and to slow or stop effective control of pollution, and have not provided a countervailing influence on many important issues.

Countervailing pressures are arising, however, to offset the kind of business pressures which produced the Hickenlooper Amendment to the Foreign Assistance Act, the Sugar Buying Acts, oil depletion allowances and import quotas and to achieve a better balanced system.[38] Except for the often ineffective or supportive privilege system of organized labor, the system of business privilege has operated largely without opposition, particularly in regard to access to government and ability to protect itself from radical policy change. Better balance can be attained if other points of view are more freely heard and carry more power and influence. Consumerism is probably a good example of a developing pressure on the system of privilege, where the outcome is likely to be a more equitable balance of influence, better legislation and safer consumer products. Socially responsible behavior should include recognition, acceptance and encouragement of this kind of change.

The impact of corporate social responsibility on lobbying activities has received little attention and is closely related to systems of privilege and access to government. Few of the leaders of business who have embraced social responsibility have given any sign that they recognize the implications for the lobbying activities of their own firms. Oil companies cannot opt for social responsibility and then lobby against all effective legislation for pollution control or campaign actively to defeat legislation that might divert small amounts of gas tax money toward research in rapid transit. Steel companies cannot embrace socially responsible behavior and then oppose the control of polluting emissions or refuse to cooperate with public officials attempting to reduce smog levels tem-

---

[38] There is a huge body of literature on this subject. An interesting recent study is Jerome Levinson and Juan de Onis, *The Alliance That Lost Its Way* (Chicago: Quadrangle Books, 1970), esp. Ch. 8.

porarily elevated to dangerous heights. This kind of lobbying and certain types of advertising will surely have to change if social retribution is to be avoided. Perhaps, in years to come, governmental envoys to the Middle East will represent the American consumer as well as the American oil companies, as more groups in society achieve the right to be heard, consulted, taken seriously, and to expect, from time to time, favorable action, as has long been the privilege of business.[39] Perhaps affected corporations will reflect a bit before taking the easy, obvious, self-serving (in the short run) stand on such proposed legislation as scenic river bills, federal highway acts, redwood national parks, food and drug quality control acts, depletion allowances, and restrictions on the use of insecticides.

Implications for the Handling of Technology

Those leaders of business who have embraced the new social responsibility have given only peripheral thought to the implications of bringing this strange and untamed social animal into their midst, nor have they noted the irreversibility of admitting even a small portion of the proverbial camel to their bastions of power and privilege. Among the most important overlooked effects of adopting a socially responsible stance is the necessity of finding new ways of handling technology. Although it is still popular in some circles to blame our environmental and other social problems on capitalism, in the face of overwhelming evidence to the contrary, our search for a basic cause can start, as Max Ways has said,[40] by tentatively picking technology as the villain. I think that most would agree that it really is not technology itself which is to blame, but rather the way in which we and other technologically advanced nations have handled technology. There must be changes in the management of technology if mankind is to survive.

The omens are clear and strong; there is no shortage of prophets, but there is still little understanding among the leaders of business of what this technology talk is all about. In a recent quarterly letter to stockholders, the president of a large utility corporation made the usual assurances of environmental concern in connection with two large nuclear power installations, both subject to public controversy, one in the planning stage and one under construction. The next two paragraphs dealt with the construction of a new research and development center, with no controversy, and two joint industry-government projects involv-

---

[39] A good discussion of the question of access can be found in David B. Truman, *The Governmental Process* (New York: Alfred A. Knopf, Inc., 1951), pp. 321-32.

[40] Max Ways, "How to Think About the Environment," *Fortune* (February 1970), 98 and 100.

ing the development of a demonstration fast breeder nuclear power plant and of coal gasification for pipeline transmission, without any show of interest in the environment whatever. The really crucial environmental issues of the future will be created, no doubt, in these three research and development projects, and others like them, but concern for potential social and environmental impacts is nowhere evident, except where controversy has already arisen. What is more, the stockholders are not the only, or even the most important, parties of interest; and there is no comparable quarterly letter to the coinhabitants of the corporation's ecological space.

Even where concern is expressed by leaders of business and government who are reputed to control technology, there is not much trust on the part of the public in what they say. As Myron Tribus of Xerox has pointed out,[41] there is a real crisis of confidence and no better evidence of it than the termination of the supersonic transport program. Majorities in Congress and large numbers of people simply did not trust the managers of technology to be responsible to society and to stop the program if the problems of noise and pollution were not solved. There is a lot more evidence, including some almost Luddite-type movements which condemn science and technology out of hand.

This is not the place to review or even to comment on the vast literature related to the better control of science and technology in order to achieve social ends, but it *is* the place to point out that the new social responsibility does impose upon business the duty to take into account the social impacts of new technology and to participate constructively in the quest for social machinery which can effectively adapt technology to the changing value and priority systems of society. The first requirement for a new method of handling technology is to bring into the screening equation factors other than the strictly economic ones. Although much has been spoken and written on the subject and many attempts made to develop a sound policy on technology, little progress has been made, except for the addition of some new terminology to the language, e.g., technology assessment. Little progress will be made until those in a position to take the leadership recognize the urgency of the problem and the fact that technology, like the economy, is neither an end in itself nor a subsystem which can operate independently of the whole. The goals, values and policies of the whole must first be established and recognized before there is much hope of stopping technology from wandering aimlessly over a ravaged landscape. "Ideally, what seems to be needed is an infusion of the spirit of technology assessment into the total fabric

---

41 Myron Tribus, "Technology and Society—The Real Issues," *Bulletin of the Atomic Scientists* (December 1971), 27.

of our thinking and way of life. . . . Certainly industry needs a technology stance of its own, if only for self-preservation. . . . But if the scientific and industrial community [*sic*] remain unequipped to sort out good uses of technology from bad, all science and engineering may suffer." [42]

Implications for Goals, Values and Ways of Thinking

Among the many abstract and less easily foreseeable, though not less important, implications of corporate social responsibility are the effects which an overt commitment to socially responsible conduct will have on certain goals, values and ways of thinking that are well established in the business community. These changes are closely intertwined and most of them inextricably linked with the other implications already discussed. Some are necessary prerequisites to truly responsible behavior; others will accompany and still others result from a course of action which has as one of its major ingredients the element of social responsibility. Only a few of the more important and more easily discerned will be mentioned here. All of these changes have begun to take place in certain portions of society, and some of them are making their first tentative appearances in the private economic sector.

Americans, and the people of other highly industrialized nations, have long been addicted to a kind of "side-effect mentality," which has permitted them to keep clear consciences while lakes, rivers and wildlife died, while cities strangled in the debris left behind by the fleeing corporate headquarters and middle class whites, while the automobile multiplied in numbers so huge that the atmosphere was fouled and local transportation brought to a halt, and while, in the case of our own country, the world image of America was decimated. All of these results were "side-effects" of decisions and actions intended for some other purpose, and labeling them "side-effects" somehow made it possible for us to escape responsibility and remorse for our conduct. We have learned to call effects "*side*-effects" when they come to us as a surprise and have discovered that the mere act of labeling, through some marvelous alchemy of the human mind, seems to have protected us from having to pay the price for our faulty forecasting, inadequate or sloppy research, or careless disregard for the impact on others. It is now very slowly occurring to us that there is really no such thing as a "*side*-effect" and that the act of attaching the label is actually an admission of failure, not a free ticket to exoneration and a clear conscience. We are just now beginning to discover that DDT appears to kill peregrine falcons just as directly and

---

42 Kiefer, "Assessing Technology Assessment."

just as surely as it did one of its original intended victims, the body louse. Social responsibility implies an abandonment of the side-effect way of thinking and requires that corporations, as well as the rest of us, stop seeking refuge behind that illusory and self-defeating shield.

Closely related to the growth goal already discussed is the idea that material progress necessarily brings with it a better life. The changes in this idea, already well advanced in society, are in large part the result of our having moved to a post-industrial or mature industrial stage where the economy may no longer be the dominant subsystem. The dissonance between the high value placed on material progress and the degraded environment we see around us every day are all too plain, as are the inconsistencies between that value and attempts to behave in a socially responsible fashion. The earlier observation that increasingly people are inclined to want to be known, not by their occupational base or material possessions, but by their cultural taste and life styles is well worth mentioning again in this connection. The younger managers coming into the corporations today are likely to bear with them these new values, but the older generations of managers will have to recognize and adjust to the new values as part of their commitment to social responsibility.

As John Kenneth Galbraith and David C. McClelland have both emphasized,[43] capitalist societies actually accepted Marx's materialistic view of history and his assertion that their conduct was governed solely by self-interest and profit. Probably nothing has been a greater barrier to socially responsible behavior on the part of businessmen than the acceptance of these views together with their ideological reinforcement found in certain social and economic theories. Research in the field of motivational psychology strongly supports a contrary view, that the primary goal of businessmen is not profit per se but a "strong desire for achievement, for doing a good job." [44] If a man spends his time thinking about doing things better, the psychologist says he has a concern for achievement. Profit has loomed large as a measure of achievement because it was simple, convenient, obvious and was accepted by society as the leading measure of success. As measures such as cultural tastes and life styles have become widespread, particularly but not exclusively among the young, they have given the businessman a socially acceptable opportunity to reassess his own motivations and values and to remove the masks from his underlying desire for achievement. Undoubt-

---

[43] John Kenneth Galbraith, *The Affluent Society* (Boston: Houghton Mifflin Company, 1958); and David C. McClelland, *The Achieving Society* (New York: The Free Press, 1967), esp. Ch. 6.

[44] David C. McClelland, "Business Drive and National Achievement," in *Organizations and Human Behavior,* ed. by Gerald D. Bell (Englewood Cliffs, N.J.: Prentice-Hall, Inc., 1967), pp. 185-86.

edly, this accounts for some of the tendency on the part of businessmen to accept the principle of social responsibility and may increase the chance that more and more businessmen will come to regard the need for solutions to social problems as opportunities for personal achievement rather than as unpleasant burdens imposed upon businessmen by the vagaries of fate.

Managerial ideologies, in contrast with traditional capitalist ideologies, appear to accommodate in some areas a wider exercise of power by the government, but careful inspection of the utterances of business spokesmen leads one to the conclusion that the managerial and traditional ideologies are really not in fact very different. Still prevalent are views of government as an interfering outside force or as a social institution subject to being manipulated by those who can gain access to its centers of power. Inherent in corporate social responsibility is a profound change in these conceptions and a clearer recognition of cooperation between business and government, not solely for the benefit of business, but as a means of solving some of our basic social and environmental problems and for the benefit of society as a whole.

There has been considerable speculation in recent years about the form our federal and state constitutions might have taken had the great corporations, as centers of political and social as well as economic power, existed at the end of the eighteenth century. It is hard to believe that they would have been ignored or not taken into account, although just what form their recognition would have taken in the drafting is not possible to determine, although there has been some experience in other countries with latter day constitutions. The *Federalist Papers* on the subject would make fascinating reading. What is now bound to come about through evolutionary processes, fueled by social responsibility and other social forces, might have appeared, or had its foundations laid, in the constitutional drafts of two centuries ago. One can say, however, that the fact the system of great corporations is not a part of the formal constitutional framework does not make it any less a part of the whole society, any less amenable to the impact of social change and social challenge, or any less obligated to conduct itself in a socially responsible fashion.

CONCLUSION

If the leaders of business continue to conceive of social responsibility as a mere euphemism for charity, a surrogate for the corporate image, a concern only for the public relations department, or simply a passing fad, they are going to fail to meet what may be one of mankind's great challenges, and will, as a price for their failure, lose their own leadership roles in society and bring about the fall of the very organizations with which they are identified. They will make the wrong decisions, using irrelevant data, inappropriate criteria and anachronistic goals, and will find inadequate solutions to the wrong problems; they will take actions which can only aggravate the real problems while producing misleading feedback for their decision-making systems.

Growing both in size and persuasiveness is a body of evidence which compels the businessman seriously to consider the possibility that social responsibility is more than an expedient response to temporary conditions. If, as now seems very likely to be the case, social responsibility appears in the eyes of future historians to have been one of the important manifestations of profound social change, leaders of business must immediately begin to see it as such and to orient their words and actions around a better view of reality. As never before in our history, it has become necessary for the private economic sector to concern itself in a major way with its own view of its role in society. If it cannot adapt itself to its new, less central, but nonetheless important role in society, it will find itself replaced by other institutions, and society may also be the loser.

It is, then, utterly essential that corporate leaders, in particular, consider the evidence and adjust their thinking to this more penetrating way of looking at events going on around them. Then and only then will they be able to assess the implications of what they see. There is not much time. Today's decisions shape the constraints within which tomorrow's decisions are made. Based on the wrong assumptions or inadequate world views, today's decisions may produce results exactly the opposite of what was intended and may shape irremediably and devastatingly the course of future events.[45] Let us not be too sanguine about the outcome under the best of circumstances. "We need not the courage of illusory optimism but the courage of almost desperation," said Gunnar Myrdal in a paper on the necessity and difficulty of planning the future.[46]

After the business leader becomes amenable to a new perception of social responsibility, he must still examine the implications of doing so. The goal of social responsibility is not responsibility but responsible social action, and society is the ultimate judge of whether social action

---

[45] Dennis L. Meadows, *The Limits to Growth* (New York: Universe Books, 1972); Jay W. Forrester, *World Dynamics* (Cambridge: Wright-Allen Press, Inc., 1971); Robert L. Heilbronner, *The Future as History* (New York: Grove Press, Inc., 1960); and Aurelio Peccei, *The Chasm Ahead* (London: The Macmillan Company, 1969).

[46] Quoted in Herbert J. Muller, *The Children of Frankenstein* (Bloomington, Ind.: Indiana University Press, 1970), p. 386.

has been responsible. The businessman cannot take lightly even the expedient view of social responsibility, because there are implications for him, and for everyone, in how he conducts himself.

Organizational and structural changes will be necessary if social awareness is to permeate all levels of the firm, if channels of communication between society and the firm are to be made more effective, and if the corporate responses to social challenge are to become timely and appropriate. Representation for some of the groups affected by corporate decisions, where feasible, appears to be a step worth serious consideration and should be experimented with. Among the more likely possibilities is the two-board system already in use in some European countries. Internal organizational shifts, possibly in a direction away from the familiar hierarchical forms, may also be in the corporate picture. Standards employed in corporate reward systems will probably have to be altered to avoid the inevitable result of having an inconsistency between goals and the incentives used to achieve them.

The avoidance of inconsistencies between goals is another important implication of the new social responsibility. The goal of rapid, continuous economic growth appears to be inconsistent with the goal of preserving the environment and enhancing the quality of life. Trade-offs may have to be worked out between the two goals, where that is practicable, and distinctions made between short-run and long-run objectives, but unusual vigilance will be necessary if we are to avoid preferences for easy short-run alternatives that impede or destroy the more basic long-run alternatives.

Admission to our traditional systems of privilege will have to be opened to more groups and broader segments of society in order that they may gain better access to power, wealth and the important decision-making centers. Rather than rigid resistance to such change, the leaders of business may find that their acceptance of a policy of social responsibility requires them to encourage and support wider sharing of the advantages they have enjoyed for generations. New attitudes toward and new ways of handling technology will need to be developed by both the public and the private sectors, and a necessary first step will be the restoring of public trust and confidence in those who manage technology. Central to the whole issue of social responsibility, at least in the public eye, is the management of technology. Ambivalence may well be the chief characteristic of the public attitude, as the SST affair seemed to demonstrate, where massive doses of patriotism are all that made the fight a close one or that keep it alive today.

Intimately interwoven with the new doctrines of social responsibility, both as causes and as implications, are certain important changes in the goals, values, ways of thinking and attitudes of business leaders.

Side-effect thinking would appear to be one of the first victims of corporate social responsibility and one of the first products of improved methods of handling technology. In the past, side-effect thinking may actually have worked against thorough research and the anticipation of the consequences of corporate conduct. Surprise results have been excused or explained and consciences assuaged by side-effect reasoning, with the result that the major argument for putting on the market a technology or product of unknown consequences or leaving on the market a suspicious product continues to be "it has *not yet* been proven harmful."

As social responsibility provides better communication between the economy and the society, changing goals and attitudes in the society at large will more quickly manifest themselves in the corporation and its conduct. Appearing already are changing perceptions of the relationship between material progress and the quality of life, changing criteria by which even the leaders of business want to be known, and different views of the role of self-interest and profit in the motivations of those engaged in business. Perhaps not as far advanced on the explicit level are the perceptions of the changing relationship between the business and government subsystems, but these will come as the phenomenon of social responsibility is more widely accepted and better understood and as it comes to play a greater and greater role in business behavior and in the decision process.

PART THREE

The Role
of
Ideology

COMMENT

One of the themes unifying the material in this book starts from the premise that ideas, values, and ideologies play important roles, not only in how a corporation responds to social pressure, but also in whether it responds at all, and in the way results of action taken in response are measured by the corporation or by society as a whole. The very title of the book suggests that some corporate responses to certain contemporary social problems, influenced and evaluated by traditional ideas, values, and ideologies, have produced results that are frustrating and confusing for corporation and community alike. Even the doctrine of social responsibility, to the extent that it is a response to contemporary pressures, is viewed, shaped, and evaluated in a highly ideological context. Some would argue, as Chatov does in the piece to follow, that social responsibility *is* an ideology. For all of these reasons and others unmentioned, it seems to us wise to take a look at the ideology of the corporation. Chatov has provided that view.

Neither his purpose nor ours is to go back over the ground covered by Sutton,[1] Monsen,[2] and others [3] during the last two decades and to describe once more the various ideologies of "business" which are

---

[1] F. X. Sutton, S. E. Harris, C. Kaysen, and J. Tobin, *The American Business Creed* (New York: Schocken Books, 1956).

[2] R. Joseph Monsen, Jr., *Modern American Capitalism: Ideologies and Issues* (Boston: Houghton Mifflin Company, 1963).

[3] For example, R. L. Heilbroner, "The View from the Top," in *The Business Establishment* (New York: John Wiley and Sons, Inc., 1964).

alleged to prevail in this country, or to have prevailed in the recent past. Our goal, instead, is to examine the theoretical constructs of ideology in a corporate setting in order to supply a reasonably firm foundation for speculations about the ideological aspects of corporate behavior. Inherent in such an effort is the necessity for taking sides in an ancient polemical contest: the function of ideology as an independent variable in social evolution. Max Weber's disagreement with Marx over the origins of the spirit of capitalism in Western society centered on this same issue, and Weber insisted that material factors, without ideology, were insufficient to explain the phenomenon and that the ideological factors themselves were at least partially independent and could not be explained solely in material terms.[4] Weber's view, to a large extent, has carried the day. Chatov's piece on ideology assumes a Weberian point of view. Weber has been criticized in turn for having left implicit the psychological origins of ideology.[5] Talcott Parsons,[6] David C. McClelland,[7] and others [8] have made attempts to provide psychological additions to Weber, and Chatov includes in his paper an interesting discussion of some possible psychoanalytical approaches to the ideology of the corporation.

It will be noticed as soon as one begins to read the Chatov essay that he also has strong views on the question of whether corporations may properly be seen as having personalities of their own, separate and distinct from the personalities of the individual human beings who, at any given time, constitute the decision-making structure of the corporation. Chatov obviously believes that there is a powerful element of continuity in corporate ideology and that there are more factors at work in shaping that ideology than the aggregate of conscious and unconscious beliefs brought into the organization by its members. Chatov does not discuss this issue explicitly, but his conclusions and his reasoning are clear from his definition of "corporate ideology," which appears very early in the essay. He does not actually personify the corporation but does urge on the reader the view that institutions and organizations do have a collective character (and ideology) produced by the inter-

---

4 Max Weber, *The Protestant Ethic and the Spirit of Capitalism,* translated by Talcott Parsons (New York: Charles Scribner's Sons, 1930).

5 N. Birnbaum, "Conflicting Interpretations of the Rise of Capitalism: Marx and Weber," *The British Journal of Sociology,* IV (June 1953), 125-41.

6 Talcott Parsons, *The Social System* (Glencoe, Ill.: The Free Press, 1951).

7 David C. McClelland, *The Achieving Society* (New York: The Free Press, 1961).

8 D. Having, *Personal Character and Cultural Milieu* (Syracuse, N.Y.: Syracuse University Press, 1948); and C. Kluckhohn, H. A. Murray, and D. M. Schneider (eds.), *Personality: In Nature, Society and Culture,* 2nd ed. (New York: Alfred A. Knopf, 1965).

actions of past and present, old and new members and among the members at any particular time. Whether this approach is truly useful and productive is left to the reader to decide, but it must be said that Chatov's comments are interesting and provocative and do appear to give some insight into the components of corporate behavior.

Because it is not intended to deal generally with the subject of ideology, Chatov's definition may not be detailed enough to provide the reader who is not well informed on the matter with the flavor of ideology in such a way as to make it possible for that reader to distinguish easily the term "ideology" from some of its close relatives like "idea," "belief," "value," "image," or "myth." While not making it a part of his definition, Chatov does emphasize the emotional content of ideology. Daniel Bell has said: "What gives ideology its force is its passion." [9] Most students of ideology would agree with this characterization, but there is more to ideology than emotion. Ideology is action-oriented, which sharply distinguishes it from most of the related terms with which it is often confused. It has been defined as the link between action and fundamental belief (Apter),[10] and Bell has described it as "the conversion of ideas into social levers." [11] Ideology includes a competitive element, too, which Chatov does make a part of his definition, but without elaboration. Many definitions state explicitly that one of the purposes of an ideology is to bestow virtuous status on the group and the members of the group which possess it and to afford the grounds for odious comparisons with competitors or the "enemy." [12] Let not the reader be misled into believing that these brief comments on ideology have overcome the "terminological vagueness" [13] with which the concept is infected. Whole volumes have been written and remain yet to be written on the subject. Perhaps, however, enough illumination has been provided to make it possible to read with pleasure and understanding the Chatov essay on the ideology of the corporation.

Lest this brief discussion of the concept of ideology has left the impression that ideology is wicked and best avoided by civilized groups, including corporations, the reader should take care to note that Chatov, near the end of his opening discussion of rational processes, comments: "The absence of an ideology means an absence of normative orientation

---

[9] Daniel Bell, *The End of Ideology* (New York: The Free Press, 1962), p. 400.

[10] David Apter, *The Politics of Modernization* (Chicago: The University of Chicago Press, 1965), p. 314.

[11] Bell, *The End of Ideology*, p. 400.

[12] Monsen, *Modern American Capitalism: Ideologies and Issues*, p. 8.

[13] George Lichtheim, *The Concept of Ideology* (New York: Vintage Books, 1967), p. 3.

—the lack of a set of 'oughts' which the corporation should follow." In other words, a group without an ideology is likely to be a group without rationality to its behavior and, when confronted with a new problem for which it has no ideological reference, is likely to become immobilized. The link between fundamental belief and action is missing. The reader should also note that, in Chatov's view, the beliefs which ideology links to action need not be announced or even held consciously. The primary goal of Chatov's essay is to examine the unconscious, psychoanalytical components of corporate ideology.

THE ROLE
OF IDEOLOGY IN
THE AMERICAN CORPORATION

Robert Chatov *

THE COMPONENTS OF CORPORATE BEHAVIOR

Corporate experience in American life may be seen as a series of conflicts and accomplishments through which the corporate business form has emerged with institutional integrity intact and with greatly enlarged functions and power. Adjusting where necessary, but preserving critical prerogatives and autonomy, the corporation is solidly entrenched as the nation's primary means of organization for planning and production.

The major price the corporation has to pay for preeminence is that, as prime agent in the management of private resources, it is a focus for the frequently conflicting expectations of a highly differentiated society with a broad and frequently irreconcilable range of values and goals. The ways in which corporations respond to the pressures placed upon them in the contemporary scene are of vital significance and have received a great deal of comment. The critical problem is how to interpret the corporation's frame of reference so that corporate responses to societal pressures are comprehensible and may therefore become predictable.

* Assistant Professor, School of Management, State University of New York at Buffalo, New York. Printed by permission of the author, who reserves all rights of further reproduction.

Perhaps the most common interpretation of the corporate perspective, simply stated, is that the corporation is motivated by rationalized self-interest as the guiding principle, constrained by what the corporation may safely do or may have to do to protect its position. Corporate behavior can then be interpreted solely as a response to outside pressures that threaten corporate values, profits, and prerogatives. Although self-interest must be recognized as an important factor in evaluating corporate behavior, when it is used as *the* single explanation, as in a pure Marxian approach, it becomes so general that in the final analysis it explains nothing.

If we reject a single explanation, it is necessary to identify the variables that do determine corporate behavior. In order to do that, it is necessary to analyze corporate behavior by differentiating between rational processes and ideological attitudes, and between conscious and unconscious motivations, with the objective of indicating when and how these factors come into play in corporate decisions and when a given factor will be the controlling one. Pragmatically, an awareness of these variables should also help corporate decision makers to realize when they are treading on dangerous ground in situations of corporate conflict with other sectors of society.

Rational Processes and Ideological Attitudes

My purpose in bringing up the "rationalized self-interest" concept of corporate behavior was only partly to illustrate its logical shortcomings. Rationality, as a decision-making process, is characterized by the weighing of all available information, alternatives, goals, and possible reactions before a decision is made. But the "rational man," like his cousin, the "reasonable man," is never found in a pure state. The same may be said of the "rational corporation." Some types of corporate decisions do, nevertheless, lend themselves more to rationality than other types, e.g., product line mixes, profit and pricing decisions, and facility locations, as opposed to decisions where feelings per se enter into the matter, e.g., whether to release to a militant minority organization complete information on the corporation's employment of minorities. Although it is likely that rationality is the basis for conventional business decisions, this should not obscure the fact that on another level the *prior* selection of an *ideology* is the controlling influence on the direction that subsequent corporate rationality takes. I define corporate ideology as the sum of conscious and unconscious beliefs held by corporate members, past and present, which affects, justifies, and defends corporate behavior. Whatever the behavior effect of a specific rationality, that particular orientation implies a corresponding, supporting ideology.

Stated differently, this rationality is based on a selected ideological assumption that leads to specific types of behavior. For example, with respect to product line mix, a rationalized self-interest orientation will probably lead to a profit-maximizing product mix decision, even if the products have to be forced through the marketing channel. A predisposition to maximize consumer preferences, on the other hand (given a fixed volume assumption), would lead to a different, probably less profitable, set of product offerings. In each case, the underlying ideology is quite different. Given the basic ideological commitment, the selection of appropriate behavior can be made rationally—self-interest, consumer interest, or whatever.

Difficulties are encountered when the corporate ideology is obscure, not thought out, or unconscious, at a time when the objectives of the corporation come into conflict with other social needs and norms. Decisions that have to be made on nonconventional business problems, e.g., disclosure of minority employee lists, are likely to fall into one of the categories mentioned above. Where there is an apparent lack of rationality in the behavior of the corporation, it suggests the total absence of an ideology or an ideology that is unstated, unadmitted, or unrecognized. The absence of an ideology means an absence of normative orientation —the lack of a set of "oughts" which the corporation should follow. Faced with a new problem for which it has no ideological referent, the corporation may become paralyzed or make a decision on the basis of a nonapplicable norm. In either event, the consequences are likely to be disastrous, which underlines the value of anticipating problems before they arise so that a conscious behavior decision can be made, based on the selected ideology. While this would solve the problem of being taken by surprise without a developed ideology, the problem of dealing with unstated, unadmitted, or unrecognized ideologies remains.

Conscious and Unconscious Ideologies

Unstated or unadmitted ideologies of which the corporation is consciously aware are of relatively limited interest since they merely imply an effort to mask embarrassing motives. While masked motives and accusations thereof give rise to a great deal of rhetoric, some legal actions, much acrimony, and a great deal of distrust, there is little new to be learned by examining the phenomena since the basic text on matters such as these was written some centuries ago by Niccolo Machiavelli.[1] There is, however, a lot of interest in ideologies, or elements of ideol-

---

[1] Niccolo Machiavelli, *The Prince,* Modern Library Edition (New York: Random House, 1950).

ogies, that are unrecognized by the holder—in this case, the corporation. When rationalized self-interest appears to be the base for corporate behavior designed to maximize profits, this is an explicit, presumably conscious, ideology. A conscious, profit-maximizing ideology would reasonably be based on a set of identifiable historical American precedents, e.g., the emergence from numerous conflict situations with enlarged powers; the adoption of selected parts of national and political values in an explicit manner; and the permissive aspect of American corporation laws. For example, as we will see, in the conscious component of corporate ideology, the history of productive achievements ranks as very important; thus, it should not be assumed that all corporate ideology is attributable to past conflict situations. However, the conscious component is only part of corporate ideology.

There is another component of corporate ideology that is largely *unconscious* (therefore, not explicit) and not primarily based on actual corporate experience, and it is one of the purposes of this paper to explore the influence and importance of the unconscious component in corporate ideology. It is well over seventy years since the basic discoveries were made about the functioning of the unconscious component of the human mind, and the way in which psychic life—which affects human interactions on a day-to-day basis—relates to family structure and ego needs and values. It seems appropriate now to incorporate explanatory psychoanalytical material into our picture of the corporation and its ideology, *in addition* to retaining what we know about other, more conscious influences such as available alternatives, perceived short- and long-run effects, rational or irrational self-interest, and charitable objectives.

The difference between conscious and unconscious thought and motivation as it refers to corporate ideology and behavior is thus stressed, and the heavily emotional content of corporate ideology is underscored. In fact, a basic thesis of this paper is that the emotional content of some business decisions vis-à-vis encounter with other sectors of society is far more important than students of corporate behavior have generally thought. The understanding of certain business–society conflicts can be assisted by becoming aware of the influence of ideological beliefs (on the part of all protagonists), some conscious, some unconscious, which can be clarified by a careful consideration of the nature of ideology.

My proposed definition for corporate ideology reflects a view of the importance of both unconscious factors and emotionalism in the corporate schema of societal interaction. I have chosen to define corporate ideology as the sum of conscious and unconscious beliefs held by corporate members that affects, justifies, and defends corporate behavior. These beliefs are conditioned partly by past and ongoing corporate experience and partly by individual psychology, which is based on environmental and cultural factors, and by psychological and genetic conditioning as reflected in and influenced by individual and family relationships. It is possible to identify the importance of some of these factors in reference to concrete corporate experience and involvements. My objective is to take some initial steps toward developing a comprehensive model of corporate ideological construction and the influences of ideology upon corporate behavior.

THE CONTENT AND ROLE OF BUSINESS IDEOLOGY

An exhaustive, highly regarded investigation into the content of the ideology of American business was published in 1956 by Francis X. Sutton and his associates: *The American Business Creed*.[2] Concentrating on large corporations, it has generally remained the basis for any substantive description of what is referred to as the "American business creed." Sutton's description is, in fact, compelling, and the substance of public policy statements made in the late 1960s and early 1970s by business leaders and/or spokesmen is reminiscent of the findings published in his book sixteen years ago. The additions that could be made today would center on business confrontations with students, radical critics, and environmentalists, but, even here, antecedents are clearly apparent in the rhetoric of the 1950s.

Sutton's Description of the American Business Creed

As Sutton found it, the American business creed is traditionally based, simple, clear-cut, certain, and relies heavily on emotional values. Selective in what it emphasizes, the creed stresses traditional, sometimes mythical, values imputed to the American system, and characterizes the businessman as hard-headed, practical, and legitimately engaged in providing essential services to society.

The traditional simplicity of the business creed frequently invokes the Protestant ethic, while also symbolically relying on the "founding fathers" approach. The creed attributes the advances of the American people to a "free" economic system dependent upon competitive characteristics for viability, via the price mechanism and supply and demand. The economic system is regarded as inherently sound, but continually threatened by outside forces, such as communism, government, or labor unions.

---

2 F. X. Sutton, S. E. Harris, C. Kaysen, and J. Tobin, *The American Business Creed* (New York: Schocken Books, 1956; paperback edition, 1962).

If the inherent structure of the American economic system is a necessary element in the business creed, the self-perception of the businessman and his role is at least as important. Humble origins are stressed, as is the myth of the small entrepreneur; the firm is seen as a team, but the prevailing ethic nevertheless remains that of individualism. The businessman sees himself as a decision maker—unemotional, practical, talented, with a hard job to do. Professional, utilitarian in outlook, dedicated, realistic, active, and devoted to material progress, the businessman carries the conviction that everyone should be judged on his merits.

The perspective of business ideology toward other sectors is important. Sutton concluded that it is basically anti-union; although collective bargaining is accepted, workers have to be saved from the forced strike. Customer sovereignty is stressed, working through the price mechanism to spur business to continual excellence. Hostility toward government is apparent, but the constitution, the judiciary, and the nation are valued symbols. Government intervention is seen as inherently evil, since it interferes with the free working of the economic system; government people are regarded as bureaucrats, politicians as weak, and government action as sterile.

In viewing his role in relation to society, the businessman frequently resorts to the symbolic values of individualism and realism, assuming that maximum satisfaction and distributive justice result from individual egotism. Progress and materialism are stressed, and these lead to a positive attitude toward the role of the businessman in carrying out his functions. The basic view starts from the legal model, stressing the right of the owner to use his property as he sees fit. But this right is not seen without responsibilities (determined by business itself) that are owed to customers, employees, stockholders, the general public, and sometimes to suppliers and other business contacts. Profits are defended as rational, justified by the votes of the consumer, and necessary for the operation of the business. The stockholder is regarded as necessary, providing the funds for the operation of the business, receiving dividends, and exercising his right to vote out management if incompetent or to show his lack of confidence by selling his stock.

● "CLASSICAL" AND "MANAGERIAL" STRAINS OF BUSINESS IDEOLOGY. The foregoing has some of the aspects of a caricature when summarized, but the ideology as stated is not adopted in toto by all businessmen. Rather, adherence to these views may be seen more as a spectrum of belief, ranging between, as Sutton describes them, the two main versions of the business creed—the "classical" and "managerial" strains. Viewing the classical version as substantially the description offered in the previous paragraphs, the managerial version is distinguished by de-emphasis of profits; accent on service and responsibility; greater acceptance of the roles of labor and government; and emphasis upon the fundamental transitions from the first part of the century, rather than the more remote, presumed "ideal" circumstances of the past. Despite the differences in degree (rather than kind) between the "classical" and "managerial" perspectives, their ideological consistencies are much more significant.

• REALITY AND THE SELECTIVITY OF BUSINESS IDEOLOGY.   Perhaps the most important similarity between the managerial and classical versions of the business creed is that both are characterized by selective avoidance or distortion of apparent facts, and both contain the same major inconsistencies.

The business creed generally avoids discussing the operation of historical forces, the advantages of geographical location, changes in society, the debt to foreign immigration, and capital and technological borrowing. Also avoided is the issue of the relative powerlessness of stockholders to affect the management of the firm or the division between profits and retained earnings. The authoritarian element of executive power is ignored, as are: the dependence of junior management upon favor from higher levels; the pleasures of high position; price fixing; inferior products; questionable selling practices; molding consumer demand; and government aid via subsidies, tax benefits, tariffs, quotas, loans, and the like.

The contradictions within business ideology indicate a significant confusion of myth with reality. The emphasis on the small entrepreneur does not fit the facts of the increasing growth in size of corporations; the self-seeking profit motive is at odds with the stress placed on service and responsibility; individualism has little place in the highly structured modern corporation; and the assertion of business ethics is frequently contradicted by business practice. Management control of the corporation is hardly democratic and is usually self-perpetuating; small shareholders have little, if any, power. Business involvement with, and frequent influence upon, government policies is at direct odds with the laissez-faire ideology so frequently postulated. Finally, the emphasis upon the achievement and superiority of the economic system is difficult to reconcile with recessions and inequitable distributions of income, privilege, and wealth.

• BUSINESS IDEOLOGY AS A COMPENSATING REACTION.   Sutton rejects the idea that the ideological avoidances and contradictions of the business creed are motivated by hypocritical self-interest. Sutton was convinced that business ideology is believed by its adherents and that the belief is based on reactions to patterned strains in the business role, i.e., these pressures and the inherent vulnerability cause the formation of compensating, defensive beliefs.

The argument runs as follows: in a basically pluralistic society, counter-ideologies are important; because the businessman's role is suspect, a consistent pattern of reaction emerges. Doubts about business assertiveness lead to the defense of beneficence; selective use of ideologies relates to needs developed by strains, oversimplification permits comprehension, and the development of symbolic opponents, e.g., intellectuals and government, serves to focus aggressive reactions. The strains in the businessman's role come from authoritarian decision making, responsibility, uncertainties, lack of legitimation, and subjection to obscure moral standards. The general anti-intellectual tradition [3] and austere values are significant; vigorous acceptance of the business role results in "strain transformation" (development of compensating ideologies) to definitions of merit and achievement, with room left for scapegoats. The need to rationalize self-interest creates the drive to accent behavior consistent with public welfare, thus exonerating the businessman from lack of social responsibility. Legitimacy is supported by the institution of private property, market place balloting is seen as a substantiation of business decisions, and competition is used as an emotional symbol. The attitude toward change is rational and institutionalized, but strain and the intolerance of external change create insecurity, for which nationalism and anti-intellectualism provide an antidote (the latter in particular can be viewed as a defense of rationality).

To summarize, Sutton viewed the business creed as basically stable and conservative; even the managerial tradition was portrayed as stable in the face of major societal changes. With respect to changes in the creed, Sutton noted that the creed had lost some ground in the face of the new egalitarianism, decline in individualism, and loss of inner direction. However, stress of adapting to the changing role of government and to the changing society was creating some danger of an ideological shift to the right.

Other Perspectives on Corporate Ideology

Other evaluations of the substance of business ideology tend to support Sutton's evaluations. R. Joseph Monsen's work sees the same variations in classical and managerial viewpoints and confirms the major points discussed by Sutton, but adds that Galbraith's idea of counter-

---

[3] Richard L. Hofstadter, *Anti-Intellectualism in American Life* (New York: Random House, 1962).

vailing power had been adopted by the managerial version of business ideology.[4]

Perhaps the major theme of, and addition to, business ideology since 1956 is the cult of social responsibility.[5] Earl F. Cheit's analysis of this phenomenon in 1964 revealed that it was a primary concern of top business leaders and often the sole topic of their important meetings, assuming the elements of a gospel. That it seemed to replace the old theme of free enterprise, he found encouraging, as a response to the new demands being made of corporate executives, while noting, *à la* Sutton, that power, income, and the tendency to behave like owners placed managers in the position of having to defend these advantages.[6] The theme of social responsibility[7] remains ascendant. A recent Committee for Economic Development publication[8] lays out a series of guidelines for managers, presses the need for the socially responsible corporation, and presents a firm, albeit optional, program. The real-world effect of the social responsibility doctrine has been questioned, relative to the actual contribution that a socially responsible corporation could make.[9]

If the idea of social responsibility has a positive potential, another element in business ideology—anti-intellectualism—probably has an equal potential on the other side of the balance sheet. The recurrent theme of anti-intellectualism in American corporate-business ideology is substantiated from widely different sources and often appears in conjunction with the content of the creed with respect to its mythical legacy from a presumably purer past. This can be seen on a literary basis; the moral of even the Horatio Alger stories has been altered (by generations of nonreaders) to be compatible with the business ideology of the rise from rags to riches via the road of hard work. This altered view is substantially incorrect, insofar as the moral of the Alger stories is concerned, since the heroes of the stories are usually rewarded with success because of their personal character, luck, and morality, in the face of adversity,

---

4 R. Joseph Monsen, Jr., *Modern American Capitalism: Ideologies and Issues* (Boston: Houghton Mifflin, 1963).

5 Clarence C. Walton, *Corporate Social Responsibilities* (Belmont, Calif.: Wadsworth Publishing Co., 1967), pp. 44-48.

6 Earl F. Cheit, "The New Place of Business," in *The Business Establishment*, ed. Earl F. Cheit (New York: John Wiley and Sons, 1964), pp. 152-92.

7 See the detailed discussion of social responsibility in Part II.

8 Committee for Economic Development, *Social Responsibilities of Business Corporations* (New York: C.E.D., 477 Madison Ave., 1971).

9 Dow Votaw and S. Prakash Sethi, "Do We Need a New Corporate Response to a Changing Social Environment?" Parts I and II, *California Management Review*, 12:1 (1969), 3-31.

rather than because of hard work. In *Andy Grant's Pluck,* e.g., the hero drops out of school because his father is impoverished by another's criminal act.[10] Performing several deeds of courage, Andy's fortunes rise when he is befriended by influential persons; he succeeds in business, pays off the mortgage on the old homestead, and is looking forward to even better days as the book ends. The story is, of course, somewhere between a morality play and *Little Orphan Annie,* but what is really significant is the attitude toward a business career versus that of an intellectual one. After three months of work in the city, Andy at seventeen already earns more than the number two administrator-teacher in his old school. Entering his twenties, Andy has made his first fortune and notes that ". . . it was lucky for me that I had to leave school. It was the beginning of my present prosperity," a dismal comment on the value of education.

From another point of view, Richard Hofstadter has indicated the pervasiveness of anti-intellectualism in the United States and shows that the business sector shares, if it did not actually develop, that perspective.[11] It ought to be mentioned, in all fairness, that intellectuals return the compliment.[12] But, in spite of a pervasive anti-intellectual framework, the American businessman has almost never fared well at the hands of novelists, and, if popular literature reflects the values of the times, it adds persuasion to the suggestion in business ideology that the businessman is on the defensive.[13] The turn-of-the-century preoccupation with the new type of business leader became a commonplace perspective during the 1930s, evolving into a rather unpersuasive portrayal of various business "supermen" in the 1950s.[14] At the same time, it became apparent that the increasing size and regimentation of American business was producing a style of "organization man," portrayed as colorless, harassed, frustrated, and unfulfilled.[15]

However, the general ethic of the public is characterized by a lack of really serious animosity toward the businessman, which makes one wonder about the heavy defensive element in business ideology. Thorstein Veblen conjectured that the emulatory instinct of the lower classes made them accept the oppressions of the rich and their values and that

---

[10] Horatio Alger, *Andy Grant's Pluck* (Philadelphia, Pa.: H. T. Coates, 1902).

[11] Richard L. Hofstadter, *Anti-Intellectualism,* pp. 233-43.

[12] *Ibid.,* pp. 233-37.

[13] *Ibid.,* pp. 233-34.

[14] Henry N. Smith, "The Search for a Capitalist Hero," in *The Business Establishment,* ed. Earl F. Cheit, pp. 77-112.

[15] William H. Whyte, Jr., *The Organization Man* (New York: Simon & Schuster, 1956); and David Riesman, *The Lonely Crowd* (New Haven, Conn.: Yale University Press, 1950).

this instinct was a cohesive force in society.[16] His explanation seems fresh and applicable today. Attacks on business are seldom attacks on privilege stemming from wealth and income, but rather attacks on its uses of power and its presumed betrayal of a "public" trust. Thus, we can conclude that American business has been accepted by the larger part of American society, in terms of the desirability of achieving high influence and wealth. In spite of sporadic attacks by disaffected intellectuals and students, and at various low points concurrent with times of economic depression, general acceptance of the corporate structure and the corporate man by society suggests that there is more to the defensiveness of the business ideology than a set of patterned strain reactions to social pressure or the "interest-cum-prestige" revision of the Sutton interpretation that was offered as an alternative by Paul Samuelson.[17] I now propose to discuss additional theoretical materials that deal with the question of ideological formation and retention.

THEORETICAL CONSTRUCTS OF IDEOLOGY

The earmark of ideologic evaluation is inescapably that it has certain elements of pathological delusion. This unhappy fact is frequently commented on and has been criticized as a perspective that unavoidably warps the evaluative impartiality of the investigator.[18] If one begins with the conviction that the ideologist suffers from an illusion, it eliminates the possibility of concluding that what the believer believes may actually be true and/or reasonable. Thus the ideological investigator may be suffering from his own ideological incapacity.[19] Although this may seem like fruitless tail-chasing, the question goes to the heart of the problem. Although my preference would be to begin to appraise ideology from the point of the reasonableness of its perceived reality, a point to which I will return later, I first plan to discuss ideology as seen by some leading theorists who have had enormous impact on their own scientific fields and/or on the course of history.

---

[16] Thorstein Veblen, *The Theory of the Leisure Class,* Modern Library Edition (New York: Random House, 1934), Chs. II and IV, esp. pp. 59–64. First published in 1899.

[17] Paul A. Samuelson, "Personal Freedoms and Economic Freedoms in the Mixed Economy," in *The Business Establishment,* ed. Earl F. Cheit.

[18] *Ibid.,* pp. 194-97; and Clifford Geertz, "Ideology as a Cultural System," in *Ideology and Discontent,* ed. David E. Apter (New York: The Free Press, 1964).

[19] Carl Mannheim, *Ideology and Utopia* (New York: Harcourt Brace, 1936), pp. 49-52. First published in 1929.

Ideology and Strain Theory

Sutton used strain theory as his basic explanation for the development of business ideology. Inherent in the use of this explanatory device for ideology is the assumption that, even if the ideologist is indulging in illusory machinations, he is blissfully unaware of it. While this does not save him from error, it does at least place him outside the range of hypocrisy. Postuated in its most complete theoretical form thus far by Talcott Parsons, with whom Sutton studied, strain theory is part of a more general format that seeks to explain the social system and its dynamics.[20] Parson's general theoretical approach has been applied to specific problems and expanded by his students.[21]

The general inspiration for strain theory comes from Freudian psychology, which is based upon the study of individuals. Parsons had taken individual psychology and generalized it to a societal setting, explaining the collective dynamics of that society in terms of how an individual would behave in the same circumstances. The argument regarding the individual's psychology is roughly as follows. An individual's expectations may be frustrated, which places a "strain" upon him presenting an adjustment problem; these expectations, or need-dispositions, which press for gratification, have been attached to some object, the relationship with which has been internalized, that is, become part of his personality structure. If his value pattern, which governs the need-disposition, is violated, he is directly frustrated; he can react in one of three ways: he can inhibit or repress the need-disposition; he can transfer the need-disposition to a new object; or he can learn to redefine his value pattern. This, in theory, reestablishes equilibrium.

The alternative to repression, transference, or redefinition of need-dispositions is a compromise solution, whereby some of the need-disposition remains and continues to be frustrated, resulting in a hostile or resentful reaction. A conflict situation may result in which no aspects of the now-ambivalent motivation can be satisfied. If no satisfactory adjustment is possible, deviant behavior may result.[22] The question of socialization and social control can be understood on the basis of adjustment to strain, which may produce anxiety, fantasy, hostile or aggressive responses,

---

20 Talcott Parsons, *The Social System* (New York: The Free Press, 1951; Free Press paperback edition, 1964).

21 Sutton, et al., *American Business Creed;* and Neil J. Smelser, *The Theory of Collective Behavior* (New York: The Free Press, 1962).

22 Parsons, *Social System,* pp. 251-56.

or defensive measures to limit the deviation from expectations and/or restore the status quo. The support necessary to relieve the strain is found in providing a sense of security which avoids a feeling of isolation. In an integrated social system where institutions play coordinated, specific roles, such as in the United States, role-expectation patterns and the coordination of individuals must be successfully combined to minimize conflict. This is usually done by establishing legitimized priorities backed by society's common-value sentiments.[23]

The position of the corporation in conflict, in a period of changing values, is readily apparent in the context of this framework. Generalizing the corporation's perspective as a set of need-dispositions that are partially frustrated by the conflicting values and powers of other groups in society, the formation of hostile responses, defensive measures to restore a status quo, the development of fantasy (reliance on mythology), and a general feeling of anxiety can be readily understood. The Parsonian framework provides a helpful approach to the ideological beliefs of the corporation but still requires augmentation, because it does not sufficiently account for pure self-interest or for more fundamental unconscious processes.

Ideology and Interest Theory

Interest theory as a concept is familiar in its simplistic form to all men, e.g., "it all comes down to whose ox is gored," and "ideological pronouncements are seen against the background of a universal struggle for advantage." [24] Developed by Marx and Engels in their early writings, interest theory reverses the Hegelian thesis that the ideas of an age determine its substance and postulates instead that ideology can be correctly understood only as the effect of basic changes in the economic system.[25] Consciousness, Marx and Engels argued, is determined by life; a national ideology is the product and self-justification of the ruling classes, who create the ruling ideas in every epoch. Furthermore, one cannot accept the word of individuals regarding their conception of ideology and beliefs, because they are subject to the false consciousness, i.e., misinterpretations, of any age. Ideology then becomes a system of beliefs produced by false consciousness, that is, people do not understand the bases of their beliefs, which are really determined by the mode of economic life. Since the ruling classes have property and social power and thus determine

---

23 *Ibid.*, pp. 297-301.

24 Geertz, "Ideology as a Cultural System," p. 52.

25 Karl Marx and Frederick Engels, *The German Ideology* (New York: International Publishers Co., 1947), esp. 3-78. (Written in 1845-1846.)

the practical-idealistic expression in the state, they also act as the ruling thinkers.[26] Thus, Marx and Engels take the Hegelian dialectic, add the ingredient of materialism, develop a general concept of social change that is based on the control of property, and use that combination to explain the beliefs and ideologies of each epoch. It is important to recognize that Marx and Engels stress that the social behavior of individuals is seen not as a function of autonomous decisions based on rational self-interest, but by their socially conditioned roles as members of an economic class.[27]

The familiar ideological contests of our time, in which competing groups seek to institutionalize their own views of reality, are evident in the context of interest theory. Its weakness is that it lacks a developed analysis of motivation—"its psychology is too anemic and its sociology too muscular." [28] That is, the psychological aspects of the theory are inadequate. With respect to an evaluation *of* and predictions *for* business ideology, interest theory supplies an explicit adjunct to the concepts introduced via strain theory; in combination, the reactions of the business firm can be seen both in terms of corporate responses to outside pressures and corporate self-interest based on a "false" set of values.

Ideology and Psychoanalytic Theory

This framework remains incomplete, however. We have not yet accounted for the power of unconscious mental processes that affect conscious attitude and behavior. Strain theory infers these processes through its conceptualization of need-dispositions but requires explicitness; interest theory deals with "false consciousness" but in a pre-Freudian sense and ignores the imperatives of bureaucracy and authority relationships that were advanced by Max Weber. These elements may now be sketched into our framework.

Ideology in the Freudian sense can be seen as the product of unconscious mental forces in the individual that consist of repressed infantile wishes and fantasies. Their power is as enormous as their range. They consist of highly charged erotic and aggressive wishes that are barred from consciousness and enactment by intracyclic censorship, but that can achieve gratification in highly complicated and disguised form. For example, the Oedipus complex, which consists of incestuous wishes toward the mother and parricidal rage against the father, may be re-

---

26 *Ibid.*, pp. 39-43.

27 Henry D. Aiken, *The Age of Ideology*, Mentor Books Edition (New York: The New American Library, 1956), p. 188.

28 Geertz, "Ideology as a Cultural System," p. 53.

solved by a child by identifying himself with the father and thus protecting himself against the fear of punishment for his repressed wishes. This "projective identification," which lies behind the phenomenon of religious awe, is the mechanism involved in association with and reliance upon charismatic leaders. The first childhood fantasy that has been distorted by repression, then, may be the first "ideology"! In this sense, Freud analyzes the development of religion as a result of infantile needs projected upon a father figure, associated with the development of supporting illusions.[29] One of the difficulties with developing this kind of an ideology, when viewed from this perspective, is that it usually results in the impoverishment of the individual personality by investing the charismatic leader with all good qualities, and viewing the related phenomenon of regarding the "childlike innocence" of the follower as the ultimate in "faithful obedience." Carrying the thought further, it can be seen that, in this respect, ideology is a means of making the individual feel less "monstrous," less alienated, less "guilt-ridden." Ideology serves to make possible some acts that would otherwise be a source of shame or guilt. Moreover, when unacceptable needs are unconscious, repressed, and a threat to the ego because of their content, there may be great difficulty in maintaining the repression. An effective means of defending the ego against the threatening content of the unconscious is to see those unconscious threats as emanating from outside the self. Thus the unconscious thought, the real source of the experience, is seen as an external reality.

This, of course, is a qualitatively different explanation for the formation of ideology than that offered by strain theory, since the latter implies a response mechanism to defend need-dispositions which may be more or less conscious, whereas a Freudian approach carries the implication that the ideologist is not aware of the delusionary aspect of his feelings. One can also see here some compatibility with the Marxian view of the formation of an ideology developing from false consciousness, which is in itself a condition of alienation.

Another important consideration in developing a satisfactory perspective on the formation and use of ideologies is the internal relationships among people in an organization and the effect that these have in their external contacts. Weber's work was concerned with social orders and those elements that affect their stability, of which systems of command and obedience were the most important.[30] Although Weber himself

29 Sigmund Freud, "The Future of an Illusion and Civilization and Its Discontents," in *The Complete Psychological Works of Sigmund Freud,* ed. James Strachy, Vol. 21 (London: Hogarth Press, 1953). First published in 1927 and 1929, respectively.

30 Donald McIntosh, "Weber and Freud: On the Nature and Source of Authority," *American Sociological Review,* 35:5 (1970), 901-11.

saw little application for psychology in sociology, a good case can be made for the introduction of the psychoanalytical framework into his theories. Weber postulated three bases for systems of domination: coercive power, mutual interest, and the recognition of the leader's commands as legitimate—all three of which play "an indispensable role." [31] Weber accented attitudes toward the supernatural as the basis for the legitimacy of all authority, for justifying and rendering obligatory all forms of social order, and for creating a feeling of enormous power and the sense of numinous authority that is invested in the charismatic leader.

On a more advanced stage of psychological development, once the inner sense of right and wrong comes into play, the superego supplies a validation of traditional authority and legitimacy. This constitutes an internalization of values or, alternately, turns prophetic charisma into bureaucratic authority. Family relationships are seen as important in this process, as already pointed out in connection with the deification of the father figure. But the family also comes into play in another important sense with respect to business ideology in relation to its national fervor, an element of great importance once we attempt to predict the nature of business response to given situations. In this sense, a nation is made up of the relationships it has to its citizens and it may be characterized in familial terms, e.g., professional rivalries are likely to be thinly disguised sibling battles—the nation viewed as a fatherland or motherland, and an officeholder regarded as a son who wields authority for the father.[32] This phenomenon may also be seen in the business corporation, where the ties among members of the firm are fostered by identifications and loyalty patterns similar to those which characterize the nation, perhaps in a form of secularized charisma.[33] The legitimization of authority is important, since it can be argued that peer relationships by themselves (sibling identifications) are insufficient to build a stable system of authority, that being possible only when there are superego identifications with the leader.

The psychoanalytical approach to the problem of business ideology offers several important additions to the information already gleaned from the strain and interest theories: it is now possible to add to that framework the knowledge that ideological formation may be based on primitive unconscious mental functioning, and that the structure of internal corporate relationships and the relationship of the corporation to other groups in society are closely connected with family relationships. Significantly, the elements of emotionality, unconscious motives, and repressions have now been included in our perspective.

---

31 *Ibid.,* p. 901.
32 *Ibid.,* p. 909.
33 *Ibid.,* p. 910.

CORPORATE IDEOLOGY AND ITS EFFECT ON
CORPORATE BEHAVIOR

Combining the perspectives offered by the strain, interest, and psychoanalytical theories results in a reasonably complete explanatory device for predicting how corporate ideology will affect corporate behavior in different circumstances. In particular, certain situations where corporate behavior heretofore appeared irrational or inexplicable may now be seen as having been determined by unconscious factors that follow a logical, understandable pattern. The application of the psychoanalytical component of corporate ideology permits the analysis of two important aspects of corporate conflict where the strain and interest theories are inadequate. These two aspects involve the way in which corporate ideology affects the corporate view of its protagonists and the way in which corporate ideology relates to the nature of a conflict between a corporation and another part of society.

Corporate Ideology and Protagonist Perception

An essential part of the corporate conscious and unconscious beliefs depends on the identity of the corporate protagonist, on how that protagonist is expected to behave, and on how the corporation should behave toward the protagonist. This stems from the fact that each corporation is unique, i.e., "corporations have behavior patterns, personalities, and styles." [34] The total personality of the corporation is summed up in its frame of reference, which together with the involvement of each participant, determines corporate perception of the "other's" behavior. The protagonist of the corporation has its own set of perceptions regarding the corporation, and the perceptions of corporation and protagonist constitute "reality" for each of the participants. In the final analysis, a corporate-society conflict may be regarded as a contest between different perceptions of "reality." Thus, what may appear to the corporation as a comprehensive set of rational beliefs may appear to the protagonist as mere hypocrisy, and to an observer as an inconsistent set of values.

The critical issue is the corporation's perception of the reality of its protagonists, which is a function of the conscious and unconscious components of its ideology. The more the corporation sees its protagonists as a unitary peer group, the less likely will be the appearance of corporate emotional feelings, rising from unconscious levels to dictate

---

[34] Samuelson, "Personal Freedoms," p. 206.

the corporate response. If the protagonists are viewed as peers, e.g., as members of the same corporate community, conflicts can be solved along familiar lines with both sides following the same set of rules. A controversy over patents, for example, is likely to go through an orderly, recognized judicial procedure to some resolution or may be settled by a rational (although possibly illegal) agreement to share markets, distribution, and profits. Emotional involvements will be evident, but will exist on a conscious level related to the actual economic stakes involved. The same may be said of an intercorporate conflict growing out of a takeover attempt.

If the protagonists are viewed as "inferior" or "dependent" groups, the emotional response of the corporation is likely to be less conciliatory or flexible. Part of the traditional antagonism of business to government in the United States, for example, probably stems from conscious and unconscious internalization of the feeling that government is "unproductive" and "obstructionist" and, thus, "inferior." From a psychological point of view, however, the government may be seen as a father figure, a concept which carries with it the corollary of unconscious antagonism on the part of the corporation. Failure of the corporation sufficiently to identify with the government, i.e., as a leader figure, prevents the build-up of a stable authority relationship between business and government. That is not to say that the failure to achieve this authority recognition is necessarily good or bad, but the absence of this relationship, i.e., the inability of the corporation to identify with the government, does provide the basis for continuing conflict. Nevertheless, as Sutton noted, business still incorporates into its ideology traditional, largely mythicized versions of patriotism, idealization of the democratic political framework, and respect for the judicial process. Relative to this ideal view, the government is seen as failing to measure up to the perceived national standard, and, in this respect, the belief of the corporation that government has largely negative value can be seen as a defense and a challenge to a superior authority. The status of business and the critical importance of its roles vis-à-vis the government in regard to production and to the political process suggest that to some extent the authority relationship that one looks for is really reversed, i.e., that the government to some important extent views business as an authority figure, rather than the other way around!

With regard to blacks and other minorities traditionally excluded from managerial corporate positions, the conscious and unconscious components can be seen fairly easily. On a conscious level, the early slave status of the black and his continuing existence on a generally low economic level aids the corporate perception of this group as dependent, nonpeer, and inferior. On a deeper, unconscious level, the "differentness" of the black because of his color makes him easily susceptible to being identified as a "stranger," and the possible focus of projected, displaced hostilities. Prejudices relating to religion and national origin work approximately the same way toward other minorities, all of which are denied sibling-peer recognition to varying degrees.

Women generally have been excluded from executive corporate posts in spite of the fact that as a group they probably own the majority of corporation stock held by individuals. The reasons for their exclusion are a complex combination of psychological, sociological, cultural, and historical factors too extensive to be dealt with in this essay. It is sufficient for the present purpose to note that women's drive for equal treatment in the corporate world has just begun and will undoubtedly accelerate in the future, presenting the corporate structure with a major area of conflict and an extremely difficult adjustment process.

If the protagonist is a unitary group, e.g., another corporation or a labor union, rather than a composite group, e.g., environmentalists or consumerists, this may have important effects in conditioning the response of the corporation at a time of conflict. Since the unitary group is easily identifiable within the corporate frame of reference, a rapid corporate response is likely to develop along conditioned lines. A composite group is less easily delineated, hence more complex to handle for the purpose of corporate responses. A "hire minorities" drive backed by City Hall, religious groups, and civil rights organizations will be more difficult for the corporation to respond to than if the drive were the creation of a single organization representing a specific minority. Initially it might appear that a composite group would be more apt to receive a negative corporate response because of its multiple objectives and lack of a clear-cut identity. However, a nonpeer, unitary group might not even get through the front doors of the executive offices, while a composite group making the same demands could perhaps obtain a hearing because of the peer qualifications of one or more of the group's participants.

The question of opponent-perception works both ways, of course, and this affects the amount of trust the parties to the encounter invest in each other. For example, it appears reasonable that corporations would display more trust and good will in dealing with environmental groups that represent a rather broad spectrum of social identifications, including many with recognizable, conservative credentials similar to those of the corporate hierarchy itself, than in dealing with students (= radicals), blacks (= dependents), or academicians (= intellectuals). The environmentalists could be expected to respond in kind to the corporation. We know from sad experience that, in warfare, treatment of the enemy depends on whether they are regarded as human (peers) or whether they are seen as *untermensch* (dependents or worse). Therefore, in forecasting future corporate conflict situations and their outcomes, the matter is more than one of just identifying the issues that are likely to arise; perhaps the most important consideration from a psychological viewpoint is identifying the parties who will press those issues. Examining the peer status of the corporation's present and future protagonists supports some speculations about corporate behavior in future encounters with other parts of society.

Summing up the influence of protagonist perception on a conflict situation as it works through corporate ideology, the following paradigm is offered for consideration: (1) Corporate ideology, consciously and unconsciously, sees its protagonists along a spectrum of social acceptability. The spectrum can be described as running from zero peer recognition, e.g., an unshaven, bushy haired, black, Jewish, radical-left student in worn army surplus clothes and boots and carrying the works of Chairman Mao (everyone can make his own nomination here) to 100 percent peer recognition, e.g., another corporation of somewhat larger size, with a better earnings record, and controlled by persons from an upper-middle-class socioeconomic group. (2) The lower a corporation rates the protagonist on the "peer-recognition" scale, the greater the influence of the unconscious component of corporate ideology, and thus the greater the chance for acrimonious nonsettlement of a dispute and a concomitant buildup of fuel for the next round of confrontations. Faced with substantially identical demands from a composite black rights group, Xerox settled the issue without problem, but Kodak engaged in a wracking confrontation.[35] Kodak saw itself with a good record of minority concern but probably also possessed an unconscious attitude of nonpeer recognition for the blacks and conveyed an attitude of condescension that often goes with charity and eliminates any chance for a dialogue between equals.

Using the peer-recognition scale, and ignoring for the moment the matter of the importance of the involved issues, it would appear that environmentalists and consumer groups have the best chance of influencing corporate activities. But it is the very middle-class essence of the environmental movement that also has stamped it nonrelevant to the blacks and a "cop-out" to the radical left. Consumerists are probably farther down the peer-acceptability scale than environmentalists, but not so far down that concessions can't be obtained from corporations, albeit under duress. Use of the courts and legislation as conflict techniques make consumerists more acceptable, and the reforms they seek

---

[35] S. Prakash Sethi, *Up Against the Corporate Wall* (Englewood Cliffs: Prentice-Hall, 1971), pp. 107-28.

probably work to corporate advantage in the long run. The truth-in-lending law, for example, was strongly opposed at first but has probably been beneficial to the firms involved in lending.

Predictions of the fate of reforms sought by minority groups, when viewed in terms of the "peer-acceptability" paradigm, are apt to be pessimistic. The likelihood of the black minority's overcoming the resistance inherent in the unconscious component of corporate ideology probably depends on how long it takes for them to achieve significant economic and political power within the overall social system. I do not foresee significant changes for the present generation. Other minority groups face similar problems but will probably remain less troublesome for corporations. The geographically localized oriental and Chicano minorities are relatively small, and Jews have maintained a quiescent attitude in spite of general exclusion from top corporate posts and from some corporations altogether.

The foregoing remarks will probably be difficult for many readers to accept, particularly members of corporate organizations who in their own view have made significant attempts to change past practices toward minority groups and who have tried to make sincere accommodation to the need for improvement in environmental and consumer-oriented practices. Certainly some corporations have made enviable progress in developing new, enlightened perspectives and practices. The analysis that I have offered is not a blanket accusation; it is intended to incorporate into our understanding of corporate behavior the idea that there are at work certain unconscious factors that affect the course of corporate operations. These unconscious factors function through the personalities of all corporate employees, but mainly through the managers and owners —the corporate hierarchy. As a colleague of mine has aptly said, "corporate employees do not leave the unconscious component of their personalities behind them in the parking lot when they go into their offices in the morning." The same is true of all of us. Feelings based on early family experiences become part of the adult personality and are worked out repeatedly in many areas of an adult's life. On another level, childhood and adult experiences also become internalized and are subsequently reflected in behavior. One wonders, in this sense, whether an affluent corporate executive living in an exclusive suburb, belonging to a country club, and sending his children to an expensive private school can possibly be capable of having or developing peer-recognition patterns that permit a meaningful inclusion of minority groups in the corporate structure, when the minorities are excluded from all other forms of peer relationships. What this query suggests is that the problem is not exclusively one of corporate ideology, but of family psychology and social structure.

However, the unconscious part of corporate ideology is not always controlling, and, when the absence of peer-recognition is not fatal to the amicable solution of a problem, the "nature of the issue" and the conscious part of corporate ideology will play more dominant roles.

Corporate Ideology, Issues, and Realities

By "the nature of the issue," in the previous paragraph, I refer to the issues in terms of the stakes involved, i.e., what the corporation can lose in terms of prerogatives, autonomy, and *ego values*. It has already been noted that emotional content is a significant part of corporate ideology and will be more influential than the pure "interests" or "strains" present in some situations. Corporations can become deeply involved on a collective psychological basis, and such emotional involvement may account for aggressive, irrational behavior. The dominant position of the corporation gives it more than a proprietary interest in its prerogatives—in familial terms, it is rather a "head of the family" position, playing a father-like role in many situations to employees and even to outsiders.

Attitudes toward the corporation tend to bear this out. Veblen noted the idealization of the powerful by the less fortunate, the tendency toward approving emulation,[36] and it seems likely that his observations are still accurate with regard to much of the public's attitude toward the corporation today. Critical attitudes shown by academics and students hardly seem typical of the general public, a conclusion suggested by the lack of support for those attitudes from other sectors when the corporation is under attack. Although many factors have tended to erode general public sympathy for the labor movement, a continuing point of their weakness is that employees are still regarded as "dependents" in their employment relationship with the corporation, hence in the unenviable position of always challenging the corporate "father." Within the corporation, strong business leadership has the effect of solidifying internal authority recognitions and identifications, a vastly different view of the faceless leaders usually perceived from the outside. Since charismatic values are associated with the office as well as the man, the corporation's organizational structure creates a flexible, compelling, psychological implication of the all-powerful father figure that is transmittable from chief executive to chief executive, thus providing a strong cohesive element. When organizational ego satisfactions are involved, and, perhaps, where significant threats develop to the leadership, the need to react defensively with some violence may occur

---

36 Veblen, *Theory of the Leisure Class.*

on an unconscious level and so provide much of the real motivation for corporate behavior.

The stakes held by corporate owners and managers in the contest to control corporate actions are enormous. The value of corporate holdings and the handsome levels of executive compensation in all of its forms are thoroughly documented, and it has been observed that hired managers behave enough like owners to make little difference in behavior patterns between the two. The powerful interests of the corporate hierarchy affect their ideological perspectives of corporate prerogatives and can be expected to foster self-serving rationalizations, particularly when historically established patterns of corporate autonomy are available. It is important to realize that many of the changes being pressed on corporate executives involve *diminutions* of their authority, while the legal and historical development of the corporation, plus the nation's traditional protection of property rights, clearly supports the continued broad exercise of corporate power by the hierarchy.

It is important to realize that the American corporation developed into its present form by following but one path out of a number of alternative paths, reaching its position through a unique series of events, none of which were by any means inevitable. Nevertheless, corporate ideology in its conscious form treats its past history as if it were almost predestined. Had some of the other alternative paths been followed, the present organization, functions, and roles of the American corporation would probably now be very different from what they are. The legal form of the corporation would be different if the drive for federal incorporation laws had been realized. Asset-size limitations could have altered the oligopolistic structure of American industry. Stricter enforcement of existing antitrust laws could have prevented the extensive use of interlocking directorates. Economic planning could have been transferred to or shared with the government. But none of these "alternative pasts" occurred, and, having achieved a level of autonomy and importance at least equal to any corporations in the world, the American corporate system and its ideology treat the present roles, including participation in a wide range of extra-business activities, as fixed. The ideologically legitimized extra-business roles include support for charitable and educational institutions, active involvement in politics, lobbying, direct influence on elected officials, and ready access to regulatory agencies. American corporations do in fact behave in a manner compatible with their own historical traditions, but this does not make them immune from criticism when they exceed their authority or fail to carry out their social mandates.

The challenges presently directed at the corporate structure and its controlling hierarchy are easier to understand when viewed as an attempt to reverse the trend toward autonomy that has continued without major interruption since the 1880s. The test of corporate performance has shifted from the utilitarian approach of a previous generation toward an emphasis on the legitimate uses of corporate power. This may be seen in the current issues facing the corporation, e.g., rights of minority shareholders, adequacy of revealed corporate financial data, responsibility of directors, the use of insider information, environmental issues, minority hiring, and rights of women. Stated another way, there has been a metamorphosis in the acceptance of the corporation from the earlier idea of utility to contemporary standards of legitimacy and responsibility.[37]

The attempt in our own time to reverse the rapid expansion of corporate power and authority is a traumatic event for the corporate hierarchy and a source of dissonance for a conscious ideology based on the mythical adaptations of the experience of the historical past. The extent of this "shock" ought not to be minimized, since it constitutes a major challenge to the reality perception of the corporation relative to its organization, functions, and roles. For several reasons, a bitter struggle can be expected from corporations to retain their present status. Existing corporate ideology supports feelings of personal worth and purpose, as well as providing enviable individual privileges, power, and wealth. Change has not been wholly lacking in the past, but the ways in which corporations are being asked to change today amount to an abrupt reversal of precedent and will be resisted. The teachings of history and psychology support this conclusion, and I would foresee a period of more intense conflict between the corporation and society in the future.

CONCLUDING REMARKS

Some recent literature indicates that corporations may be subject to change under pressure from new internal and external sources. Charles A. Reich has popularized the notion that the influx into corporations of socially oriented youth will change corporate ideology.[38] Daniel Bell has suggested that, as the nation matures, new emphasis and agreement on goals will produce important changes in the means

---

[37] James Willard Hurst, *The Legitimacy of the Business Corporation in the Law of the U.S., 1790-1970* (Charlottesville: The University Press of Virginia, 1970), 109-11.

[38] Charles A. Reich, *The Greening of America* (New York: Random House, 1970).

of resolving present social conflicts.[39] Both views suggest a long-run process, and are based on a somewhat utopian approach. Youth *may* save the situation, but it is unclear whether socially oriented youth are entering the corporate world, and there is no accurate forecast of what will happen to *their* ideology once they become part of that world.

As far as a concern with long-range goals is concerned, one could make the argument that long-range goals are usually a part of the resolution of social conflict, and that the important thing to look for is a *change* in those goals. In any case, corporate ideology is likely to opt for a maintenance of the status quo. This conclusion is important, because it suggests that little of real substance in a societal sense can be expected of the apparent commitment to corporate social responsibility, as long as responsibility is determined and implemented by the corporation itself. Since the discretionary scope of the corporation is what is presently being questioned, the issue of corporate social responsibility may be superfluous, and the analysis of corporate behavior may properly be directed to the real issue: the legitimate uses of corporate power.[40]

It is in the analysis of corporate legitimacy that the understanding of the nature and effects of corporate ideology is most useful. This review of corporate ideology has indicated that corporations have personalities which reflect the conscious and unconscious values of the corporate hierarchy and that the hierarchy is unaware of the unconscious aspect of its motivations, but finds it useful to assume rationality as the basis for all decisions. When conflict situations become predominantly emotional, the corporate unconscious is likely to prevail in directing corporate decisions but will always attribute the decision to a rational process. A corporation acting on the basis of unconscious motivation may pose a threat to the social system because of the far-reaching consequences of its acts, e.g., the continuing exclusion of minorities and women from corporate participation. Thus, it is appropriate that corporations be required to account for their behavior through the process of public examination.

The structure of corporate ideology in its conscious and unconscious components is extremely rigid and too ingrained to be likely to change without a great deal of pressure. Perhaps one of the most crucial problems is the inability of the hierarchy to question its assumptions regarding the role of the corporation. This leads to the conclusion that, if corporate behavior is to become more flexible in the future, it will

---

39 Daniel Bell, "The Corporation and Society in the 1970's," *Public Interest,* 42 (Summer 1971), 5-31.

40 See a different view of this matter in Part II.

not result from the application of present ideology or from expected changes in that in the near future. Business ideology reflects personal ideology, but changes in personal ideology do not occur without the opportunity for reexamination of personal motivation that is associated with long, tedious, and not always successful individual therapy. In any event, it is unrealistic to imagine that the corporate hierarchy will engage in such a self-examination. The chances for a revision of corporate ideology based on a sophisticated, scholarly reappraisal of American corporate history by the hierarchy is no more likely than mass therapy.

The question is not what will create a change in corporate ideology, but whether change is possible at all. Solidification of corporate ideology in its present form may lead to a series of social encounters that take us over a cliff, and there have been societies that have gone over cliffs because their institutional structures and supporting ideologies became petrified. The question of whether American institutional structures have frozen is beyond the scope of this article. Nevertheless, the answer to that question requires an understanding of the nature and effect of ideology. In the short *and* the long run, I would see the greatest possibility for change in corporate ideology stemming from continuing confrontations of the corporation with other areas of society. This does not need to mean bombs and broken windows, but rather face-to-face encounters where one group is required to defend its behavior relative to the interests of another group. Some of the issues that will provide this arena are presently with us: pollution, minority relations, attitudes toward women, and corporate influence upon the political structure. Other issues are around the corner: corporate internal employment policies, free speech within the corporation,[41] rigid systems of authority relations, and the use of corporate assets to influence public opinion. All involve the permissible exercise of the right of private property ownership, and it is reasonable to expect that some of these issues will eventually be resolved, as others have in the past. The present generation of the corporate hierarchy will react negatively to these issues and perhaps real progress *will* have to await the presence of a new generation. Thomas Kuhn notes that holders of older scientific paradigms don't discard them in favor of newer paradigms, but that new ideas become accepted as the older generation of scientists die out.[42] The same may be true of businessmen. Thus, it may be that real changes in corporate ideology will be a function of both confrontations and time.

---

41 See Part IV.

42 Thomas S. Kuhn, *The Structure of Scientific Revolutions* (Chicago: University of Chicago Press, 1962).

PART FOUR

The Corporation
and
The Individual

COMMENT

Traditional values and ideologies are nowhere more frustrated and no-where produce more dissonance than with respect to the relationship between the corporation and those groups which are vitally affected by its activities. Whether the groups affected are employees, consumers, lenders, suppliers, or those who share the same air, water, and tax fund, the received model of the corporation, together with its conventional values and ideologies, is in conflict with rapidly changing views of the corporation itself and of its relationships to these groups. "New voices" are pressing to be heard; new standards of corporate behavior are being urged; new principles are pushing their way in among the old. But there is nothing new about an encounter between traditional values and change. That clash is as old as human society. Yet there is something different about the speed of social change today and about the bewild-ering array of forms in which it appears. Traditional values and ideolo-gies are probably being met now with more rapid and more varied change than ever before in history. The corporation, because of its prominent role in our society, is in the very forefront of the conflict.

Basic to all of the changes bearing in upon the modern corporation is a changing view of the social role of the corporation itself. It seems no longer to be possible to regard the great corporation as a strictly economic institution operated for the exclusive benefit of its "owners," and it is likely that most corporate leaders are altering their perceptions of the corporation in this respect. Yet, to alter one's perceptions in one respect is not immediately to see all the implications and all the changes

77

which may ultimately become necessary as a result of so doing. Corporate leaders and the rest of society, for many years to come, will be searching and groping for the meaning and implications of these changes.

The particular area which we have selected for treatment in Part IV is concerned with the impact of the new view of the corporation upon traditional concepts of the duties of loyalty and obedience of the employee to his employer. This subject is a subcategory of a subcategory, no matter how one may choose to organize the material, but it is especially appropriate for inclusion here, for several reasons, not the least of which is the availability of Professor Blumberg's excellent article. Most important, however, are its implications for changes in the organization of corporations, a subject afforded considerable prominence in Part II, and its potential for bringing about far-reaching changes in legal concepts. Another reason for singling it out is that it is now in a rather early stage of development, and most of its dimensions can be described without unwieldy commitments of time, space, or detail. Furthermore, its intimate relationship with new concepts of social responsibility and with the dynamics of corporate ideology, together with the informative way in which it illustrates the confrontation between traditional values and contemporary problems, makes it a particularly meaningful part of this book. While Part IV concerns itself with the individual as a part of the internal structure of the corporation, Part V will examine two external groups whose relationships to the corporation have substantially altered in recent years but whose changing roles are again illustrative of the impact of the new view of the corporation.

Although the subject of the employee's duty of loyalty and obedience is relatively well defined and of manageable size, the issue is actually very complex, whether one is speaking legally or socially. Its trails lead to the Constitution, to concepts of property and ownership, to deeply rooted beliefs about the relationship between master and servant, to varying concepts of man himself, and, not least of all, to the socially responsible conduct of the corporate employer. Neither in this "comment" nor in Blumberg's article are all of these traced thoroughly or even identified. The volume of literature and court decisions in this area is growing very rapidly, but much still remains to be explored.

One of the paradoxes of modern American society is found in the fact that one of our most important institutions, whose actions may affect more profoundly the lives of more people than the actions of the state, whose role in governance, if exceeded at all, is exceeded only by the state, is not explicitly a part of the governing framework laid down in the Constitution or subject to the limitations there imposed. It has been speculated that were the federal Constitution being drafted today, it could not help but take expressly into account the role of the modern corporation. Certainly one result of the absence of this recognition in our Constitution is the attempt through court decisions to define the status of corporate activities under the Constitution through such doctrines as "public interest," or "public function," or "public figure." In *Marsh* v. *Alabama*,[1] for example, the Supreme Court ruled that where a corporation had assumed such "public functions" as owning and operating a town, it came under the purview of certain constitutional limitations, including those having to do with free speech. The theory apparently was that operating a town constituted "state action" and subjected the corporation to appropriate limitations in this regard.

Other factors come to bear here, and the reader may want to explore them on his own. One of the most important of them is a phenomenon documented by many observers who see a blurring of the line between public and private authority in the industrial system or an "emerging partnership" between business and government.[2] If these developments are taking place and continue to do so, determined efforts to bring about judicial expansion of the concept of state action may become unnecessary. One cannot say where all of this will lead, as far as the relationship between the individual and the corporation is concerned, but there does appear to be a strong trend toward a closer association between business and government and toward a frank recognition of that change. Wholly apart from any manifest trend which may be involved are the observations by such people as Galbraith, Dahl, and Hacker that to draw sharp distinctions between a large corporation on one hand and a state government on the other, on the basis of their "publicness" and "privateness," may not make very much sense.[3]

Some recent cases have made it reasonably clear that governmental employers cannot deny their employees freedom of speech.[4] An important question now at issue is: When can corporate employees complain that their constitutional right to freedom of speech has been denied them by their employer? [5] Many traditional values and ideologies will be shaken before this question is answered, but the process has already begun. The then traditional values with respect to the free speech rights of govern-

---

[1] 326 U.S. 501 (1946).

[2] See J. K. Galbraith, *The New Industrial State* (Boston: Houghton Mifflin Co., 1967), Ch. XXVI; Robert Dahl, *After the Revolution?* (New Haven: Yale University Press, 1970), p. 120; Andrew Hacker, ed., *The Corporation Take-Over* (Garden City, New York: Anchor Books, 1965), Ch. 1.

[3] *Ibid.*

[4] See especially *Pickering* v. *Board of Education*, 391 U.S. 563 (1968).

[5] Kenneth D. Walters in an as yet unpublished Ph.D. dissertation does an excellent job of exploring this issue; "Freedom of Speech in the Modern Corporation," Graduate School of Business Administration, University of California, Berkeley, 1972.

mental employees were undoubtedly expressed by Justice Holmes in 1892 when he uttered his famous dictum in *McAuliffe* v. *Mayor of New Bedford* to the effect that a discharged policeman

> may have a constitutional right to talk politics, but he has no constitutional right to be a policeman. There are few employments for hire in which the servant does not agree to suspend his constitutional right of free speech, as well as of idleness, by the implied terms of his contract.[6]

But, in 1968, "the Supreme Court put to rest such outgrown shibboleths." [7]

The traditional values with regard to corporate employees are even more deeply imbedded in our culture, however, and the effect of their collision with a changing society will be more shattering. Just barely starting to erode is the traditional ideology which holds that, absent specific law or contract provision, an employee may be discharged for good cause, bad cause, or no cause at all. Disloyalty to the employer or to the employer's interest has been described as "private treason." [8] Yet other currents are at work in society. Some priorities, including certain constitutional rights, are being placed ahead of economic and property interests, and some organizational theorists are even suggesting that such rigid concepts of organizational loyalty may only guarantee bureaucratic totalitarianism.[9] Mason Haire has urged on us a "new concept of man" which would have profound impacts on traditional duties of employee loyalty and obedience.[10] Richard Eells [11] and Jay W. Forrester [12] have both proposed new kinds of corporate constitutionalism which include strong elements of free speech and other fundamental rights.

Developments in the area of free speech for governmental employees underline the conclusion that while confusion and frustration usually accompany clashes between traditional values and contemporary social

---

6 155 Mass. 216, 220, 29 N.E. 517-518 (1892).

7 *London* v. *Florida Department of Health,* 448 F.2d 456 (1971), in referring to the Supreme Court's decision in *Pickering* v. *Board of Education,* 391 U.S. 563 (1968).

8 *Wise* v. *Southern Pacific Co.,* 272 Cal. App. 2d 257, 268 (1969).

9 Clark Kerr, *Labor and Management in Industrial Society* (Garden City, New York: Anchor Books, 1964), p. 82; Philip Selznick, *Law, Society, and Industrial Justice* (Russell Sage Foundation, 1969), pp. 41-43.

10 Mason Haire, "The Concept of Power and the Concept of Man," in *Social Science Approaches to Business Behavior,* George B. Strother, ed. (Homewood, Illinois: Richard D. Irwin, Inc., 1962).

11 Richard Eells, *The Government of Corporations* (New York: The Free Press, 1962).

12 Jay W. Forrester, "A New Corporate Design," *Industrial Management Review,* Vol. VII (Fall 1965).

problems, the ultimate result need be neither frustrating nor irresponsible. As Walters has pointed out:

> . . . the courts have creatively and responsibly dealt with the problems of formulating a policy of freedom of speech for employees in modern bureaucracies. The policy reflects a concern for the individual employee's rights to free speech, but also recognizes the legitimate requirements of organization.[13]

Obviously, the courts will not be the only dynamic factor involved in the evolution of the relation between the great corporation and its individual employees, but they will probably play an important role in mitigating the trauma of change as well as helping to bring about change.

Professor Blumberg uses as the core of his discussion the right of the employee of the large public corporation to take action adverse to the interests of his employer in response to the employee's view as to the proper social responsibility of his corporate employer. His point of departure is Ralph Nader's recent "whistle-blowing" proposal and two episodes involving Eastern Airlines and the Polaroid Corporation. Blumberg's primary concern is with the extent to which the new interest in a responsibility to society has changed the nature of the employee's obligations to his employer. Although Blumberg's approach is largely a legal one, his interests, knowledge, and expertise are clearly much broader than the law, and his conclusions have a bearing on the social, political, organizational, and personal aspects of the problem as well.

---

[13] Walters, *op. cit. supra* at note 5, ch. 10, p. 2.

CORPORATE RESPONSIBILITY AND THE EMPLOYEE'S DUTY
OF LOYALTY AND OBEDIENCE:
A PRELIMINARY INQUIRY

Phillip I. Blumberg *

I. INTRODUCTION

The nature of the American corporate world is changing, reflecting changing concepts of the objectives, role and responsibilities of business. The public corporation as a social and economic organization is undergoing a process of re-examination which has not yet run its course, and the ultimate outcome of which one may still not safely predict. There is general acceptance of the concept of corporate social responsibility with the major public corporation assuming a role of increasing significance in social problem solving. Although highly controversial and not generally accepted, there is also increasing expression of a new view of the large American corporation as a social institution to achieve social objectives, rather than as an economic institution to be operated for economic objectives for the benefit of shareholders. It is inevitable, therefore, that as a corollary, new views will also emerge with respect to the changing relationship between the corporation and the groups vitally affected by it, particularly its employees, as well as such other groups as consumers, suppliers, and the public generally.

II. THREE RECENT DEVELOPMENTS

This article constitutes a preliminary inquiry into aspects of a problem that the author believes will become an area of dynamic change in the corporate organization and in time will produce significant change in established legal concepts. It is concerned with the impact of the new view of the corporation upon traditional concepts of the duties of loyalty and obedience of the employee to his employer, firmly recognized in the law of agency. This impact has been illustrated by a number of recent developments, which have a common core: the right of the employee of the large public corporation to take action adverse to the interests of

---

* Professor of Law, Boston University School of Law. Reprinted from *Oklahoma Law Review*, Vol. 24, Number 3, August 1971, with permission of author and publisher. Copyright 1971. A few paragraphs of text and most footnotes have been omitted.

his employer in response to the employee's view as to the proper social responsibility of his corporate employer.

A. The "Public Interest Disclosure" Proposal

The outstanding example, which will serve as the major topic of this article, is the recent appeal of Mr. Ralph Nader that "professional" employees of corporations, as well as of government, disclose to private agencies information about their "employers' policies or practices that they consider harmful to public or consumer interests." [1] Mr. Nader simultaneously announced the establishment of a "Clearing House for Professional Responsibility" to solicit and receive such reports and to encourage what Mr. Nader termed "responsible whistle-blowing" by scientists, engineers, and other professional employees, and to protect employees acting as informants or tipsters from retaliation by employers. Mr. Nader originally stated his program in terms of professionalism: professional ethics should take precedence over loyalty to employers when the public interest is at stake. Although this initial statement rested on an appeal to a professional responsibility, Mr. Nader's broad reference to harm to "public or consumer interests" was apparently restricted to cases where the employer's behavior was "illegal, hazardous, or unconscionable." [2]

Subsequently, Mr. Nader substantially broadened the scope of his appeal for disclosure of confidential information by employees. He included all employees, not merely professional employees, and extended the area of disclosure to a wide range of information, going far beyond the original restrictions of unprofessional conduct or "illegal, hazardous, or unconscionable" behavior. The *New York Times* reported:

> One way Nader sees to alleviate the problem of individual responsibility in the bureaucracies of both the Government and corporations is to turn what he calls "whistle blowing" into an honorable action. "A whistle blower," says Nader, "is anyone in any organization who draws a line on his own account where responsibility to society transcends responsibility to his organization." [3]

---

1 *New York Times,* Jan. 27, 1971, p. 32, col. 3.

2 *New York Times,* Jan. 15, 1971, p. 43, col. 2,

3 *New York Times,* Mar. 21, 1971, § 6, p. 16, col. 5. For a detailed account of the experiences of nine "whistle blowers" honored at a conference sponsored by Mr. Nader, see Branch, "Courage Without Esteem: Profiles In Whistle Blowing," *Washington Monthly,* May 1971, p. 23. It may be noted that only one of the case studies involved a corporation and that particular case pertained to a government-financed project in Peru.

Thus, the test has become a personal decision by each employee "where responsibility to society transcends responsibility to his organization." It is clear that Mr. Nader wishes to encourage the "corporate leak" to facilitate efforts of so-called "public interest" organizations in publicizing actions by the major power centers in the society—whether governmental or corporate—not deemed to be in the public interest.

In brief, any person in any organization, who disagrees with a decision of his superiors in the social or environmental area is encouraged to continue the campaign (which he lost, or in which he did not have an opportunity to participate within his own organization) in the public arena via disclosure to a "public interest" organization.

Mr. James M. Roche, Chairman of General Motors Corporation, promptly attacked the proposal, stating:

> Some of the enemies of business now encourage an employee to be disloyal to the enterprise. They want to create suspicion and disharmony and pry into the proprietary interests of the business. However this is labelled—industrial espionage, whistle blowing or professional responsibility—it is another tactic for spreading disunity and creating conflict.[4]

Thus, the question arises: What is the duty of the employee to his employer? To what extent, if any, has a heightened sense of a responsibility to society—on the employee level as well as on the corporate level—changed the nature of the employee's obligations to his employer?

B. Eastern Airlines

Another example involves Eastern Airlines. The airline's procedure required pilots shortly after takeoff to jettison in the atmosphere about three gallons of excess fuel in holding tanks remaining from the previous run. A senior pilot of thirty years' experience had repeatedly requested the draining of the tanks on the ground by mechanics because of his concern of the impact of the practice on air pollution. Eastern management had refused. The pilot thereupon violated the regulation and had the kerosene drained while on the ground. Eastern maintained that "each of its 3,700 pilots cannot make his own rules" and discharged the pilot. After considerable publicity (and pressure from the Airline Pilots Association), Eastern reinstated the pilot. It subsequently went further and announced that it was endeavoring to have manufacturers develop engines to eliminate the problem by allowing excess fuel to return to the regular fuel tanks.[5]

---

4 *New York Times,* Mar. 26, 1971, p. 53, col. 5.

5 *Time,* Nov. 2, 1970, p. 40; *Boston Globe,* Nov. 8, 1970, p. 2, col. 3.

C. Polaroid Corporation

A third example relates to the efforts of what appears to be a small number of black employees of Polaroid Corporation, calling themselves the Polaroid Revolutionary Workers Movement, to force Polaroid to cease doing business in South Africa by "confrontation" techniques including a boycott of Polaroid products and by picketing, disruptions and demonstrations. Polaroid responded on a number of levels, including the use of an advisory committee of employees, including black employees, who visited South Africa. The aspect of the episode with which we are concerned is the action of Polaroid management in eventually suspending one of the leaders of the Movement without pay for her "persistent activities in fomenting public disapproval" of the firm and for being "involved in a deliberate campaign calculated to damage the well being" of the company.[6]

Still another reflection of changing views as to the traditional duties of loyalty and obedience of employees is the following glimpse of the corporate future depicted in Mr. Anthony Athos' article in the *Harvard Business Review* entitled "Is the Corporation Next to Die?"

> "Within five years a president of a major corporation will be locked out of his office by his junior executives," remarked George Koch, president of the Grocery Manufacturers Association, not long ago. The very idea would have seemed outrageous and impossible only a few years ago . . . the situation is rapidly becoming ripe for the kind of action Koch predicts.[7]

The foregoing illustrations of the present and possible future world of the corporate employee require a reexamination of the traditional fundamental concepts of the employer-employee relationship: the employee's duties of loyalty and obedience to the employer, and the employer's freedom to discharge an employee. They reflect a new view of responsibility—a view that the employee's duty as a citizen transcends his duties as employee. This is a companion view to the basic tenet of the "public interest proxy campaign," such as Campaign GM, that the shareholder's interest as a citizen transcends his interest as a shareholder, and that he should act primarily for the good of the country—i.e., the

---

[6] *Boston Globe,* Oct. 18, 1970, p. 64, col. 2, Nov. 1, 1970, p. B-31, col. 3, Nov. 25, 1970, p. 7, Feb. 11, 1971, p. 3, col. 1; *New York Times,* Jan. 13, 1971, p. 9, col. 1, p. 23, Feb. 21, 1971, p. 17, col. 1; *Business Week,* Nov. 14, 1970, p. 32; *Newsweek,* Jan. 25, 1971.

[7] Athos, "Is the Corporation Next to Die?" *Harvard Business Review,* Mar.–Apr. 1970, pp. 49-50.

public interest—rather than for the good of the company.[8] These examples may also involve a different concept, the view that employees should play a part in the corporate decision-making process, at least in issues of public concern involving questions of corporate social responsibility.

These views—so profoundly changed from traditional values—reflect the politicalization of the corporation, which the author has discussed elsewhere.[9]

III. THE RESTATEMENT OF AGENCY

A review of the relevant provisions of the *Restatement of Agency* provides an obvious starting point for consideration of the new view of the role and duties of the employee.[10]

A. The Duty of Obedience

Section 383 and *Section 385* state the agent's duty to obey the principal. Section 385(1) imposes upon the agent "a duty to obey all reasonable directions" of the principal.[11] Comment *a* points out:

> In determining whether or not the orders of the principal to the agent are reasonable . . . *business or professional ethics* . . . are considered. [emphasis added]

Comment *a* continues:

> In no event would it be implied that an agent has a duty to perform acts which . . . are *illegal or unethical. . . .* [emphasis added]

Thus, Comment *a* expressly excludes matters contrary to "business or professional ethics" or "illegal or unethical" acts from those which an agent would be required to perform. This frees the agent from participation in such behavior and authorizes him to withdraw from the agency relation if the principal persists. It in no way authorizes him to disclose such directions of the principal, or not to comply with

---

8 See Schwartz, "The Public-Interest Proxy Contest: Reflections on Campaign GM," *Michigan Law Review* 69 (1971): 419, 480; *Campaign GM Round I,* proxy statement dated Nov. 19, 1970, pp. 1, 2.

9 Blumberg, "The Politicalization of the Corporation," *Business Lawyer* 26 (1971): 1551.

10 For the purposes of this paper, "agent" should be regarded as interchangeable with "employee."

11 *Restatement (Second) of Agency* (1958), § 385(1) (hereinafter cited as *Restatement*).

an instruction of the principal not to disclose any information about the principal's affairs, even in those cases where he is privileged not to perform in accordance with the principal's instructions. The duty exists not only so long as the agent remains an agent but continues after the agency has been terminated as well.

Section 385(2) provides:

> (2) Unless he is privileged to protect his own or another's interests, an agent is subject to a duty not to act in matters entrusted to him on account of the principal contrary to the directions of the principal. . . .

The Comments make it clear that "an interest" which the agent is privileged to protect refers only to an economic interest, such as a lien or his business reputation. There is no suggestion that an interest which "he is privileged to protect" includes the public interest.

B. The Duty of Loyalty

Section 387 expresses the general principle that:

> an agent is subject to a duty to his principal to act solely for the benefit of the principal in all matters connected with his agency.

Comment *b* emphasizes the high degree of the duties of loyalty of the agent by stating that they "are the same as those of a trustee to his beneficiaries." It provides, however, that:

> The agent is also under a duty not to act or speak disloyally . . . except in the protection of his own interests or those of others. He is not, however, necessarily prevented from acting in good faith outside his employment in a manner which injuriously affects his principal's business.

and provides the following illustration:

> 3. A, employed by P, a life insurance company, in good faith advocates legislation which would require a change in the policies issued by the company. A has violated no duty to P.

Thus, the agent is free to act "in good faith outside his employment," even in a manner which injures his principal's business, but is subject to a duty identical with that of a trustee with respect to "all matters connected with his agency." Under the comment and illustration, the General Motors employee may campaign in good faith for legislation imposing costly antipollution or product safety controls on automobile manufacturers, but he occupies a position equivalent to a

trustee with respect to information about General Motors operations
which he has acquired in the course, or on account, of his employment.

Section 394 prohibits the agent from acting:

> for persons whose interests conflict with those of the principal in
> matters in which the agent is employed.

The numerous examples in the comments relate to competitors or
adverse parties in commercial transactions or parties with adverse claims
and make it plain that the reference to conflicting "interests" means
economic interests.

C. The Duty of Confidentiality

Section 395 imposes a duty upon the agent:

> not to use or to communicate information confidentially given him
> by the principal or acquired by him during the course of or on ac-
> count of his agency . . . to the injury of the principal, on his own
> account or on behalf of another . . . unless the information is a
> matter of general knowledge.

Comment *a* emphasizes that the agency relation "permits and
requires great freedom of communication between the principal and
the agent." It expands the agent's duty by stating that the agent:

> also has a duty not to use information acquired by him as agent . . .
> for any purpose likely to cause his principal harm or to interfere
> with his business, although it is information not connected with the
> subject matter of his agency.

Comment *b* extends the duty beyond "confidential" communications to "information which the agent should know his principal would
not care to have revealed to others." Both Comments *a* and *b* refer to
protection of the principal against competition, but it is clear that this
is merely one of the interests of the principal protected by the section.

Comment *f* creates a privilege, significantly enough for a public,
not an economic, interest:

> An agent is privileged to reveal information confidentially acquired
> . . . in the protection of a superior interest of himself or of a third
> person. Thus, if the confidential information is to the effect that the
> principal is committing or is about to commit a crime, the agent is
> under no duty not to reveal it.

This is the only illustration in the *Restatement* that the term "interest"
may embrace something of a noneconomic nature. The public interest

in law enforcement is deemed a "superior interest" giving rise to a privilege to reveal otherwise confidential information.

If construed to include disclosure to any person, and not solely to law enforcement agencies, Comment *f* would support the "public interest disclosure" proposal to the extent it relates to "illegal" matters, without regard to the nature or seriousness of the offense. Section 395, Comment *f*, however, refers only to commission of a "crime." This contrasts with Section 385 (1) relating to the duty of obedience which refers not only to "illegal" but also to "unethical" acts and to "business or professional ethics." The inclusion of these latter elements in Section 385(1) and their omission in Section 395 would indicate that the release of confidential information privileged under Section 395 does not extend beyond criminal acts.

Although Section 395 refers only to the agent's use or communication of information "on his own account or on behalf of another" and does not literally prohibit use or communication of such information for the benefit of the public, Comment *a* prohibits such use "for any purpose likely to cause his principal harm or to interfere with his business." Comment *a* thus would appear to expand the duty of the agent beyond acts "on his own account or on behalf of another" to include disclosures made to advance the "public interest," which were not related to commission of a "crime" privileged under Comment *f*.

D. Privileged Conduct

Section 411 makes "illegality" a defense for an agent's nonperformance. Comment *d* extends the defense to acts:

> which are criminal . . . [or] although not criminal, are so contrary to public policy that an agreement to perform them will not be enforced.

This follows the common-law rule that the principal cannot complain of the agent's failure to enter into agreements which would have been unenforceable, since even if the agent had performed, the principal would not have been able to enforce the agreement made by the agent.[12]

Section 411, referring to "illegality" or acts which are "criminal" or "contrary to public policy" closely, but not precisely, follows Section 385(1), Comment *a*, which refers to "illegal or unethical" acts. Both

---

12 *Thomas Cheshire and Co.* v. *Vaughan Bros. and Co.* [1920] 3 K.B. 240 (C.A. 1920); *Cohen* v. *Kittell*, 22 Q.B.D. 680 (1889); *Webster* v. *DeTastet*, 7 Term Rep. 157 (1797); see F. Tiffany, *Handbook of the Law of Principal and Agent*, 2nd ed. (1924), p. 376; W. Paley, *Law of Principal and Agency* (1856), p. 8.

Sections 411 and 385(2) dealing with the agent's privileged refusal to act contrast with Section 395 dealing with privileged disclosure which is restricted solely to "crime." [13]

Section 418 confirms the exception contained in Section 385 that:

> An agent is privileged to protect interests of his own which are superior to those of the principal, even though he does so at the expense of the principal's interests or in disobedience to his orders.

Again, the crucial question is the meaning to be ascribed to "interests." Comment *a* contains the usual emphasis on the agent's economic interests. As in the case of Section 385(2), Section 418, Comment *a* permits the agent to perform a contract unenforceable under the Statute of Frauds "to protect his financial interests or reputation" or to protect "a security interest in the principal's goods."

Comment *a* also provides that:

> Similarly the agent has no duty to commit a tort or a minor crime at the command of the principal.

This reference to "tort or a minor crime" may be compared with the references to "illegal or unethical" acts in Section 385(1), Comment *a,* and to acts which are "criminal" or "contrary to public policy" in Section 411 dealing with essentially the same problem.

In summary, except in the single area of "crime," the *Restatement* provides no support for the view that the employee may disclose non-public information about his employer acquired as a result of the employment relationship in order to promote the superior interest of society. While prohibiting affirmative acts of the employee such as disclosure, the *Restatement* relieves the employee of any duty to obey or act for the employer not only in the case of "crime" or "illegality" but also in case of "unethical acts" or acts "contrary to public policy" or constituting a tort.

The duties of obedience, loyalty, and confidentiality enunciated by the *Restatement* and the carefully circumscribed privileged exceptions clearly proscribe the "public interest disclosure" proposal suggested by Mr. Nader. We must recognize, however, that the *Restatement* drawn from the common-law cases is drafted in terms of economic activity, economic motivation, and economic advantage and formulates duties of loyalty and obedience for the agent to prevent the agent's own economic interests from impairing his judgment, zeal, or single-minded devotion

---

[13] It is possible to envision an act which is "illegal" but not a "crime." There is no indication that the draftsmen of the *Restatement* were attempting to make such a distinction.

to the furtherance of his principal's economic interests. The reference in section 395, Comment *f* permitting the agent to disclose confidential information concerning a criminal act committed or planned by the principal is the sole exception to a system of analysis that is otherwise exclusively concerned with matters relating to the economic position of the parties. Thus, the question may fairly be asked to what extent the *Restatement* and the common-law decisions are useful in the analysis of a proposal that rests on the concept of an agent's primary obligation as a citizen to the society, transcending his economic duty to the principal.

Are doctrines resting on a policy of protecting the economic position of the principal against impairment by reason of an agent's effort to achieve economic gain properly applicable to the employee who releases nonpublic information about his employer without intent to obtain economic advantage for himself—and in fact at considerable economic risk to himself—and motivated by a desire to promote the public good rather than to injure the principal (although such injury may in fact result)?

The duties of loyalty and obedience on the part of the agent are unquestionably central to the agency relationship, irrespective of economic considerations. But these duties, as the *Restatement* itself recognizes, have limitations. To paraphrase Mr. Justice Frankfurter's well-known admonition: [14] To say that an agent has duties of loyalty and obedience only begins analysis; it gives direction to further inquiry. It is thus not enough to say that the agent has duties of loyalty and obedience which will be impaired. One must inquire more deeply and ascertain the outer perimeter of the agent's obligations by balancing the conflicting considerations. On this critical question of how far the duties of loyalty and obedience extend, the *Restatement* enunciating the traditional rules in their economic setting provides limited guidance.

IV. THE ENGLISH VIEW OF UNAUTHORIZED DISCLOSURE

In contrast to the *Restatement of Agency,* a 1967 English case, *Initial Services, Ltd.* v. *Putterill,*[15] provides substantial support for the "public interest disclosure" proposal. The *Initial Services* case involved the acts of a sales manager of a linen supply firm who gave two-weeks

---

14 See Mr. Justice Frankfurter in *SEC* v. *Chenery Corp.,* 318 U.S. 80, 85-86, 63 S.Ct. 454, 458, 87 L.Ed. 626, 632 (1943).

15 [1967] 3 W.L.R. 1032, 84 *Law Quarterly Review* 8 (1968).

notice and left employment on August 31, 1966, taking with him documents belonging to his employer. He delivered the documents to report-
ers for the *Daily Mail* [16] and disclosed that the employer was participating with competitors in price-fixing and was deceiving the public by
asserting in circulars to customers that price increases were necessary to
offset a newly imposed tax whereas they were in fact producing substantially increased profits for the firm. On September 1, 1966, these facts
appeared in a front-page story in the *Daily Mail;* a follow-up story appeared on September 2, 1966.

In suing on September 2, 1966 for damages for breach of confidential information, injunctive relief and return of the documents, the linen
supply firm contended that every employment relationship implied an
obligation upon the employee not to disclose information or documents
received in confidence.

The employee defended on the grounds that the price-fixing agreement was subject to the Restrictive Trade Practice Act, 1956, and should
have been registered under the Act, that the agreement should have been
referred to the Monopolies Commission pursuant to the Monopolies and
Merger Act, 1965, and that the circulars to customers were misleading to
the public, and that, therefore, disclosure to advance the public interest
was not actionable.

The opinions in *Initial Services* must be read in the procedural
context. The case arose on the pleadings, and Lord Salmon pointed out
that "in order to succeed . . . the plaintiff would have to satisfy the
court that this defense is unarguable and has no chance of succeeding."
The Court was not so persuaded and sent the case back for trial. The
language in the opinions, however, provides substantial support for the
"public interest disclosure" proposal. The recognition that the privilege
to disclose confidential information is not restricted to "crime or fraud,"
but includes "inquiry" and Lord Denning's test of the "public interest"
in disclosure of the employer's conduct move well beyond the confines
of the *Restatement of Agency* in the direction of the "public interest
disclosure" proposal. Further, the opinions of Lords Salmon and Winn
indicating that disclosure, if justified, could be made to others than
governmental authorities supports the utilization of a "public interest
clearing house" as the conduit for disclosure.

---

[16] The facts of the *Initial Services* case in this respect resemble two actions
against Drew Pearson involving his use of confidential documents disclosed by the
plaintiff's employee: *Pearson* v. *Dodd,* 410 F.2d 701 (D.C. Cir. 1969) (*cert. denied*) 395
U.S. 947, 89 S.Ct. 2021, 23 L.Ed.2d 465 (1969) (damages denied); and *Liberty Lobby,
Inc.* v. *Pearson,* 261 F. Supp. 726 (D.D.C. 1966) (injunction denied). Neither case considered the liability, if any, of the employee.

It should be noted, however, that the conduct which was disclosed in the *Initial Services* case included: (a) a price-fixing agreement which a statute required to be disclosed in any event so that the defendants' acts were not only implementing the public policy underlying the statute but arguably did not involve confidential information at all; and (b) false circulars to customers, which the Court readily found to be at least arguable as an iniquitous trade practice.

Thus, the facts of the case stop well short of the "responsibility to society" used by Mr. Nader as a bench mark, but an extension of the perimeters of "crime or fraud" to "inquiry" and the introduction of a concept of the "public interest" would clearly widen substantially the area of permissible disclosure.

In reviewing the *Initial Services* case, an English commentator noted:

> The effect of this case will be to put at risk all employers whose conduct is against the public interest and it will protect all employees who take reasonable steps to safeguard this public interest by making the "iniquity" known. The employer who uses sharp practices . . . may well have cause to rue his honest servants.[17]

Whether the Court of Appeal would have reached the same conclusion after trial and whether the opinions of the judges will be followed by American courts remain open questions.

V. MISPRISION OF FELONY

The recognition of Section 395, Comment *f,* of the *Restatement* that the duty of confidentiality does not prevent the agent from releasing confidential information about his employer's actual or potential criminal conduct rests on the citizen's responsibility for law enforcement. At the common law, a person who saw the commission of a felony or knew that a felony had been committed and possessed information that would lead to apprehension of the offender and failed to communicate such information to the proper authorities was guilty of a misdemeanor known as misprision of felony.

For decades, this common-law offense was regarded as "practically obsolete"[18] or even "non-existent,"[19] and the federal act adopted in

---

[17] See North, "Further Disclosures of Confidential Information," *Journal of Business Law,* 1968, p. 39.

[18] J. Stephen, *History of Criminal Law* (1883), p. 238.

[19] *United States* v. *Worcester,* 190 F. Supp. 548, 565-66 (D. Mass. 1960).

1790 making the offense a statutory crime was moribund.[20] In recent years, however, the doctrine has demonstrated considerable vitality. Following six successful prosecutions in England [21] and one in Australia [22] in the period from 1938 to 1961, the House of Lords in the *Sykes* case [23] ended further debate by upholding the existence of the offense as a common-law crime. Similarly, there have been numerous recent cases under the federal statute as well.[24]

In jurisdictions where proof of affirmative concealment is not regarded as an element of the offense, the philosophy underlying the misprision of felony doctrine expresses a principle of public policy that supports the "public interest disclosure" proposal. Both rest on the social importance of citizens aiding law enforcement agencies through the reporting of crime. Unlike agency law where it is necessary to find a privilege justifying the disclosure, the doctrine of misprision of felony manifests a public policy, supported by penal sanction, creating a duty to disclose.

VI. OTHER JUDICIAL EXPERIENCE

A brief examination of fundamental tort and equity doctrines may provide further guidance. From the enactment of the Ordinance of Labourers in 1349, the English law regarded inducement of a servant to leave the service of his master as wrongful. After a period of uncertainty, the doctrine was subsequently extended by the common law to breach

---

20 In 1934, it was noted that in 144 years the federal act had come before the courts on only two occasions. See *Bratton* v. *United States*, 73 F.2d 795, 797 (10th Cir. 1934).

21 *R.* v. *Aberg* [1947], 1 All E.R. 601; *R.* v. *Wilde, Criminal Law Review*, 1960, pp. 116-20 (Leeds Assizes Dec. 7-14, 1959), and four unreported cases referred to by counsel and in Lord Denning's opinion in the *Sykes* case, infra n. 23, pp. 544, 560: *Rex* v. *Barnett* (Cent. Crim. Ct., Jan. 17, 1952); *Rex* v. *Casserley, The Times* (London), May 28, 1938, p. 7, col. 5 (Cent. Crim. Ct.); *Rex* v. *Prothero* (Salop Assizes, June 24, 1949); *Rex* v. *Tapp* (Hampshire Summer Assizes, July 23, 1952); see Allen, "Misprision," *Law Quarterly Review* 78 (1962): 40.

22 *R.* v. *Crimmons* [1959], Vict. 270. In *R.* v. *Semenick* [1955] 15 W.W.R. (n.s.) 333 (Brit. Colum. Ct. App. 1955), a Canadian court held misprision of felony not a part of Canadian criminal law. The court was influenced by the statutory elimination of the distinction between felonies and misdemeanors.

23 *Sykes* v. *Director of Pub. Prosecutions* [1962] A.C. 528 (1961).

24 E.g., *Sullivan* v. *United States*, 411 F.2d 556 (10th Cir. 1969); *United States* v. *King*, 402 F.2d 694 (9th Cir. 1968); *United States* v. *Norman*, 391 F.2d 212 (6th Cir. 1968) (*cert. denied*), 390 U.S. 1014, 88 S.Ct. 1265, 19 L.Ed.2d 186 (1968); *Neal* v. *U.S.*, 102 F.2d 643 (8th Cir. 1939); *United States* v. *Thornton*, 178 F. Supp. 42 (E.D.N.Y. 1959); *United States* v. *Sullivan*, 284 F. Supp. 579 (D. Okla 1968]; see *Lancey* v. *United States*, 356 F.2d 407 (9th Cir. 1966) (*cert. denied*), 385 U.S. 922, 87 S.Ct. 234, 17 L.Ed.2d 145 (1967).

of personal service contracts and ultimately to inducement of breach of contracts generally. It is established therefore that any inducement of an agent to violate his contractual obligations to his principal is tortious. Although the authorities are divided where the contract or agency is at will, there are signs that the courts are extending liability to this area as well. Similarly, courts are prepared to enjoin third parties from the use of any information that has been imparted to them or is being used in breach of the agent's duty to keep such information confidential, even though the third party has not committed the tort of inducing the breach. In this area, it is not relevant whether the employment was at will, or indeed has already terminated, since the conduct in issue is the use of wrongfully obtained information.

However, in at least one case, where the motivation was to aid the public and not for economic advantage, conduct—otherwise wrongful—was held to be justified.[25] In *Brimelow* v. *Casson,* an English Court held that a party inducing a breach of contract out of a sense of duty to the public at large had not committed a tort. This decision involved trade unions inducing a breach by a theatre manager of a contract with a touring theatrical company which was paying such low wages that chorus girls were compelled to live in immorality under circumstances that the Court described as a "terrible and revolting tragedy." The Court referred to the union's duty "to the public" as well as to its members. In view of the very unusual nature of the case and the labor relations element, the *Brimelow* decision constitutes an isolated exception. It does illustrate, however, that familiar legal concepts grounded on economic foundations may suddenly become irrelevant when noneconomic conduct is under review.

Other English courts have stated in dicta that interference with contract may be justified when the defendant was acting under a duty rather than for protection of his economic interests.

Professors Harper and James emphasize that a privilege justifying otherwise tortious interference with the contractual relations of others reflects a "general social policy" and will exist "if the interest which he seeks to advance is superior to the interest invaded in social importance." [26] They quote Professor Carpenter's comment that "The defendant may be privileged to invade the interest of the plaintiff although it is not for the protection or furtherance of any interest of his own, if the invasion is in furtherance of a social interest of greater public import than is the social interest involved in the protection of the plaintiff's

---

[25] *Brimelow* v. *Casson* [1924] 1 Ch. 302 (1923), 38 *Harvard Law Review* 115 (1924). See G. Fridman, *Modern Law of Employment* (1963), pp. 581-82.

[26] See Harper and James, *Law of Torts* (1956), p. 514.

individual interest." [27] Thus, in referring to the *Brimelow* case, Professors Harper and James state "social and economic facts were weighed in determining whether the defendant's purpose was to promote another person or groups or of society in general." They describe the test of liability to be "balancing the conflicting interests of the plaintiff and the defendant and assessing the value which society places upon them." [28]

Section 767(e) of the *Restatement of Torts* specifies that in determining whether otherwise tortious inducement to breach of contract is privileged, important factors include "the social interests in protecting the expectancy on the one hand and the actor's freedom of action on the other hand."

Thus, tort law, extending over a full range of human conduct, has embraced a system of values for determining liability which is enunciated in broad social terms, in contrast to the more specialized area of agency law, where the articulation of the underlying considerations is almost exclusively in economic terms. However, one may inquire whether there really is, or should be, any different standard for liability in the two areas, and whether the preoccupation with economic interests in the agency law merely is a reflection of the way problems for. decision have arisen in that more specialized field. In brief, tort law introduces considerations of social interests, which would appear applicable to the agency field as well, and which on preliminary review would appear to provide support for the "public interest disclosure" proposal.

What are the implications of the materials reviewed thus far? What is the balance of conflicting considerations with respect to the relative social costs and benefits arising from encouraging employee disobedience and disloyalty with respect to employer conduct deemed socially irresponsible by an employee?

Although the employee may be motivated by the public interest rather than economic gain, the employer will undoubtedly incur economic loss from the employee's conduct. Changes in airline operating procedures to reduce impact on the environment will result in higher costs. Elimination of South African business will mean a loss of South African profits. As for the disclosure proposal, the inability to conduct business operations without concern that corporate information may become a matter of public knowledge will impose an economic burden on the corporation forced to restructure its organization and operations to reduce the possibility and extent of "leaks." Management will become more cumbersome and less efficient. Suspicion as to the source of leaks

---

[27] See Carpenter, "Interference with Contract Relations," 41 *Harvard Law Review* 728, 745.

[28] See Harper and James, *supra* note 26, at 516; Carpenter, *supra* note 27.

and the extent of company "loyalty," as well as the security measures that such concerns necessarily involve, will inevitably mean a loss of human values within the organization, invidious distinctions between those with security clearance and those without it, and a general impairment of group identification, group loyalty, and morale.

Further, it must also be recognized that implementation of the disclosure proposal will rest on the individual judgments of innumerable employees seeking to draw the difficult line "where responsibility to the society transcends responsibility to his organization." Inevitably, a number of such judgments will be unjustified, resting on partial information, misinformation, or misunderstanding. Other judgments will involve improper motivation, reflecting a desire to injure the employer for reasons that could range across the entire spectrum of cause for employee dissatisfaction, or stem from political considerations. Even wtih the best of faith and intentions, can the members of the Polaroid Revolutionary Workers Movement really be objective in drawing the line between their concept of social responsibility and responsibility to Polaroid?

Thus, the costs of the proposal are unquestionably serious in light of the indisputable value of protecting the principal's right to the undivided loyalty and obedience of his agent without which it· is hard to conceive of an efficient, harmonious enterprise. What then is the offsetting social gain and the ultimate justification?

VII. THE VIEW OF THE CORPORATION AS A POLITICAL INSTITUTION

Presumably, the basis for the proposal for unauthorized disclosure of corporate conduct that is regarded as socially irresponsible rests on a judgment as to the crucial social importance of controlling the important centers of power in the nation. The disclosure proposal would appear to be another variation on Mr. Nader's theme that the large public corporation is a political institution in which forces not represented in the traditional decision-making process of the corporation, such as the public generally, should participate in the decision-making process. This theme was clearly articulated in Campaign GM where its counsel acknowledged that a major objective of the Campaign was to involve the public—not merely shareholders—in the corporate decision.[29]

When the references to "professionalism" or "illegal, hazardous or unconscionable" activity are removed, this is the real basis of the proposal that corporate employees become informers, ready to act whenever

---

29 See Schwartz, *op. cit. supra* note 8, at 485.

they believe their responsibility to society requires disclosure of aspects of their employer's activities which they do not deem to be in the public interest. Emphasizing the view that the public corporation is a political institution, Mr. Nader has also called for "the popularization" of the corporation and the election of five directors out of twenty by the public —not shareholders—in a national election.[30] The adaptation of the tolerated, if not accepted, practice of the government "leak" to corporate affairs is a simple corollary of this view.

Even without accepting the implications that Mr. Nader draws from the conclusion, it is clear that his view of the large public corporation as a political institution is in many respects sound.

If the validity of the disclosure proposal rests on the changing nature of the major public corporation into a political institution with government-like qualities, it becomes appropriate to review the duties of obedience, loyalty, and confidentiality of the government employee.

VIII. THE GOVERNMENT EMPLOYEE

The cases involving the discharge or suspension of government employees for public criticism of the policies or administration of the governmental agencies in which they have been employed provide insight into the degree of importance to be accorded to the employee's duties of obedience and loyalty. The problem presented is the extent to which the government employee loses his constitutional right to free speech with respect to issues of public importance because he has accepted public employment.[31]

In the leading case of *Pickering* v. *Board of Education*,[32] the Supreme Court held that in the absence of "proof of false statements knowingly or recklessly made by him, a teacher's exercise of his right to speak on issues of public importance may not furnish the basis for his dismissal from public employment." [33] The Court made it plain that "teachers may [not] constitutionally be compelled to relinquish the First Amendment rights they would otherwise enjoy as citizens to comment on matters of public interest in connection with the operation of the public schools

---

30 *New York Times,* Jan. 24, 1971, § 3, p. 1, col. 3.

31 See Van Alstyne, "The Constitutional Rights of Public Employees: A Comment on the Inappropriate Use of an Old Analogy," *U.C.L.A. Law Review* 16 (1969) 751; Note, "The First Amendment and Public Employees: Time Marches On," *Georgetown Law Journal* 57 (1968): 134.

32 391 U.S. 563, 88 S.Ct. 1731, 20 L.Ed.2d 811 (1968).

33 *Ibid.,* p. 574, 88 S.Ct. p. 1738, 20 L.Ed.2d p. 821.

in which they work." [34] In reaching its conclusion, the Court recognized that it had "to arrive at a balance between the interests of the teacher, as a citizen, in commenting on matters of public concern and the interest of the State, as an employer, in promoting the efficiency of the public services it performs through its employees." [35] The significance of the *Pickering* decision is the relatively unimportant role it assigned to "the interest of the State, as an employer" and to the teacher's duty of loyalty and obedience to the school board and the superintendent of schools. The Court left no doubt that in the balance of interests, freedom of speech for government employees was deemed so important that it outweighed any general duty of loyalty and obedience to the public employer and that following the rule established in the *New York Times* case,[36] even false statements were protected so long as they were not "knowingly or recklessly made."

Thus, the Court emphasized the degree of intimacy of relationship required before the government employee's right of free public comment would be lost. It stated: "Appellant's employment relationships with the Board and, to a somewhat lesser extent, with the superintendent are not the kind of close working relationships for which it can persuasively be claimed that personal loyalty and confidence are necessary to their proper functioning." [37] The Court further noted:

> It is possible to conceive of some positions in public employment in which the need for confidentiality is so great that even completely correct public statements might furnish a permissible ground for dismissal. Likewise, positions in public employment in which the relationship between superior and subordinate is of such a personal and intimate nature that certain forms of public criticism of the superior by the subordinate would seriously undermine the effectiveness of the working relationship between them can also be imagined. We intimate no views as to how we would resolve any specific instances of such situations, but merely note that significantly different considerations would be involved in such cases.[38]

In *Meehan* v. *Macy,* involving a Canal Zone policeman who was discharged for criticizing the Governor's personnel policies during a

---

34 *Ibid.*, p. 568, 88 S.Ct. p. 1734, 20 L.Ed.2d p. 817.

35 *Ibid.* The decision is a far cry from the celebrated statement of Mr. Justice Holmes almost 80 years ago that "The petitioner may have a constitutional right to talk politics but he has no constitutional right to be a policeman." See *McAuliffe* v. *City of New Bedford,* 155 Mass. 216, 220, 29 N.E. 517 (1892).

36 *New York Times Co.* v. *Sullivan,* 376 U.S. 254, 279-80, 84 S.Ct. 710, 725–26, 11 L.Ed.2d 686, 706-7 (1964).

37 391 U.S. 563, 570, 88 S.Ct. 1731, 1735, 20 L.Ed.2d 811, 818 (1968).

38 *Ibid.*, p. 570, n. 3, 88 S.Ct. p. 1735, n. 3, 20 L.Ed.2d p. 818, n. 3.

period of rioting by Panamanian students protesting American "colonialism," the Court of Appeals noted that "the situation in the Canal Zone was tense and official apprehension of renewed rioting was reasonable" and upheld the discharge.[39] The Court emphasized that "such uninhibited public speech by Government employees [may produce] intolerable disharmony, inefficiency, dissension and even chaos." [40] The importance of these elements in the quieter context of a domestic dispute over school affairs was not regarded so highly by the Supreme Court in the *Pickering* case.

A number of state decisions involving school personnel and firemen have similarly reinstated municipal employees discharged or suspended for public criticism of their superiors or their agencies, except where the employee's public criticism was held to disrupt or impair the public service. It may be questioned in the light of the *Pickering* decision whether the latter limitation will persist except in unusual cases.

The first and fourteenth amendments do not apply, at least not thus far, to American corporations, however large their size, however powerful their impact on the American society and citizens, and however governmental-like they may be in their functions. Thus, the *Pickering* and related cases resting on the constitutional protection of the first and fourteenth amendments are not applicable; the cases cannot be extended to limit the right of the private employer to discharge the private employee unprotected by employment contract or collective bargaining agreement. They do, however, ascribe a profound value to the employee's right as citizen to speak out on matters of public importance, which transcends the government employer's claim to loyalty and obedience. In the *Pickering* case, the Court singled out as possible exceptions only the isolated cases of a "great" need for confidentiality of relationship (not of information) or of a "personal and intimate" association between the employee and his superior, and even in these cases, the Court carefully reserved the matter for future decision.

Thus, with respect to the balance between the private employee's position as a citizen and the private employer's claim to loyalty and obedience, the *Pickering* case supports the view that traditional concepts as to loyalty and obedience may have to yield to permit employees to fulfill their role as citizens. This is the foundation for the disclosure proposal—the importance to the nation of encouraging citizens interested in working for a better society to place their interests as citizens above the interests of their employer. If governmental agencies may, notwith-

---

39 392 F.2d 822, 832 (D.C. Cir. 1968) *modified on rehearing,* 425 F.2d 469 (D.C. Cir. 1968) *modification aff'd en banc,* 425 F.2d 472 (D.C. Cir. 1969).

40 392 F.2d p. 833.

standing such public criticism by government employees, function effectively in the view of the Court, why should not the major corporation be able to do the same? With increasing recognition of the "blurring" of the line of difference between the so-called "public" and "private" sectors and the increasing resemblance of employee relations in government service to those in private industry, the implications of the *Pickering* decision for the major public corporation become even more pronounced.

In considering the rights of government employees, it is essential to distinguish sharply between the expression of critical conclusions or opinions and the unauthorized disclosure of confidential information. *Pickering* and the other public employment cases have involved only public employees, who have expressed critical opinions about governmental policy or officials, relying on already public information. None of the cases has involved the disclosure of *information,* as distinct from the expression of *opinion.* The disclosure proposal relates to the transmittal of information, which by definition is nonpublic, which in many cases may be privileged, which may have been submitted to the governmental agency on the understanding that it remain confidential, and the disclosure of which may be prohibited by statute or agency regulation.

Where the courts have dealt with opinion, they have been concerned with the delicate constitutional balance between the employee's right to express his opinions on public issues, like any other citizen, and the need of the government to function effectively. They have, therefore, discussed the significance of such matters as the impact of the opinion on the functioning of the agency, the extent to which the opinion would impair the confidentiality of the employment relation, or the extent to which it might indicate the unfitness of the employee. By accepting government employment, the employee has not forfeited his right to express his opinion on public issues as a citizen. He has not, however, acquired any additional right to disobey procedures intended to keep nonpublic information confidential. The disclosure of nonpublic information has no relation to the protection of the right of free speech which he possesses outside of his relation to governmental employment.

This distinction is emphasized by the Federal Freedom of Information Act,[41] which includes the following exemptions, among others:

Exemption (4): "trade secrets and commercial information obtained from a person and privileged or confidential"; and

Exemption (5): "intra-agency or inter-agency memorandums or

---

[41] U.S.C. § 552(b) (1967).

letters which would not be available by law to a party other than an agency in litigation with the agency."

As explained by the Court in *Ackerly* v. *Ley*,[42]

> The basis of Exemption (5), as of the privilege which antedated it, is the free and uninhibited exchange and communication of opinions, ideas, and points of view—a procedure as essential to the wise functioning of a big government as it is to any organized human effort. In the Federal Establishment, as in General Motors or any other hierarchical giant, there are enough incentives as it is for playing it safe and listing with the wind; Congress clearly did not propose to add to them the threat of cross-examination in a public tribunal.

The Freedom of Information Act, where applicable, relates solely to records available for public inspection. It does not authorize personnel to make disclosures. On the contrary, existing prohibitions of unauthorized disclosure remain in force. The Freedom of Information Act thus represents Congressional recognition of the importance of preserving an essential area of confidentiality of information in the effective functioning of the governmental organization.

In *The Price of Dependency,* Professor O'Neil takes a different view of the problem of the "leak" by the governmental employee. He observes:

> The balance to be struck in such a case is a difficult one. Surely the government has some interest in keeping the information confidential, . . . until a time when it will be least damaging to the public confidence. Equally clearly, however, sanctions against public employees who speak the truth should not be lightly permitted. . . . Perhaps what is required when the charge is one of leaking the truth is a test approximating the "clear and present danger" test applicable to criminal prosecutions against spoken and written attacks upon the government. Thus a dismissal would require proof that divulgence of the information . . . did pose a very substantial threat to the security of the state. That would be a difficult burden to meet. . . .[43]

This failure to distinguish between critical opinion and unauthorized disclosure of information is believed ill-founded. The line between statements of opinion and of disclosure of nonpublic information may blur and on occasion not be easy to draw. Nevertheless, it is difficult to conclude that implementation of the public employee's right to free speech requires elimination of such a distinction or that in *Pickering,* the Court had any intention of doing so.

If there is no basis in the cases dealing with the government em-

---

[42] 420 F.2d 1336, 1341 (D.C. Cir. 1969).

[43] See O'Neil, *Price of Dependency* (1970), p. 100.

ployee thus far supporting the right of disclosure of nonpublic information, however public spirited the employee's intentions may be, the legal right of the corporate employee to do so is similarly doubtful. Thus, in the end, the view of the major public corporation as a political institution provides no support on the legal level for the disclosure proposal.

It is possible, however, to argue for a less restricted standard for disclosure by corporate employees than that applicable to government employees. In democratic society, the existence of the opposition party provides a counter-balance to the administration, and the opposition may be relied upon to look after the public interest in any controversy. The public employee need not feel that he must act to protect the public interest himself. In the corporation run by management not effectively subject to shareholder control, appeal by an employee to the public generally may be the only available alternative for the protection of the public interest, and the forces for disclosure may therefore be stronger. Further, unlike government, the corporation has institutional objectives other than the promotion of the public interest and disclosure may be essential to protect the public interest.

In addition to the question of the applicable rules, one must not lose sight of the practicalities of the situation. Notwithstanding statute and agency regulations, governmental "leaks" have persisted and appear to play a role of some usefulness in the shaping of opinion and the determination of public policy. Government personnel involved may be disciplined in the rare cases where they are identified, but if the political considerations involved are important enough, the political groups whose ends have been served by the "leak" support their source.

In the political arena, it is clear that the role of the "leak" is accepted both within and without the administrative structure.[44] All the while, the business of government continues to be conducted. The only question for debate relates to the political interests which are served by a particular "leak." In the political arena, the rules to the contrary are clear, but the practice continues. Is there any reason to suppose that the corporate world would be different? If vital public interests are involved, or seem to be involved to the individual in question, some corporate employees will no doubt respond to an impelling drive to

---

[44] See D. Cater, *The Fourth Branch of Government* (1959), pp. 112-141 for a thoughtful review of the "leak" in the federal government.

The recent publication of the so-called "Pentagon papers" by the *New York Times, Washington Post,* and other papers and the ensuing litigation, *New York Times Co.* v. *United States,* 39 U.S.L. Week 4879 (U.S. June 30, 1971), among other things, has resulted in considerable discussion of "leaks" of governmental information, particularly classified information.

continue the issue in the public arena, for the very reasons which moti-
vate government employees in similar cases to do the same.

In short, the major corporation may well anticipate an unhappy
future where corporate "leaks" in the area of social responsibility will
become not uncommon, and the corporation, like the government, will
have to learn to live with this unwelcome development.

IX. THE CHANGING ROLE OF THE
CORPORATE EMPLOYEE

Underlying the problem is the concept of the proper position of
the employee of the major corporation. In the balance of the conflicting
rights of the government employee as citizen and the objective of government for efficient administration, the courts have placed a lesser
value on the traditional duties of loyalty and obedience and have sub-
ordinated these duties to the employee's right of free speech in order to
enable the employee to play a role as a citizen in matters of public controversy. Similarly, one may inquire whether, in time, erosion of the
traditional employer-employee relation and the traditional concepts of
loyalty and obedience will not also occur within the major American
corporation.

A. The Developing Law

The basic problem goes to the employer's right of discharge of an
employee who is publicly acting contrary to the interests of the employer: the Polaroid worker picketing in protest of Polaroid's alleged
involvement with apartheid; the Eastern Airlines pilot disobeying standard operating procedures for dumping excess kerosene in the atmosphere instead of draining it on the ground; the automobile worker
who protests the shipment of allegedly unsafe cars from his employer's
factory; or the employee who "leaks" nonpublic information in accordance with the "public interest disclosure" proposal.

At common law, the employer's freedom to discharge was absolute.
Over the years, this right of discharge has been increasingly restricted
by statute and by collective bargaining agreements, but the basic principle of the employer's legal right to discharge, although challenged on
the theoretical level, is still unimpaired.

In *NLRB* v. *Local Union No. 1229*,[45] the Supreme Court held that
the discharge of striking employees of a television station because of

---

45 346 U.S. 464, 74 S.Ct. 172, 98 L.Ed. 195 (1953).

their attack on the station for poor programming and service did not constitute an "unfair labor practice" under the National Labor Relations Act. The employees' effort to discredit the employer's business, as distinct from his labor practices, was held "such detrimental disloyalty" as to constitute "just cause" for discharge.

Accepting without discussion the employer's absolute right of discharge, except as limited by statute, the Court emphasized "the importance of enforcing individual plant discipline and of maintaining loyalty." Insofar as the limited purposes of the National Labor Relations Act were concerned, the Court stated: "There is no more elemental cause for discharge of an employee than disloyalty to his employer," and upheld the employer's right to discharge for "insubordination, disobedience, or disloyalty." [46]

Discharge of employees for causes not related to unionization has been upheld under the National Labor Relations Act, including such "offenses" as being a member or sympathizer of the Communist Party, or invoking the protection of the fifth amendment at a Congressional hearing or refusing to complete a defense agency security questionnaire. Discharge for testifying under subpoena against the employer in a criminal proceeding has also been upheld. On the other hand, a review of arbitration awards in this area has concluded that these activities were not normally regarded as constituting "just cause" under collective agreements and that some "resulting adverse effect upon the employment relationship which makes the retention of the employee a detriment to the company" was required.

In an illuminating article,[47] Dean Blades has reexamined the traditional concept of employment at will and the employer's traditional power to discharge the employee at any time for any reason (or indeed for no reason) and has suggested that in time the doctrine—already hedged in by statute and collective bargaining agreements—will be modified, possibly by the legislatures, perhaps by the courts, to protect the employee against discharge for exercise of those personal rights which have no legitimate connection with the employment relationship.

It is noteworthy that even Dean Blades who has ventured boldly to foresee limitations on the employer's right of discharge has restricted himself to two areas: the protection of the employee against improper employer influence over the area of the employee's life unrelated to the employer; and safeguards to enable the employee as a practical matter to

---

[46] 346 U.S. p. 472, 74 S.Ct. p. 176, 98 L.Ed. p. 202. See *NLRB* v. *Jones and Laughlin Steel Corp.*, 301 U.S. 1, 45-46, 57 S.Ct. 615, 628, 81 L.Ed. 893, 915-17 (1936).

[47] See Blades, "Employment at Will *v.* Individual Freedom: Or Limiting the Abusive Exercise of Employer Power," 67 *Columbia Law Review* 1404 (1967).

insist on those rights already theoretically granted him under agency law not to be an unwilling participant in immoral, unlawful, or unprofessional activity. Dean Blades further recognizes that "[t]here may even be occasions when an employee's public utterances on controversial subjects can be considered incompatible with his professional position and the duty of loyalty he owes to his employer." [48]

Thus, even this proposed transformation of employee status from its traditional role of employment at will would only restrict the employer from "overreaching domination" which is "clearly not justified by the employer's legitimate concerns." It would not protect the Polaroid employee, or the Eastern Airlines pilot, or the employee of the giant automobile corporation making unauthorized disclosure to a "public interest clearing house."

Professor Blumrosen has similarly suggested that the employer's unrestricted right of discharge has been changed so drastically by a "complex network of contract and statutory provisions" and the "restraints on that freedom are now so extensive that the principle itself is in question, and the United States' legal system may be moving toward a general requirement of just cause and fair dealing between employer and employee." He can offer no authority, however, to support this conclusion insofar as it relates to employees not protected by collective agreements or by statute.[49]

Where a collective agreement covers the employee, the requirement of "just cause" for discharge and other provisions have been construed in the rough and tumble of the labor arbitration process to afford significantly greater protection to the employee than indicated by the traditional statements in the older legal authorities. The living law has progressed beyond the law in the books. This, no doubt, underlies Professor Blumrosen's conclusion as to the movement of the law in this area. A new view of the corporation and of the role of the employee will also undoubtedly result in further modification of the concept of "just cause" under collective agreements.

In a changing society with changing values, long-prevailing views on social relationships will inevitably change as well. Thus, the suggestion that the employee of the major corporation has certain rights and duties as a citizen which transcend his traditional obligations as an employee may find increasing support although the suggestion conflicts with long-accepted legal doctrines.

---

48 *Ibid.*, pp. 1406, 1408-09.

49 See Blumrosen, "Employer Discipline: United States Report," *Rutgers Law Review* 18 (1964): 428.

If the public school teacher can be protected against discharge for public criticism including allegedly false statements concerning the school board and the school superintendent, is it too much to suggest that a similar protection may develop in time for the employee of one of America's giant corporations who publicly challenges the conduct of his employer in a sphere of public interest? In the absence of constitutional protection for the corporate employee, unlike the governmental employee, the question is whether new law—whether created by statute, judicial decision, arbitration award, or collective agreement—will develop in the future to reach a similar result.

In any such analysis, the nature of the employee's conduct is fundamental.

Participation in public controversy involving the employer through the exercise of free speech presents the most appealing case for extension of employee rights. In the light of the balance-of-interests expressed in the *Pickering* case on the constitutional level, should the Polaroid employee be free, without fear of retaliation, to urge publicly that American corporations, including Polaroid, cease doing business in the Union of South Africa or Greece or the Soviet Union, if he so chooses? Should his duty of loyalty and obedience be so construed as to deprive him of his right to speak out on public issues? Although courts may not uphold such a position at the present time, will not changing social values likely produce such a conclusion in the law of the future? On the other hand, is there justification for the Polaroid employee joining in a concerted campaign to injure his employer through an organized boycott of its products? Does this involve free speech or economic warfare?

The Eastern Airlines case rests on the reasonableness of the employer's instructions in the light of the intense public concern with environmental abuse. Even today, one might inquire whether in arbitration under a labor agreement permitting discharge only for "just cause," an arbitrator would hold that such conduct, however disobedient, justified discharge, or whether some lesser penalty such as reinstatement without back pay might not be deemed appropriate.

In view of the absence of theoretical support for any right of unauthorized disclosure on the governmental level or of any relationship between such conduct and the employee's right to conduct himself like any other citizen, it is hard to visualize the development of a legal right of unauthorized disclosure for the corporate employee. Further, there is the additional hurdle of the decisions under the National Labor Relations Act that the use or disclosure of confidential information is just cause for discharge for the limited purposes of the statute, even when related to unionization activities.

B. The Dynamics of the Public Climate

As one moves from the theoretical level to the practical level, one may inquire whether the employer's right of discharge has not already been impaired at least in those cases where public sympathy is squarely behind the employee, as in the case of the Eastern Airlines pilot who placed his concern with air pollution above obedience to company regulations. The rules of law may condemn such activity as a clear breach of the duty of loyalty and obedience. The corporation may be tempted to exercise its right of discharge, but its freedom of action (without regard to obligations under any union contract) will be severely restricted by the climate of public opinion which may well have been significantly influenced by the publicity attending the affair.

In the arena of public opinion, the issue will involve the merits of the conduct of the employee, not whether the conduct was contrary to instructions. In the Eastern Airlines case, the intentional violation of regulations and the impracticability of allowing each of the 3,700 Eastern Airlines pilots to "make his own rules" were not the issues before the public. The subject of the public debate was the impact of the Eastern Airlines practice on air pollution. Unless the corporation can prevail in the battle for public opinion on the merits of the conduct in issue, it must yield to public clamor or face the consequences of unfavorable public reaction. Moreover, if the employer is unionized, it is unlikely that the union efforts on behalf of the employee will be limited to the legal question of whether the conduct constitutes "just cause" for discharge under the collective agreement.

At this stage, whatever the traditional legal doctrines, the corporation's right of discharge may be illusory. The major corporation must recognize that it has become a public institution and must respond to the public climate of opinion. Thus, whether or not the major corporation in the law of the future comes to be regarded as a quasi-governmental body for some purpose, it operates today as a political as well as economic institution, subject to political behavior by those affected by it and to public debate over those of its actions which attain public visibility.

The pervasive public concern with corporate social responsibility will unquestionably lead to employee response to an appeal for disclosures of confidential information tending to show corporate participation in the creation of social or environmental problems. It is only realistic, therefore, to anticipate the appearance of the government-type "leak" in the major corporation. Whether or not it violates traditional agency concepts, a "public interest clearing house" may be expected to transact considerable business. Aggrieved employers are hardly going to feel free to resort to theoretically available legal or equitable remedies for redress so long as the unauthorized disclosures relate to "antisocial" conduct and do not reflect economic motivation. The corporation that is guilty of environmental abuse reported to the "clearing house" will not be well-advised to compound its conduct by instituting action against the "clearing house" or the employee (if it can identify him) and thereby assure even greater adverse publicity with respect to its objectionable environmental activities.

The "corporate leak" will join the "government leak" and serve the same political purposes. Whatever the incidental cost, business will survive, as has government, and indeed wrongful though it may be, the possibility of such a "leak" may serve a useful therapeutic or preventative function. Nevertheless, it may be well to review some of the inevitable aspects of the "public-interest disclosure" proposal. An official of the Federal Highway Safety Bureau commented in the *New York Times:* "Many a night I've spent late at the office trying to 'Nader-proof' a regulation. The pipelines this guy has into this agency are unbelievable." [50]

Fortune similarly reports:

> Both reporters and professional politicians find him [Mr. Nader] extremely useful. "Nader has become the fifth branch of government if you count the press as fourth," says a Senate aide who has worked with Nader often in drafting legislation. "He knows all the newspaper deadlines and how to get in touch with anybody anytime. By his own hard work he has developed a network of sources in every arm of government. And believe me, no Senator turns down those calls from Ralph. He will say he's got some stuff and it's good, and the Senator can take the credit." [51]

Once the duty of loyalty yields to the primacy of what the individual in question regards as the "public interest," the door is open to widespread abuse.

In a society accustomed to governmental "leaks"—deliberately instigated by an administration as trial balloons as well as by bureaucrats dissatisfied with administrative decision—extension of the conduct described above to the corporate area will be merely more of the same, part of a tolerated pattern in a political world, embracing the major corporation as well as government. At the same time, it sharply poses

---

[50] Duscha, "Stop! In the Public Interest," *New York Times,* Mar. 21, 1971, § 6, p. 4, col. 5.

[51] Armstrong, "The Passion that Rules Ralph Nader," *Fortune,* May 1971, pp. 144, 145.

the question of the desirability of encouraging the spread of such patterns of violation of the concepts of loyalty and obedience from government to major business. The proposal for disclosure to private groups —however disinterested their objective or public-spirited their purpose— seems an excessive and dangerous response [52] to the problem of subordinating to social controls the tremendous economic and social power of the major public corporations.

The problem of unauthorized disclosure inevitably has political overtones. The significance of the erosion of the employee's traditional duties of loyalty, obedience, and confidentiality may be better appreciated if the problem is viewed in a setting that does not involve issues of social and environmental responsibility that are currently matters of such deep national concern. Such a setting may be found in the case of the university communities which are increasingly troubled by reports that the Federal Bureau of Information, the military, or the local police has been maintaining surveillance over campus activities. In some cases, university staff personnel, such as security officers and switchboard operators, apparently on an individual basis, have been supplying information about faculty, students, and campus activities. These university employees have made apparently unauthorized disclosure of nonpublic information in response to the appeals of government officials for information to enable them to discharge their concept of their public law enforcement responsibilities. No doubt, these employees were responding to their personal views of their social responsibility to cooperate with the "authorities." This problem has created deep concern at many institutions. Thus, at Swarthmore College, President Robert D. Cross responded by warning faculty, students, and staff that "those who divulged confidential information not demanded by law or college policy risked dismissal." [53]

In brief, unauthorized disclosure of confidential information presents serious problems for any organization; the matter can hardly be allowed to rest on each individual employee's decision as to the nature of his responsibilities to society and to his employer.

C. Alternatives to Unauthorized Disclosure

Other alternatives to reach the same objective without the same corrosive effect on personnel and the same potential for private abuse are available. These involve the use of governmental machinery with

---

[52] The possible disclosure of what the employer may regard as trade secrets further aggravates the problem.

[53] *Chronicle of Higher Education,* May 31, 1971, p. 1, col. 1.

governmental safeguards with respect to the use of information received.

1. Traditional doctrines of agency law recognize the privilege of employees to report violations of law to proper governmental authorities.[54] Private vigilante efforts should not be essential to achieve effective administration. "Public interest" groups would seem better advised to continue to concentrate their attention on improving the efficiency and effectiveness of the regulatory processes.[55]

2. Another alternative is to extend further the growing statutory and administrative requirements of disclosure of conduct in areas of social responsibility.[56] Examples include the Employer Information Report EEO-1 on minority employment practices filed with the federal Equal Employment Opportunity Commission,[57] the Affirmative Action Compliance Program filed with the Office of Federal Contract Compliance,[58] the water pollution data filed under the Federal Water Pollution Control Act,[59] and the reports on work-related deaths, injuries and illnesses under the Federal Occupational Safety and Health Act.[60] Enforcement of such matters by public agencies under public standards and with public personnel and safeguards would serve the basic object without the serious disadvantages involved in the "public-interest disclosure" proposal.

3. Still another alternative is the development of the so-called social audit or a systematic quantitative (and possibly qualitative) review of a corporation's activities in the area of social responsibility. This proposal, suggested almost twenty years ago,[61] has been gathering

---

54 *Restatement* § 395, comment *f.* "Code of Ethics for Government Service," *House Doc. 103,* 86th Cong., 1st sess. (1958): "Any person in government service should . . . (xi) Expose corruption wherever discovered."

55 See, e.g., studies produced under auspices of the Center for Study of Responsible Law: J. Turner, *The Chemical Feast* (1970); J. Esposito, *The Vanishing Air* (1970); R. Fellmeth, *The Interstate Commerce Omission* (1970); H. Wellford, "Sowing the Wind: Pesticides, Meat and the Public Interest," *Wall Street Journal,* July 19, 1971, p. 9, col. 2; *New York Times,* July 18, 1971, § 1, p. 45, col. 3.

56 Thus, the Securities and Exchange Commission was asked by the Project on Corporate Responsibility and the Natural Resources Defense Council to require disclosure of minority employment and pollution control activities in reports under the 1933 and 1934 acts. *New York Times,* June 10, 1971, p. 25, col. 4. The Commission subsequently required disclosure of environmental requirements or legal proceedings under civil rights statutes which might have a material effect on the corporation. Securities Act Release No. 5170, Securities and Exchange Act Release No. 9252, July 19, 1971, *Commerce Clearing House Federal Securities Law Reporter* para. 78, 150.

57 29 C.F.R. § 1602.7 (1971).

58 41 C.F.R. § 60-1.40(a) (1971).

59 18 C.F.R. § 607.3(a) (1971).

60 P.L. 91-596, § 8(c), (g); see *Wall Street Journal,* May 21, 1971, p. 23, col. 3.

61 See H. Bowen, *Social Responsibilities of the Businessman,* p. 251 *ff.* (1953).

increasing attention and strength with a number of institutions and corporations endeavoring to develop a satisfactory methodolgy. Such disclosure and evaluation seem an inevitable product of the forces making for greater corporate participation in the solution of social and environmental problems. Development will obviously take some time. In the meanwhile, "public interest" groups and others have proposed resolutions calling for wider disclosure in this area for consideration at the annual meetings of such corporations as General Motors Corporation, Honeywell, Inc., American Metal Climax, Inc., Kennecott Copper Corporation, Phelps Dodge Corporation, and Gulf Oil Corporation.

D. Protection against Discharge

Another aspect of the proposal for a "public interest clearing house" has considerable merit. This is the objective to provide protection through exposure to public opinion for corporate employees discharged for refusal to participate in illegal, immoral, or unprofessional acts. Involving no breach of confidentiality, this is a laudable effort to translate into reality the theoretical legal rights of the employee recognized at common law and in the *Restatement of Agency* in the face of the grave economic inequality between the individual employee and the giant corporate employer. Such an effort should receive the support of all interested in raising the standards of industrial morality.

The related objective of assuring employee rights to participate in the public discussion of corporate conduct, including that of their employer, may also be achieved through extension of employee protection in collective bargaining agreements. As public concern over the social implications of corporate conduct continues to increase, and as more employees feel an individual sense of responsibility by reason of their identification with their employer and its activities, it is not unlikely that protection of employee freedom of speech and even of unauthorized disclosure to advance the "public interest" will increasingly become topics both at the collective bargaining table and in arbitration proceedings over the meaning of "just cause."

An example of the power of the trade union is provided by Mr. Nader:

> For example, the Fisher Body inspector who, five years ago, turned over information to me about defective welding of Chevrolet bodies, after the plant manager and all his other bosses told him to forget it, is still on the job. Why? Because he is a union member. Had he been an engineer, or a scientist, or a lawyer or any nonunion person, G.M. could have showed him the door at 5 p.m. and he would have had no rights.[62]

---

[62] *New York Times,* Jan. 24, 1971, § 3, p. 1, col. 6.

Statutory relief is another possible method to achieve appropriate protection for the rights of employees covering unionized and nonunionized employees alike. Antidiscrimination employment statutes already prohibit discrimination on the basis of "race, color, religion, sex, or national origin," age, or union membership. They might well be extended to make unlawful discrimination for political, social, or economic views even when publicly expressed in opposition to an employer's policy. Similarly, statutory prohibition of discharge for refusal to participate in acts that are illegal or contrary to established canons of professional ethics, or for cooperation with governmental law-enforcement, legislative or executive agencies, deserves serious consideration.

X. CONCLUSION

The duties of loyalty and obedience are essential in the conduct of any enterprise—public or private. Yet, they do not serve as a basis to deprive government employees of their rights as citizens to participate in public debate and criticism of their governmental employer and should not be utilized to deprive corporate employees of similar rights.

As employee attitudes and actions reflect the increased public concern with social and environmental problems and the proper role of the corporation in participating in their solution, traditional doctrines of the employee's duties of loyalty and obedience and the employer's right of discharge will undergo increasing change. The pressure of "public interest" stockholder groups for increased corporate social responsibility will also be reflected by employees. At some point in the process, disagreement with management policies is inevitable. When the employees persist in their disagreement and the disagreement becomes public, an erosion of the traditional view of the duties of loyalty and obedience will have occurred. Yet, this hardly seems a fundamental problem for the corporation or undesirable from the point of view of the larger society. The real question is to establish civilized perimeters of permissible conduct that will not silence employees from expressing themselves on the public implications of their employers' activities in the social and environmental arena and at the same time will not introduce elements of breach of confidentiality and impairment of loyalty that will materially impair the functioning of the corporation itself. A balancing of interests, not a blind reiteration of traditional doctrines, is required. It is hoped that this preliminary review will suggest some possible solutions to the problem.

PART FIVE

The Corporation
and Other
Social Institutions

COMMENT

Where Part IV devoted attention to certain aspects of the relationship between the corporation and its employees, as a group and as individuals affected by the corporation's activities, Part V concentrates upon the relationship between the corporation and two other social institutions: the church and the state. The theme remains the same as it was in the earlier portions of this book, and both authors have as their goal the better illumination of the clash between traditional values and ideologies, on one hand, and contemporary social issues, on the other.

The church was chosen as one of the two institutions to be considered here because the nature of its contacts with the corporation is undergoing marked change, and because the church is bringing to bear upon the corporation certain types of social pressure which the corporation is not accustomed to having imposed on it from that source. It might be said that the church-corporation relationship has, until recent years, called upon the church for a largely passive role as recipient of corporate largesse and sometime provider of moral legitimacy and spiritual refuge. Although that role probably will continue to persist for many years to come, the role of social critic and wielder of worldly power has now come to supplement the earlier one and to confront the corporation from an unexpected quarter. It may be that, in some sense, the corporation has now come to play the passive role.

The relationship between corporation and state is also undergoing change, but to characterize it as a change of the state's role from passive to aggressive would be misleading and inaccurate. The change is one of a very different nature. Where the corporation, for all practical purposes, has been able to disregard the church in the past, as far as substantive influence on the corporation's activities is concerned, the state has never been that easily ignored and corporation and state have often been vigorous antagonists. The change—if one dares to characterize it in a phrase—is more a matter of reducing antagonism and creating an atmosphere of partnership than it is a tendency toward intensified conflict.

Sethi, who authored the essay on the church, analyzes the corporation–church conflict in a systems context. He identifies and describes the sources of the conflict and the forms it takes within the constraints imposed by three basic assumptions: that the corporation and the church are two subsystems of a whole social system, that each subsystem has several constituent institutions (or subsystems) of its own, and that a subsystem's character is multidimensional. In order better to come to grips with the new conflict between church and corporation, and to lay the foundation for the use of an "action-reaction flow chart" to clarify the tactics and the impact of tactics employed by aggressive elements in the church, Sethi first analyzes the conflict in three distinct but interrelated dimensions. Those dimensions are the value sets of the two subsystems, historical changes in the value sets, and the impact of these two elements on the organizational and structural development of the subsystems.

Sethi concludes that the church's new stance carries with it certain risks that the church may endanger or weaken its traditional role in society if it pushes too far its new role as worldly protagonist. Even if the battle is won, says Sethi, will the church then be able to resume its role as shepherd of *all* souls, including those it may so recently have excoriated? The collision between traditional values and contemporary social problems may irreversibly destroy the values without having provided a substitute. Sethi also notes that the wrong kind of response by the corporation to the attacks being leveled by the church may stimulate the attackers to more radical and more destructive tactics and increase the difficulty of an eventual return by the church to its traditional and valuable social posture.

In the second essay in Part V, Votaw takes a different approach to the analysis of relationships between social institutions by examining the special role of the state in closing the gap between traditional business concepts and reality. The state is viewed, at least in part, as a positive element in the resolution of the conflict between traditional corporate values and contemporary social problems. It is clear that there are many other perspectives in which the relationship between the corporation and the state might be viewed, but this one possesses the attribute of focusing on the clash between accepted values and new social pressures, the very essence of the "corporate dilemma."

It has been said that it is probably not possible to design a social system that could safely depend upon the responsible behavior of its business leaders to preserve the environment and solve social problems. In other words, there are many more social institutions than economic ones which must participate if the environment is to be preserved and social problems solved. At the present time, the great corporation is under pressure from many directions to make its problem-solving talents and its power available in the social and ecological arena; the corporate system is under attack for itself having created some of the problems or for having failed to anticipate or solve these problems. Corporations are responding to the challenges in many different ways. Whatever form the responses take, however, corporations have discovered that many of their traditional concepts, values, and ideologies are at odds with the realities that confront them. It is in this gap between concepts and reality that Votaw feels the state is capable of a constructive role. Not only can the state fill the gap, he alleges, but it can also narrow it. The essay which follows contains both a theoretical analysis of the proposition and examples of situations where the state has actually played out these roles.

Because the essay was written for a workshop on "business" and the state, the word "business" has been used in situations where "corporation" might otherwise have been appropriate. In most instances, the meaning will not in any way be damaged or concealed if "business" is read "corporation."

THE CORPORATION AND THE CHURCH:
INSTITUTIONAL CONFLICT AND SOCIAL RESPONSIBILITY
IN A PERIOD OF TRANSITION

S. Prakash Sethi *

> "But you were always a good man of business, Jacob. . . ."
>
> "Business!" cried the Ghost, wringing its hands again. "Man-
> kind was my business. The common welfare was my business. . . .
> The dealings of my trade were but a drop of water in the compre-
> hensive ocean of my business."
>
> CHARLES DICKENS in *A Christmas Carol*

Business corporations have been buffeted by many a wind of discontent
for their performance, or lack thereof, in the interest of society as a
whole. Discontent has stemmed primarily from government, consumer
groups, and the intelligentsia. To these recently has been added the
voice of the church, a potentially more ominous opponent which, until
recently, had stayed out of the fray. Church [1] involvement in the current socioeconomic conflicts raises serious questions of a philosophical
and sociopolitical nature for society generally and of a strategic and
tactical nature for corporations specifically.

THE NATURE AND EXTENT OF THE CONFLICT

Involvement by the church in issues relating to business institutions and other elements of society has been fairly widespread, affecting
all types of business organizations and engaging practically all levels
of the church hierarchy and most of its constituent units. It would be
hard to find any major confrontation between business and some other
group during the past few years in which the church was not directly
or indirectly involved.[2]

The concern and apprehension of the affected institutions are

---

* Associate Professor of Business Administration, University of California,
Berkeley. A slightly different and summarized version of this essay appeared in the Fall
1972 *California Management Review* and is reprinted with permission.

[1] "Church" has been defined here as all organized Christian religious bodies in
the United States.

[2] For some case studies, see S. Prakash Sethi, *Up Against the Corporate Wall:
Modern Corporations and Social Issues of the Seventies* (Englewood Cliffs, N.J.:
Prentice-Hall, Inc., 1971).

well founded. Church bodies have always wielded significant social, political, and economic power. For instance, they were a prime force behind prohibition laws and have been quite successful in blocking or slowing liberalized abortion laws in many states. The church's economic power also makes it a powerful adversary when it decides to cast its lot with antimanagement forces in proxy fights.[3]

The increased activities of the church during the past few years have caused considerable discord within the church itself and met with strong opposition from outside. This, combined with the continuous decline in church attendance, raises serious questions about the long-run implications of the church's role in society. Assuming the church's right to intervene in issues involving social injustices, how far can the church pursue this goal without impairing its other objectives? A radical shift in the nature of its activities may have a profound influence on the distribution of power in society and may permanently alter our social system; it may also affect the church's character and alter its organizational structure in a manner that may not be totally desirable for either the church or society.

SOURCES OF BUSINESS–CHURCH CONFLICT

To understand the nature and source of church involvement, we must recognize that:

1. Business and the church are two subsystems of the overall social system.
2. Each subsystem has its own constituent institutions, and members of those units have a three-tier system of allegiance—institutions, subsystem, and whole system.
3. A subsystem's character is thus multidimensional.

The subsystems operate within the overall system. They attempt to maximize social power for their membership by influencing the goals of the overall system and by competing with other subsystems for greater social power. A dynamic social system is constantly under pressure to change. This pressure may result from changing needs of society as a whole or changes in the expectations of a given subsystem's membership. Societal needs may change due to external pressures, technological advances, and changes in the composition of the population. These may

---

[3] According to a recent estimate, seven major Protestant denominations owned more than $155 million worth of stock in fifteen of the largest U.S. corporations—IBM, Standard Oil of New Jersey, Texaco, Mobil Oil, Gulf Oil, IT&T, Honeywell, General Motors, Ford, DuPont, AT&T, General Electric, United Aircraft, International Nickel, Celanese Corp. *Grapevine* (New York: Joint Strategy and Action Committee, Inc., 1971).

reduce the demand for the services of a given subsystem, thereby increasing the pressure of other subsystems whose services are in greater demand. Invariably, however, the subsystem seeks to maintain itself by incorporating new functions, thus setting the stage for conflict with other subsystems.

Conflicts between business and the church may arise because (1) the "relevance" of the current goals and functions of any of these subsystems has diminished due to changes in the overall society; and (2) the organizational structure and decision-making processes of these subsystems are unable to respond to a changing external environment. To understand the nature and source of business–church conflict, it seems desirable to analyze the phenomenon on three distinct but interrelated dimensions—the value sets of the subsystems, evolutionary (historical) changes in these value sets, and organizational developments.

DIFFERING VALUE SETS

The value set of every subsystem has a conceptual core that is different from other subsystems. Although all subsystems and institutions must relate to each other in terms of their value sets (goals), the value set's conceptual core must maintain its definitely bounded location in conceptual space. New interpretations or synthetic supplementations and extensions do not cause the conceptual core to disintegrate or its boundaries to be effaced, but rather make them more readily recognized. It is only when the conceptual core (and not the value set) completely loses its relevance to the constituent members of the subsystem or to society-at-large that the subsystem begins to disintegrate. It becomes a prey to other subsystems seeking to expand their social power by incorporating some elements of the value set of the disintegrating subsystem into their own value sets.

The value set of the business subsystem has been dominated by the pursuit of individual gain in a competitive society where the goals of the overall system are assumed to be the sum total of the goals of the individuals in it. When every individual is allowed to pursue his goals to the best of his ability, it is argued, the social welfare is thereby maximized. The possibly negative side effects of this pursuit of business goals—private affluence vs. public penury, unequal distribution of income, a significant proportion of the population consistently on welfare and unable to find jobs, or damage to the natural environment—are considered the price society must pay for overall growth and expansion. Business regards the economic welfare of individuals to be the primary goal of society. Since business believes that maximum freedom for the pursuit of individual self-interest, as represented in private voluntary economic institutions, leads to maximum social welfare, it considers the objectives of the business subsystem to be similar to those of the society.

The church regards itself as the guardian of the human soul and the human spirit. Since the church believes these spiritual needs to be of primary concern to man, it considers its value set to be more in congruence with the overall objectives of society than that of any other subsystem—including business. A problem arises, however, when the church is confronted with the realities of the economic life of human beings. Should the church just tend to the soul and leave matters of the body for the individual to take care of himself? The church has in the past attempted to solve this dilemma by its ideas of the "holiness of the poor" and "the blessed community," the latter placing a high value on equality and personal participation in both the congregation and society.[4]

On the face of it, the church's presumption of the supreme relevance of its value set for the overall system, coupled with its theological emphasis on the fate of the poor and disenfranchised, should mean an inexorable business–church conflict. But until now, this conflict has been largely avoided by providing a contextual fit to the religious dogma. The causes leading to the current conflict may therefore be seen in terms of a reinterpretation of the dogma to make it theologically and contextually relevant to modern man. Since this quest for relevance demands a redistribution of power between and within subsystems, conflicts are inevitable.

HISTORICAL CHANGES

The Corporation

The large business corporation, as we know it today, is relatively young when measured in terms of the growth of social institutions and is unique in character. The twentieth century corporation differs from its predecessors of two centuries ago, which were created by special charter from the state and were limited both in purpose and life span. The modern corporation transcends the finite life cycle of its entrepreneurial creators or current owners. Its continuity has attracted a cadre of professional managers whose commitment to its survival is paramount. Freed from the limitations of size, resources, and life span im-

---

4 Harvey G. Cox, "The 'New Breed' in American Churches: Sources of Social Activism in American Religion," *Daedalus* (Winter 1967), 135-49.

posed on the individually owned and run organization, the great corporation of today has emerged as a social institution of broad power with lines of social accountability which are at best ineffective and at worse nonexistent. Some of the social effects of the large corporation's increased dominance of the American economic system have not been altogether desirable from the viewpoint of either the corporation or society-at-large.

1. The large corporation, under professional management, has divorced itself from the needs of the communities where it operates. Although it professes to be a good "corporate citizen," obeying the laws of the communities and nations where it operates, its economic muscle plays an important part in delaying, weakening, or blocking those laws that it considers inimical to its interests.

2. Business institutions have always had preferred positions in the economies of the nations, especially the U.S., which operate under the general assumptions of private property and a free and competitive market economy. Such a high priority would be reasonable in a society where the prime concern of the overall system is to provide for the basic physical needs of its members. Since business is the primary tool for achieving a nation's economic objectives, it is accorded maximum latitude and discretion in performing its basic function of producing goods and services. However, as Chamberlain points out, this high degree of autonomy permits business to treat society itself—the system of which it is a part—as a field of exploitation for its own ends.[5] Its large economic resources make possible significant control of demand and price administration. To free itself of competition and uncertainty, it channels consumer demand to specific goods and services.

This increased social power makes today's corporation insensitive to social and political changes in society until they become serious and require drastic action. Its single-minded preoccupation with achieving its goals has brought about a conflict situation between business and other social subsystems. The private affluence in the midst of public poverty, to use Galbraith's terminology, has had its costs in the deterioration of our physical and social environment. Furthermore, an affluent society is no longer willing to assign the same high priority as before to economic objectives.

3. In a sense, business suffers from guilt by association. Although public bodies contribute their share to social ills, business invariably gets the major part of the blame. This is because economic values have

---

[5] Neil W. Chamberlain, *Enterprise and Environment: The Firm in Time and Place* (New York: McGraw-Hill Book Company, Inc., 1968), pp. 104-5.

predominated in American society, and business corporations have tried constantly to encourage this identification. Furthermore, business institutions have been slow to recognize changes in the environment and in social objectives, with the result that they have either ignored or resisted these environmental changes, with consequent injury to both the business institutions and the social system.

The Church

Church and secular history intersect, and church constitutions are not unlike those of more mundane corporations. The church, then, may be a "peculiar" institution, but it is certainly not "unique." It is a social institution created by man and, as such, resembles other human institutions. Through the years, the intensity of expectation from the *original* doctrinal system was replaced by an emphasis on the church as the keeper of the keys to the Kingdom, whose specially called and ordained clergy were charged with the responsibility of transmitting doctrine, administering the sacraments, and maintaining pious behavior through instruction, discipline, and a punishment and reward system that made allowances for individual behavior in the "real" world.

The Renaissance, the Reformation, the Enlightenment, the Industrial Revolution, and the coming of the secular city have changed this picture drastically. But anyone who is surprised at the church's lethargy on issues of social justice must remind himself that the essentially "spiritual" view of the church's primary task among men is still dominant in the minds of the majority of churchgoers. The fundamentalists' prime concern is "saving souls," and social action is viewed as a dangerous distraction. With orthodox mainstream churchmen, social justice can only come from men whose minds and hearts have been rightly oriented through the grace supplied by the church, and it will come more or less automatically once enough individual men and women have been infused with faith. More sophisticated and liberal churchmen fear: (1) an avowed departure from the traditionally sacred symbols, and (2) a vague (but stubborn) feeling that there must be something wrong with the church's use of power tactics—especially if ill will and even violence are caused in the process.

The contemporary Christian social reformer or Christian radical is not the first to reinterpret the tradition to justify active participation in the affairs of the world. American Christianity has never suffered from the conviction that the church should have nothing to do with worldly matters and nothing to say about them. New England Puritanism attempted to set up a theocracy, and the sectarian denominations have always sought to legislate morality in selected areas of human activity.[6]

The establishment of a secular nation posed certain problems for the church in America. Devoid of power to coerce the citizenry into following certain value sets, the church began to reinterpret its operational strategies in terms of the prevailing spiritual expectations of the secular society. With the rise of capitalism, the idea of the poor being especially dear to God was transformed into their being those who had lost favor with God and deserved compassion. Virtue was transferred to the rich who were seen as rewarded for their Christian deeds, and this "spiritual" view clearly did not include protecting the rights of fellow human beings if they happen to be Indians or blacks and were in the path of Christian progress and expansion. As Martin E. Marty, the noted church historian, points out:

> The young nation and its churches did not lack advocates of what today would be called genocide. Using instruments of war, disease, and degradation, the conquerors cut into the native population. . . . For all these policies, American consciences had been informed and soothed by Protestant spokesmen, lay and clerical, who assured the United States that it could clear space by removing or exterminating natives, and this could be all in line with laws of nature and will of God.[7]

Nor was the fate of black Americans any better. For a very large minority, the American slogans of "Biblical Exodus" and "deliverance from tyranny and slavery" were merely expressive of vague promise and desperate hope. As noted by Marty:

> They [the black Americans] had not been rescued or liberated. And when these black Americans would evoke the symbols of Exodus, they looked subversive to those around them. . . . The Protestant Empire was built at the expense of black inhabitants. They were either to be overlooked, intentionally neglected, enslaved, expatriated or terminated.[8]

The decades immediately following the independence saw the elevation of evangelism into a kind of national church or religion. The Protestants developed elaborate organizational forms, rites, and rituals—e.g., denominations, local churches, and Sunday schools. These developments were not, however, without costs. To develop *specialized forms* and sustain these organizations, the church concentrated its activities

---

6 Martin E. Marty, *Righteous Empire: The Protestant Experience in America* (New York: Dial Press, 1971), pp. 67-88.

7 *Ibid.,* p. 12.

8 *Ibid.,* p. 24.

into narrower areas and had to "abandon involvement in area after area of men's lives. . . . So the evangelical churches as churches were increasingly content with the business of saving souls, rescuing individuals out of the world, and ministering to private, familial, and leisure worlds." In their need to secure followers, the church denominations became rather like "price fixers sharing a single market," where various denominations were like essentially similar brands of a product seeking spurious distinctions. Unable to claim universal and absolute truth, the churches chose to market themselves as guardians of public morals. "That way they gained clients among the rising, competitive middle classes—but only at the cost of adopting the prejudices and defending the privileges of their clients." [9]

Why has the situation now changed? Here, again, the same forces come into play that have raised doubts about the validity of the historical role of business institutions. The rapidly changing technological nature of society and the composition of its body politic have caused a serious erosion in church membership. Concomitantly, the broad disparity of wealth between rich and poor, and the inability of the poor to burst their bonds of poverty, have raised questions about the adequacy of the church's "politically neutral social service" concept of its role in society.

The church has been severely indicted in this context. Margaret Mead states that "Christian institutions continue to follow an inappropriate, inadequate, and no longer relevant style of individual Christian charity; in doing so, they surrender to the secular world . . . the wider goals of feeding the hungry, caring for the sick, and protecting the poor." [10]

The situation is further complicated by the church of the poor—formerly the Irish, the Italians, or the Polish, but now the blacks and the urban poor. To the latter the church is not simply a group of poor people with a common faith or identical doctrinal convictions. It is an institutional extension of an ethnic community which must fulfill many functions beyond its strictly religious and liturgical purposes—functions fulfilled for the rest of society by secular, social, economic, and political institutions. This divergence in goals among various segments of the church, coupled with its inability to make a dent in the persistent stream of poverty and social injustice, caused the church to examine anew its role in society and to re-evaluate its policies vis à vis other social institutions—notably business. At the same time, the inevitable rigidities in

---

9 *Ibid.*, pp. 68-69.

10 Margaret Mead, "Introduction," in *Christians in a Technological Era*, ed. Hugh C. White, Jr. (New York: Seaburg Press, 1964), p. 17.

organization structures and large bureaucracies allowed some elements to use radical techniques to force various subsystems into operational strategies which the majority neither intended nor wanted.

ORGANIZATIONAL STRUCTURES AND
DECISION-MAKING PROCESSES

The conflict between business and church may also be attributed to the growth in size and influence of the two subsystems and the problems this bigness entails.

Institutions give concrete form to the perceptions and perspectives of their members. However, in a constantly changing world this becomes a problem. To keep their relative social power within the overall system and maintain control over their membership, institutions enforce these perceptions and perspectives on the world long after they have become obsolete. Part of the system's crisis is due to the manifestations of the established subsystems of what their value sets are *supposed to be* rather than what they *ought to be*. The problem is that large institutions are difficult to mold. Individuals divide their interests among various institutions and constantly shift their allegiances to reflect their changing needs. To the institutions involved, these constant shifts in their members' allegiance produce risk and uncertainty which they constantly try to control. The dilemma of society is that while it needs these institutions, it must suffer because of the institutions' unwillingness to contract and expand in response to changing social needs. Large corporations and unions may offset each other's power in determining the economic aspects of an individual's life; organized church and secular education institutions may balance their influence on the development of human thought; and organized parties may offer individual, alternative, political ideologies by which they can govern themselves. Thus, although subsystems may protect individuals from totalitarianism and even from the possibility of ascent to power of one subsystem, they do not guard against the excesses of the institution to which individuals belong. To do so would be to restrict the power of the institution and, therefore, would be contrary to its own interests.

Nevertheless, to adapt to a constantly changing society, institutions must develop more and more complicated forms of organization to survive and grow. Hierarchy is indigenous to all institutions, and their ability to survive depends in part on the viability of the particular hierarchical structure they adopt. Large organizations put severe strains on manpower that is innovative, entrepreneurial, and capable of independent decision making at various hierarchical levels. On the other hand, there is an infinitely large number of tasks that requires decisions to be made only from a finite number of predetermined choices. Under stable conditions, therefore, the success of an organization and the organization man depends largely on how far decision making can be routinized so that—given a set of circumstances—the organizational bureaucracy will respond predictably and acceptably. The institution uses its large size and power to slow down changes in the external environment that may necessitate an increase in the number of innovative decisions—be they pollution control, minority hiring, dissatisfaction of the parishioners, or pressures for social intervention—to be made at the lower echelons of the hierarchy.

Information Gap

An asset in a stable environment may become a liability in a changing and dynamic environment, however. An organization geared to maintaining efficient operations develops rigid structures for information flow and decision making at the expense of flexibility that might be needed in unusual situations. The leadership tends to see the new pressures in the old environmental background and tries to deal with them through traditional channels. The "expert" in the organization sees every new issue in his own conceptual framework—and in the process filters out as irrelevant those pieces of information that do not fit in his frame of reference. Yet this information may be the critical piece needed for the appropriate decision to be made.

The implications of this situation, for both the corporations and the church, are not hard to see. Because of their own perceptual biases, they tend to see the "factual data" in their own way and develop strategies which not only do not fit the situation but that bring them in conflict with each other. Further, the misinterpretation extends not only to the external data but also to the strategies of the two subsystems. The result is that although failure of the given strategies may be due to their inherent inadequacy, the situation is worsened because the strategies are in conflict with each other.

Institutional Relevance

Allied to the problem of a communication gap as it affects the internal decision-making structure of the institutions in a subsystem is the problem of the institution's relevance to the life and vitality of society as a whole. Although the structural form of an institution should be dynamic and reflect its changing external environment and its adaptation to those changes, this does not always happen. Real-life institutions become self-perpetuating and are intolerant of rival institutions and of internal dissension. They appeal for unity against some real or imagined external enemy, with little or no regard for the needs and aspirations of dissidents. The leadership controls the organization and its heirs by its manipulation of organization procedures, control of funds, and information inflow and outflow.

Leadership independence, together with an impersonal bureaucracy, has certain weaknesses and strengths from the viewpoint of the specific institutions and subsystems involved and for the overall system in general.

THE WEAKNESS.   To maintain their position, the leadership tends to appeal to the emotions and common prejudices of the group in power, thereby suppressing the legitimate claims of the dissenting minority within the institution and subsystem. This situation is readily apparent for both corporations and the church in terms of the current social malaise. Corporations, while concentrating significant economic power and exercising substantial control on the market mechanism, continuously pay lip service to the free market system. At the same time, they ask for government subsidies (taxpayers' money) to help them in commercial enterprises (Boeing for the SST) or to bail them out of their financial predicaments (Penn Central, Lockheed). Or, they ask for rate increases (airlines) and protection from foreign competition (textiles, shoes). At the same time, they also warn the public of the danger of too much governmental control of private enterprise! They spend billions of dollars on advertising to convince the consumer that one brand is superior to another and then make style or cosmetic changes to increase the product's obsolescence. They deride the "misguided minority" among the consumers, the public officials who expect too much too soon of the business corporations, and those who ask corporations to improve their products, to refrain from polluting our environment, and to cooperate in correcting some of the other social ills. They insist on being judged only by the traditional criterion of economic performance.

The situation is not much different in the case of the church. By and large, the church is still not aggressively involved in the problems of urban America, the poor, and the blacks. According to Harvey Cox, "The Gods of traditional religion live on as private fetishes or the patrons of congenial groups, but they play no role whatever in the public life of the secular metropolis." [11] Graydon E. McClellan calls the suburban church an institution that has "luxuriant irrelevancy flowing out of its

---

[11] Cox, "The 'New Breed' in American Churches," p. 2.

magnificent institutionalism." [12] Or, to quote Martin E. Marty:

> The massive silhouette the churches (Catholic as well as Protestant)
> create on the American skyline is that of a self-preservative institu-
> tionalism. The clergyman exists as a promoter of the organization.
> Most of its outlines and means of garnering loyalties are seen to
> parallel the mechanisms employed by labor unions, management or-
> ganizations, service clubs. Since the institutional self-interest pre-
> occupies the churches and does not serve the community, it seems to
> incarnate irrelevance.[13]

This disregard of constituency results in two kinds of consequences:
(1) Some of the members refuse to go along, there is resistance and rebellion by the governed, and the growth of counter organizations to
challenge the established powers. The unresolved conflict of these powers
gradually erodes the internal harmony of the institution and often results
in a formal rupture of the constitutional relationships. (2) Dissident
groups fall out of the established institutions but stay within the subsystems. The tolerance of the large institutions for these small organizations wears thin, however, once they grow in number and the mavericks
attack not only large institutions within the subsystem but other subsystems as well. Weakened by internal discord, these large institutions
can ill afford the displeasure and anger of other subsystems. They move
to repress and eliminate the mavericks or take the offensive against other
subsystems in an effort to unite the dissident elements within the subsystem behind them. The ensuing struggle for power becomes quite
disruptive for the individuals, institutions, and subsystems involved. The
analogy in this analysis and the current social malaise and conflicts involving business corporations and the elements of the church is too apparent to need further elaboration.

THE STRENGTHS. The giant institutions—be they corporations,
churches, or government bodies—cannot survive without large bureaucracies staffed by professional managers and experts. Through their technical competence and control of information, these experts play a much
more important role in the initiation and execution of institutional policies than the "representative leaders" of the institutions. These professionals do not consider themselves accountable *only* to the owners of
the organization—shareholders of the corporation or members of the

---

12 Graydon E. McClellan, "The Ministry," in *New Frontiers of Christianity*,
ed. Ralph C. Raughley, Jr. (New York: Association Press, 1962), p. 130.
13 Martin E. Marty, *Second Chance for American Protestants* (New York: Harper
& Row, 1963), p. 65.

church—but develop a wider set of goals for themselves that may be at odds with the immediate objectives of the organization. A professional has a greater stake in the long-run success of the organization, and his code of ethics may demand a different performance standard than is desired by the principals of the organization. His peer group consists of other professionals similarly placed in other organizations. His goals and performance standards are thus likely to be influenced more by those who are external to his organization than by the representative leaders within it.

The power of bureaucrats is apparent in the conduct of large organizations—including corporations and the church—and, in large measure, is legitimized by law, custom, and de facto control of decision-making processes. The professional bureaucrat provides the institution with its forward thrust, bringing it in line with the expectations and future orientation of the overall social system and, at the same time, possibly incurring the wrath of the institution's body politic. He ensures institutional survival by narrowing the gap between the members' and society's perception of their roles. Thus, corporate management declares dividends in line with the growth of the organization, contributes to charity, supports higher education, participates in community activities, and performs other acts of good corporate citizenship—all of which may be contrary to the interests of current stockholders. In the church, the specialized ministries and missions, nationally funded and therefore independent of the local parishes, have been in the vanguard of social activism—e.g. the Urban Ministry in the case of Kodak-FIGHT in Rochester and the California Migrant Ministry in the case of Cesar Chavez and the grape growers.[14]

We may say, then, that conflicts between business and the church have stemmed primarily from the recent massive changes in our society. The dislocations and tensions caused by these changes have uprooted the traditional spheres of influence of various institutions and subsystems and have altered the patterns of allegiance to institutions, location of various social functions, norms of social and political behavior, and, above all, the source and diffusion of political power.

The situation has been compounded by the rising doubts that the value sets of the business and church subsystems are relevant. The social legitimacy of private business was found in a refuge from the totalitarian excess of political and economic power in the hands of a few feudal lords. The modern corporation has perpetuated the myth of individual ownership under the guise of private associations of individuals and

---

[14] Sethi, *Up Against the Corporate Wall*, pp. 324-39.

their capital. Thus, although the atomization of economic power has been maintained in form, it has been all but eliminated in substance.

Similarly, the church finds that its old myth of defining the Christian God and His function as problem-solver is irrelevant for today's Western man, surrounded as he is by a new myth of the rational and scientific universe. It must, therefore, define the gospel in secular terms and translate it into empirical and ethical terms. To redefine their value sets and search for a new social relevance, business and the church must both venture outside their traditional areas and activities. In their search for new approaches, each is likely to encroach on the other's sphere of influence and may pursue courses of action that will hinder the other's pursuit of its own activities. The direction and intensity of conflicts are likely to be influenced by tradition and custom and by the relative freedom and willingness of the professional bureaucracies to seek out new functions, new approaches, and new perspectives for their institutions and subsystems.

ACTION AND REACTION

Our choice of the church as the perspective from which to analyze the business–church confrontation is deliberate because, as we shall see, of the two, business has been the passive party and its responses mainly defensive.

Most churchmen now accept the legitimacy of the church's role "to help the poor" and contribute to the "growth of the blessed community" through social action. There the agreement ends. The debate, now concerned with the questions of church strategy and tactics, is by no means simple. At one end of the spectrum are those who believe in the social relevancy of the church and insist that it should be *actively* involved in the struggles of today's poor. At the other end are those who believe that the church should love these people without becoming involved in the political aspects of their problems.[15] The question is: Should the church be pragmatic in its confrontation and reach for the possible, or spin its wheels aimlessly—however moral the intent and sophisticated the rationale? Should the church insist not only on accepting the good but the possible? The choice of strategies is largely a function of (i) theological orientation and historical developments of various church denominations, and (ii) the currently prevailing fads among the professional reformers.

---

15 Cox, "The 'New Breed' in American Churches," p. 136.

Institutional Differences

Traditionalists are likely to be more or less apathetic about social reform until and unless they are convinced that a value, an institution, or a practice they perceive as sacred is being threatened. Since the American free enterprise system today is thought to be the antithesis of "atheistic Communism," an aura of sacredness attaches to business. If ecclesiastical agencies catalyze a social-reform movement unappealing to business leaders, conservative churchmen will probably do whatever they can to purge both policy makers and supporters and to defeat the undesirable policies.

Reformers and radicals are the groups of churchmen most likely to be catalysts of change and supporters of action instigated by others. They make things easier for themselves by setting up new organizational entities where they can call their own programming shots without clearing them with established governing structures. The line officers of the Establishment, of course, are often glad to cooperate with such innovations because this frequently makes both innovators and bureaucrats happier than they might be were they dwelling under the same organizational roof. Reformers prefer comparatively nondisruptive programs, such as resolutions, campaigns for jobs or job training, or raising money. Radicals add confrontation to these tactics. They use demonstrations or acts of dramatic sabotage to provoke the repressive reaction they hope will radicalize the consciousness and consciences of both reformers and respectables.

The "New Breed" of clergymen, to use Cox's terminology, sharply criticizes the traditional programs of churches and mission societies and advocates using the church's resources for politically active mobilization of the poor and the disenfranchised. "They speak unapologetically of the struggle for power in the city and the churches' responsibility to enter into the struggle on the side of the exploited and powerless." [16] That the New Breed has succeeded in radicalizing reformers can be seen from some of the position papers and policy statements issued by the National Council of Churches between 1963 and 1968. Among other things, the Council advocated the use of economic power to eliminate discrimination against minorities and pointed out that freedom from financial pressure is just as important as civil liberties. It suggested that inasmuch as the church wields tremendous economic power through its expenditure of many billions of dollars annually, it can refuse to pur-

---

[16] *Ibid.*, p. 138.

chase goods and services in the marketplace wherever there is blatant evidence of injustice and abuse. Further, it advised that the possibility of violence resulting from these economic pressures should not lead to the cessation of or opposition to such action.

Professional Reformers

The professional reformer is a member of an organization—university, foundation, welfare group, government agency (dealing with the poor, the weak, and the socially deprived), and the church—whose primary concern is correcting alleged inadequacies in the prevailing social system. The professional reformer claims a higher fidelity to his principles than to his employer. However, to be successful in his own eyes and in those of his peer group, he must persuade his organization's leadership that his suggested program is in the vanguard of a reform movement destined to be pursued by other similarly oriented organizations. This is possible only if his program is not too far afield of the current thinking of other social reformers who are also trying to persuade their organizations to commit resources to a similar program.

This consensus program develops as a result of a continuous exchange of ideas between professional reforms and their need for peer-group acceptance. Over time, interaction produces almost identical and simultaneous reform suggestions by different institutions. These "fads" appear in waves of high intensity and peak out in a relatively short time. Moreover, they are not necessarily the result of careful analysis of a given problem. They may be emotional responses to a social conflict that achieves national prominence or notoriety for reasons quite unconnected to the problem's long-term importance or to its appropriate corrective action. Thus, in his effort to remain in the mainstream of reform movement, the professional reformer may commit his organization's resources to a wrong cause, at a wrong time, and in a manner that may impair the long-term efficiency—or even survival—of the organization without solving the problem at all. Having failed, all the reformer has to do is pick up his "intellectual tools," brand the organization and leadership reactionary, move on to another organization, and propagate another reform at another place—often with similar results. This is indeed ironic because the professional bureaucrat is indispensable to the future of his organization. He provides the necessary link between the expectations of the organization's members and those of the rest of society.

The recent history of church involvement in social action demonstrates this point. The church-related professional reformer, despite his radicalism, has only followed rather than initiated any of the social movements of the early sixties, whether it was civil rights marches,[17] school desegregation, free-speech movements, the Vietnam war, or corporate social responsibility. The church-related social reformer has avoided taking part in a social protest movement until it has become "respectable" with his peer group and has then dragged the church into it, although the body politic was unprepared for it and many other issues could have been pursued with higher returns in terms of social good. Suppose the church wants to be socially relevant, wants to do something good for the community. Civil rights is an obvious area, but other, less dramatic areas—e.g. the consumer issue—would not alienate the parish. Why wouldn't the churches give several thousand dollars to provide consumer reports and list such merchandising problems as safety factors, truth-in-lending, truth-in-packaging, deceptive advertising, and pricing that would help both blacks and whites? Or, why didn't the church take the initiative in arranging local protests against pollution or for conservation? Why does the church invariably respond to outside pressures? Why, if functionalism is a stance of the church, is there no response to pressures from within or no long-range planning to identify those pressures? Or, if the quest is for social relevance, if declining attendance is a survival problem, and if civil rights issues tend to be divisive, what is there in the system that keeps it from responding in its best self-interest?

This dichotomy in the needs of the institution and the programs it pursues can be explained in the essentially divergent outlook and objectives of the two levels of the church hierarchy—the program staff (professional reformers) and the parish priest. At the parish level, areas of social action are worked out in consultation with the regular churchgoers. Thus, programs such as water or air pollution are likely to be avoided because culprits and victims are in the same group, or the alleged culprits are the mainstay of parish support. Such programs as youth activities are therefore emphasized and controversial issues are avoided.

The program staff members do not trust either the suburban churchgoers (most of whom are white) or their parish priest and cannot count on their support. They seek out only those programs that have the backing of other institutions and professional reformers, thus accounting for their tunnel vision on the kinds of programs to pursue. As one church staffer candidly remarked:

> A great deal of deception takes place between program strategists in denominations and their suburban parish constituencies. The people

---

[17] One might argue that since Martin Luther King spearheaded the civil rights marches, the church has indeed been in the forefront of this movement. However, we believe that Dr. King's participation was due more to the ethnocentric value of the issue than to his role as a professional reformer.

in the suburbs have been seen as the pawns from whom funds must be diverted for black empowerment by any means necessary. The scope of this dilemma is seen at the point of the Kerner Report's identification of suburban white racism as the prime cause of black problems in this country and the almost absolute inability of church denominational program strategists to begin to deal with suburban consistencies in light of this reality. They have sufficiently alienated this group that it would not listen to anything they had to say even now when the program strategists have come to realize that this is the key group around which change must be built to deal with the problem of institutional racism.[18]

Tactics

We now turn our attention to the tactics used by various elements of the church in confronting business corporations and to the corporate responses. For clarity and ease of comprehension, the situation is presented in an Action-Reaction Flow Chart (Figure 1). An analysis of this flow chart reveals the following points:

(1) Church involvement at the organizational level is limited to moderate-liberal Protestant denominations and is concentrated in two areas: (a) to seek redress for the problems of the poor and minority groups, and (b) to pressure corporations into greater involvement in such issues of national import as conservation. Church support is comparatively modest in both areas, but it is gradually increasing. The leadership is still somewhat hesitant about direct confrontations on a broad scale and is more inclined to follow other groups, both in the intensity of participation and in the choice of tactics.

(2) Individual clergymen of the New Breed are the most deeply involved. This signifies that (a) the denominational leadership lacks control over the activities of rank and file workers and (b) a growing number of clergymen are dissatisfied with the national church leadership's stance on broad social issues involving business corporations.

(3) The New Breed appears flexibly adept at using a variety of tactics. They tackle issues at all three levels and attack corporations at any vulnerable point. The New Breed is arrogant toward other groups and displays a militant sense of righteousness cloaked in an aura of a holy crusade. Their actions sometimes border on lunacy; in the pursuit of means, the ends get lost in the shuffle. Most of the social issues are complex and not amenable to rapid solutions. Since it is impossible to sustain a high emotional pitch among the followers, the New Breed tends to leap from issue to issue, leaving a vortex of social turmoil in its wake.

---

18 Interview with Reverend Robert Terry at the Detroit Industrial Mission, December 14, 1970.

FIGURE 1

Action-Reaction Flow Chart

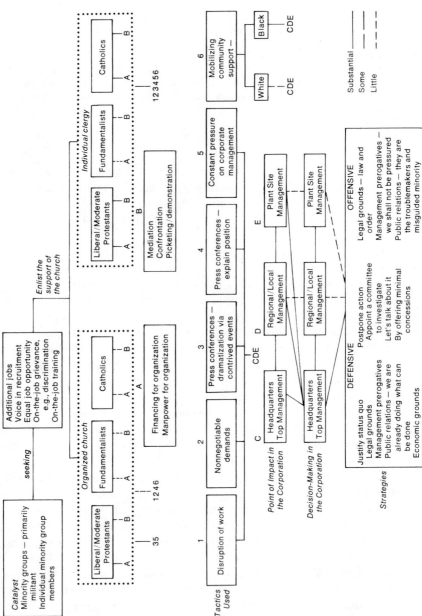

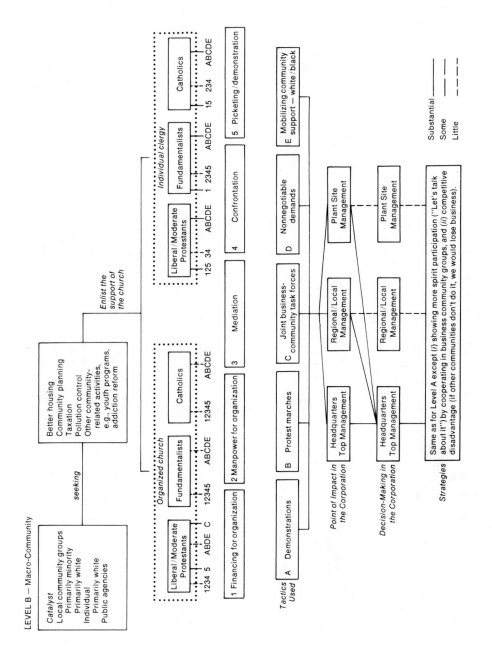

LEVEL B — Macro-Community

Catalyst
Local community groups
 Primarily minority
 Primarily white
Individual
 Primarily white
Public agencies

seeking

Better housing
Community planning
Taxation
Pollution control
Other community-
related activities,
e.g., youth programs,
addiction reform

Enlist the support of the church

Organized church

Liberal/Moderate Protestants	Fundamentalists	Catholics
1234 5 ABDE C	12345 ABCDE	12345 ABCDE

Individual clergy

Liberal/Moderate Protestants	Fundamentalists	Catholics
125 34 ABCDE	1 2345 ABCDE	15 234 ABCDE

1 Financing for organization	2 Manpower for organization	3 Mediation	4 Confrontation	5 Picketing/demonstration

Tactics Used

A Demonstrations	B Protest marches	C Joint business-community task forces	D Nonnegotiable demands	E Mobilizing community support — white/black

Point of Impact in the Corporation

Headquarters Top Management	Regional/Local Management	Plant Site Management

Decision-Making in the Corporation

Headquarters Top Management	Regional/Local Management	Plant Site Management

Strategies

Same as for Level A except (i) showing more spirit participation ("Let's talk about it") by cooperating in business community groups, and (ii) competitive disadvantage (if other communities don't do it, we would lose business).

Substantial ———
Some — — —
Little - - - -

137

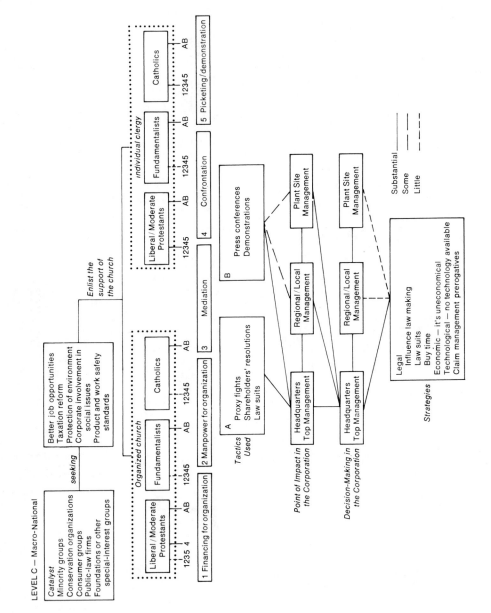

LEVEL C — Macro-National

Catalyst
Minority groups
Conservation organizations
Consumer groups
Public-law firms
Foundations or other
special-interest groups

seeking

Better job opportunities
Taxation reform
Protection of environment
Corporate involvement in
social issues
Product and work safety
standards

*Enlist the
support of
the church*

Organized church

Liberal / Moderate
Protestants
1235 4   AB

Fundamentalists
12345   AB

Catholics
12345   AB

individual clergy

Liberal / Moderate
Protestants
12345   AB

Fundamentalists
12345   AB

Catholics
12345   AB

1 Financing for organization
2 Manpower for organization
3 Mediation
4 Confrontation
5 Picketing/demonstration

*Tactics
Used*

A
Proxy fights
Shareholders' resolutions
Law suits

B
Press conferences
Demonstrations

*Point of Impact in
the Corporation*

Headquarters
Top Management
Regional / Local
Management
Plant Site
Management

*Decision-Making in
the Corporation*

Headquarters
Top Management
Regional / Local
Management
Plant Site
Management

Legal
Influence law making
Law suits
Buy time
Economic — it's uneconomical
Technological — no technology available
Claim management prerogatives

Strategies

Substantial ————
Some — — —
Little — - — -

138

By appealing to emotion rather than logic, and by resorting to rhetoric instead of reason, the New Breed raises the expectations of the alleged victims. However, when the problems cannot be solved quickly, the victims become even more frustrated and violence-prone. Similarly, "oppressors" presented with nonnegotiable demands which they cannot meet may become suspicious of the demanders and resist even legitimate requests more strongly.

(4) Business corporations display two distinct responses to confrontation tactics. First, all decisionmaking tends to be centralized at the top. Thus, issues tend to assume the broadened scope of national importance; personalities become involved; solutions become difficult, if not impossible. Corporations cannot avoid this type of behavior altogether. The nature of corporate activity leaves the lower-echelon management either untrained to handle problems involving external variables or hesitant to take the risks of making such decisions in the face of the organization's reward system.[19]

Second, corporations limit themselves to three responses—legal, industrial relations bargaining, and public relations. Since the corporate leadership still believes in the legitimacy of the goals of the business subsystem, all new issues are seen in their old framework, which is irrelevant under present circumstances. It resorts usually to those strategies that will postpone the day of reckoning, pass the blame on to someone else, or cast doubt on the integrity of their adversaries and discredit the legitimacy of their claims. Thus, problems do not get solved—they become bigger and more difficult; people do not love corporations—they increasingly distrust them; adversaries are not mollified—they become more militant.

PEERING THROUGH THE LOOKING GLASS

Business–church conflicts may appear to be isolated incidents when viewed through the eyes of the system itself or those of the parties immediately involved. However, when strung together temporally and contextually, they assume a new dimension which must be analyzed for its long-run consequences for both the institutions and the entire social system. Where the struggle is between established institutions fighting for their sense of identity and raison d'être, where the rules of the game change constantly, and where the shock waves extend far beyond the combatants and the combat zone, there are no victors—only losers—and no one emerges unscathed. Social institutions evolve over decades,

---

[19] See further elaboration of these points in Part VI.

and often centuries of work by a society and their subjection to sharp and abrupt changes should not be taken lightly. Over time, established institutions become so well integrated in a society that it is impossible to study and predict the many ways in which they affect our lives. Any radical change based on current needs and emotional pressures may irreparably damage these institutions and thereby do society more harm than good. Change must come. What is argued here is not the need for change, but its nature and direction and the process by which it is effected. The institutions are partly to blame; they precipitated the crises by refusing to change with the times. More important, they blocked those avenues for orderly and peaceful change which existed within the social system when the probable change was not to their advantage.

The church has always recognized the need to alleviate human misery and suffering, whatever its cause. However, the church's *modus operandi* has been to deal through prayer, charity, and service rather than by economic pressures or other direct actions. Church involvement in the community's internal affairs through militancy, power plays, and pressure tactics is likely to expose the church and its clergy to the kinds of stress with which they are not as yet prepared to cope. The solution of social problems is necessarily a result of compromises among various social groups. The clergy's active participation in community problems generates resentment among the target groups. Under these circumstances, it is extremely difficult, if not impossible, for the church to provide spiritual guidance to those who resent church involvement in what they consider nonchurch affairs.

There is, furthermore, no guarantee that such involvement is a blessing, even for the poor in general and minority groups in particular. The minority groups not only have causes, but leaders professing to support them. The church may unwittingly support certain leaders who do not agree with church philosophy or strategies on these issues. Furthermore, these leaders may not even be acceptable to a large majority of the people they are supposedly representing.

Another problem is the future. If a time comes when the church and other like-minded institutions have succeeded in fully integrating American society, and everyone has equal opportunities for personal advancement, what would be the role of the church under those circumstances? Affluence does not lessen the need for spiritual guidance or comfort for the soul. Would the church be able to resume its role as shepherd of *all* souls, not just those of the oppressed? Would those groups against whom the church had worked as an activist accept the church as their spiritual guide, or would they simply come to regard it as one of many pressure groups in the social system?

Nor is the attack on either business or the church, in terms of bigness being bad, likely to be fruitful. Large-scale organization is a necessary condition for the functioning of a complex and technologically oriented society. Large organizations—public and private—are merely part of the social fallout of scientific discovery and technological advance. People must learn to live with them and comprehend them in all their baffling ways. Nevertheless, size of an organization for its own sake—and without regard to its relevance to the needs of the people who create it and for whose services it exists—should be discouraged. When organizations get too big and cease to serve their constituents, they are destined to slow death because they cannot survive in the new climate.

The reformers are guilty of oversimplification by equating the alleged faults of business to bigness. It is one thing to say that bigness in business is an important cause of its social dysfunctioning, but it is quite another to say that it is the prime cause of *all* of its faults.

Business corporations still offer one of the more promising instruments for effecting necessary social changes provided they are used judiciously and without seriously undermining their basic strengths. There is much to be said for the diffusion of power and decision making in private hands *if we can broaden the basis of their governance and widen the criteria by which we measure their social usefulness.*

Unfortunately, my short-term prognosis is pessimistic. While the institutional church is moving at a somewhat faster pace to internalize the changing expectations of the society, all but a few business corporations have stubbornly refused to concede the need for a change in their social role in society, the need to share power with new and emerging groups, and to recognize that the social consequences of their private actions must be incorporated in their decisionmaking processes. By being stubborn they have given the militants additional arguments to use in support of radical, often thoughtless, and potentially destructive tactics. Looking farther into the future, I am not afraid that the business establishment will not change nor that the nation will not adjust and find a new course agreeable to its citizens. What I do fear is the severe damage to our social system that may be wrought in the process of adjustment by the anti-establishment forces—perhaps the most intelligent in history but, ironically, unable to articulate persuasive arguments to support their positions.

TRADITIONAL BUSINESS CONCEPTS VERSUS REALITY:
THE ROLE OF THE STATE
IN THE GAP BETWEEN

Dow Votaw *

INTRODUCTION

> I was put into jail as I was going to the shoemaker's to get a shoe which was mended. When I was let out the next morning, I proceeded to finish my errand, and, having put on my mended shoe, joined a huckleberry party, who were impatient to put themselves under my conduct; and in half an hour—for the horse was soon tackled—was in the midst of a huckleberry field, on one of our highest hills, two miles off, and then the State was nowhere to be seen.
>
> THOREAU, *Essay on Civil Disobedience*

Thoreau's bucolic view of the unobtrusive ideal state has long been fallen from repute. Even the less-than-ideal state that treated Thoreau to his overnight imprisonment, for failing to pay his poll tax, seems bucolic and passive when measured against modern experience. The era when the roles of the state could be described or conceived, in minimum essential terms of maintaining public peace and tranquility and protecting against foreign trespasses has vanished, probably never to return. Our society, largely through perceived necessity, has accepted into its culture the pervasive state, whose roles are myriad, often personal, and invariably penetrating. Every sector of society feels the impacts, both good and bad, of the many-functioned state. If Thoreau's huckleberry field is not now an urban subdivision or a factory site, it is because the state has saved it from that unhappy end.

The state today plays many roles with regard to American business. Untold pages have been written on the roles of the state as regulator, industrial manager, supplier, purveyor of information and service, insurer, and guarantor. Hardly anyone is surprised these days to hear the state described as planner, arbitrator, stabilizer, or forecaster. No longer can one reasonably deny the tremendous impact that the state, in its role as customer, has upon business and upon the whole society. Depending in part on the eyes of the beholder, the state is protector and op-

* This essay is a revised and updated version of one prepared for a Workshop on Business and the State, held at Berkeley, California in September 1966, under the auspices of the Ford Foundation. Permission to use it here has been granted. Some of the text and many of the footnotes have been omitted.

142

pressor, a source of stimulation and of discouragement, a supplier and a customer, an insurer and a creator of risks, a policeman, a Santa Claus, and a pickpocket.

The protection of our continental economy has become one of the major objectives of American law and politics, and, thus, a role of the state. Major responsibility for full employment has been assumed by the state.[1] In some ways, too, the state still plays a passive role as an instrument of business; to Walton Hamilton, the "politics of industry" consisted in large part of the gradual drift of the regulatory boards and commissions into the hands of those whose activities were to be controlled, thus providing business with an instrument of its own policy and a shield against state interference.[2] Another Hamilton, a century and a half earlier, wrote that it was one of the primary roles of the state to dispense largesse to business.[3]

Each of these roles is important, each a proper subject for scholarly inquiry, yet each lacks the broad, basic scope of interest that would justify its being singled out here, and these roles as a group are much too formidable an array to be conformed to our limitations of time and space. Instead, let us devote our time to the conceptualization of certain basic roles which are, at the same time, fundamental issues of political philosophy and ideology. These roles are tied closely to the very concept of the state, to legal philosophy, and to the dynamic social changes that are now so profoundly affecting our lives. In essence, these are the roles of the state growing out of our continuing and accelerating preoccupation with the gap between existential chaos and conceptual order. These roles are not new. From the earliest stages of human society, the state was undoubtedly involved in the manipulation of fetish and taboo.

An important change appears to be taking place with regard to the business-state dichotomy. In place of a virtual "separation of business and state" and in preference to a "good we—bad they" alignment, a case is made that a partnership is arising where both partners recognize a unity of goal and a coincidence of certain values and philosophies. If, in fact, such a change is taking place, it seems likely that the roles of the state will be much affected, both in focus and in scope, and the basic conceptualization of the relationship between business and state will necessarily change.

There is nothing new in the idea of a partnership between business

---

[1] Employment Act of 1946, 15 U.S.C. 1021.

[2] Walton Hamilton, *The Politics of Industry* (New York: Alfred A. Knopf, Inc., 1957); see also Grant McConnell, *Private Power and American Democracy* (New York: Alfred A. Knopf, Inc., 1966).

[3] Alexander Hamilton, *Report on the Subject of Manufactures.*

and the state. Mercantilism was such a partnership, of a sort, and the Fascist and National Socialist societies included elaborate arrangements for cooperation between business and the state. There are many other examples. But there is something new about the partnership that now appears to be emerging. It is neither a shotgun wedding nor a marriage of convenience. Instead, it seems to be an intellectual match as a result of the parties' having common goals, interests, and expectations. The "establishment," not a power elite, may have replaced the confrontation of business and state. Whatever the nature and extent of this change in relationship and whatever our perception of it, whatever alterations occur in our concepts as a result, the role of the state as a major factor in helping to resolve the conflicts between the material world which business inhabits and the inherited ideology that guides its footsteps remains. Perhaps, brief attention paid to this role of the state will help us better to understand the nature and meaning of the emerging partnership.

Every reflective person is aware of the tendency of human beings to see patterns where there are none, to inject orderly concepts into situations where chaos prevails, and to find cause and effect in random events.[4] The human mind cannot tolerate chaos. Its marvelous faculties of synthesis, deduction, and speculation can only operate in an orderly conceptual framework. The basic function of the mind is to order the chaos of reality, to build a rational conceptual world on which the mind can obtain a firm hold. The mind cannot deal with accidents until it multiplies them infinitely, arranges them in orderly groups, and constructs a concept about them.

Yet the existential world *is* chaotic. The order that men see in their world is not the real world at all but only the result of concepts that appear to order reality. Furthermore, there are often many different concepts competing for the honor of supplying order to the world about us. Worse yet, the existential world never holds still long enough for men effectively to close the gap between it and their concepts of it. Medieval man, without posing that as his goal, came as close as man ever has to closing the gap, but even the glacial flow of the medieval world was too fast for man's concepts. To put it mildly, the problem of closing the gap is more difficult today, when the existential world is changing more in a decade than it did in several medieval centuries and with ever-accelerating speed.

The gap can never close completely, but man must always strive to close it or else surrender to a life of total fantasy. One of the dominant problems of human existence is that of narrowing this gap between

---

[4] See Louis J. Halle, *The Society of Man* (New York: Harper & Row, 1966), pp. 27-29.

existential chaos and conceptual order. Man recognizes that he has a two-fold purchase upon it. Not only may concepts be adjusted to observed reality, but man may also seek to conform reality to his concepts, for man's concepts of the real world do have an effect upon that world. One need only take an airplane flight over the United States, or over almost any part of the world today, to see concrete evidence of the influence of concept on reality.

BASIC CONCEPTS

Concepts of the State

One observer claims to have collected 145 definitions of "state," [5] and he may have stopped counting—not because he has exhausted the list, but because the task finally began to bore him. There are other political scientists who feel that "state" is not a meaningful concept for political theory and is, at best, no more than an illustration of one kind of political phenomenon.[6] Fortunately, we do not have to concern ourselves with the subtleties which the specialists must face, but we do have our problems. There are many different ways of conceptualizing the state. Some of us may be influenced by Thoreau's poetic view of the state. Others would, I suppose, try another tack and see the state in the light of Hegelian, or neo-Hegelian, doctrine, which elevates the state into the positive embodiment of the "absolute spirit," the highest development of human society; but that approach today produces images of storm troopers and midnight knocks and is, emotionally, less acceptable than it once was. "The State," says Max Weber, "is an association that claims the monopoly of the legitimate use of violence, and cannot be defined in any other manner." [7] Such a definition leaves too much unspoken, but it can be useful. Or, we can accept de Juvenel's concept (borrowed from St. Augustine) that "the state is in essence the result of the successes achieved by a band of brigands." [8] If we stop here, our conclusions are determined by the premise, and there is really very little more that one can say.

On the other hand, we may be persuaded by Marx and Engels that the "modern state is nothing but a committee for managing the com-

---

[5] C. H. Titus, "A Nomenclature in Political Science," *American Political Science Review*, 25 (1931), 45.

[6] David Easton, *The Political System* (New York: Alfred A. Knopf, 1953), p. 113.

[7] Quoted in Sebastian de Grazia, *The Political Community* (Chicago: University of Chicago Press, Phoenix Edition, 1963), p. 84.

[8] Bertrand de Juvenel, *On Power* (Boston: Beacon Press, 1962), p. 100.

mon affairs of the entire bourgeois class," [9] in which case our discussion of the role of the state is somewhat circumscribed and made more difficult. The state that Marx substituted for the unacceptable executive committee of the bourgeoisie has never been approached in reality and still confronts his disciples with challenging problems of reconciliation. Neither the dictatorship of the proletariat nor the withering away of the state is anywhere perceptible and, in reality, the Communist state is no less monolithic and the absolute state no less unrestrainedly glorified than under the Hegelians.

Modern democratic society is neither Marxian nor Hegelian in pattern. One need read only a few pages of Galbraith's *American Capitalism* [10] or Lilienthal's *Big Business* [11] to be persuaded that Hegel is not the architect of American concepts. Observation of the playing and balancing of social forces covering wide ranges of class and status groups and of the reasonably accessible machinery available for replacing a force that may momentarily achieve dominance make it equally clear that Marxist theories are not pervasive. One widely held view in a democratic society sees the state as the social institution through which conflicts among interest groups, including the state, achieve balance or reach equilibrium and are translated into authoritative decisions. Madison and Hamilton, for example, saw the state as an arena of opposing interests.

Is our democratic state, then, only a mindless averaging of the power of various organized social forces that strive to translate their own values into general values? I think that we are forced to concede that the state is something more than this, having at least a "reserve function," in Friedmann's term,[12] that expresses and articulates national policies and sentiments that do not appear to arise from organized pressure groups, or, at the minimum, an "integrating function." [13] Certainly, legislators and judges, especially Supreme Court justices, have not habitually framed legislation and decisions as though they regarded American society only as a "seething mass of impersonal forces" to be held in check and balanced one against the other. The computing machine is one of the important elements at work in a democratic society, but the state is more than that.

---

[9] *The Communist Manifesto* (1847).

[10] J. K. Galbraith, *American Capitalism* (Boston: Houghton Mifflin Company, 1956).

[11] David Lilienthal, *Big Business: A New Era* (New York: Harper and Brothers, 1953).

[12] W. Friedmann, *Law in a Changing Society* (Berkeley: University of California Press, 1959), p. 301.

[13] R. M. MacIver, *The Web of Government,* rev. ed. (New York: The Free Press, 1965), p. 43.

What is the principal concern of the state? Is it, as it became in Rome two thousand years ago, the distribution of bread, oil, and wine to the inhabitants? This is clearly not what is now meant when we speak of the "reserve function" that exists above and beyond the mindless averaging of social pressures. Frankfurter saw the state as one of the energies, one of the foremost promoters, of civilization.[14] The reserve function consists, in part, of national policies and sentiments manifested in times of crisis, not wholly as a result of conflicting expressions and pressures by organized groups, as, for example, the prohibition of commercially profitable transactions with enemies or potential enemies, the prevention of undue profiteering in times of scarcity, and limitations on strikes of more than local importance. "But it is not only the occasional spurt that makes the state something more than the point of balance between contending social forces . . . it is an irreducible minimum of articulated demands of public opinion at a given time. . . ." [15] The "irreducible minimum" may include certain welfare functions, standards of conduct and morality, reconciling the gap between concept and reality, and other aspects of state responsibility, the composition of which may change with the passage of time.

It would be incorrect and misleading to suggest that in a free society the state is the only source of ethical imperatives or of leadership in the gap between the two worlds. It is the thesis of this paper that the state is an important source, especially with regard to business, but it cannot be overlooked that major elements of the common morality and of reconciliation have their origins in the public at large, in business, and in many other social, political and cultural groups. In this connection, the primary role of the state is, after all, the interpretation of certain aspects of the conceptual world, not its creation.

Because the Marxian and Hegelian extremes seem clearly not to be characteristic of American democratic society and because the interplay of divergent social forces does not alone appear to explain the observed activity of the state, we must accept a conceptualization that includes a reserve function whose scope may at times encompass mediating activities in the gap between the two worlds. Even were we to deny the reserve function, however, and to rely exclusively upon the mindless averaging of social forces within our society, the roles of the state in this area would not be proscribed. Dominant pressures would prevail and still seek to close the gap. The broader conception of the state enhances the scope of state action and facilitates the trends that appear to be taking place to-

---

[14] Felix Frankfurter, *The Public and Its Government* (Boston: Beacon Press, 1964), pp. 24-25.

[15] Friedmann, *Law in a Changing Society*, p. 302.

ward a wider participation by the state in the resolution of these issues. With such a conception of the state, in other words, the philosophical climate is more favorable for extensive state involvement with discrepancies between concept and reality and likely to be more aware of what it is doing.

It does no harm, for most purposes, to look upon and speak of the "state," or "business," as though it were a single being or entity which thinks and acts and plays roles. Such fictions are valuable aids to discussion as long as they are recognized for what they are. To pause from time to time for a reminder that the state consists of people, groups of people, and of other institutions and organizations which also consist of people is necessary to rational thinking about the state. How these people and their institutions and organizations arrive at policies and carry them out in action is beyond the scope of this paper, but it is always wise to remind one's self that the state is not really a single being but a concept used to describe a very complex social situation. The state has its internal conflicts, its leaders and its followers; the human and institutional members of the state are subject to influence from inside and outside, and they play a huge variety of interlocking roles. The state, in a real sense, is a process by which all these individuals and groups screen, interpret, and balance a host of competing views, add certain elements peculiar to the process, and come up with conclusions, policies, or guides for action. We then speak of the result as having come from the "state."

Care should be taken also, for purposes of conceptualization, not to fall into the error, common even in a democracy, of looking upon "state" and "government" as *outside* forces, rising from an environment or existing in a context wholly different from the environment and context associated with "business." Not only do "state" and "business" appear in essentially the same environment and context but are, in our discussion here, parts of the same drama, the roles in which we are about to examine. The roles of the state are in part determined by business, and certainly the responses of business to a role played by the state are as important as the role itself.

"Business" does not raise conceptual difficulties comparable with those already discussed. "Business" describes the major economic functions of society, whether carried on privately or by the state. However, this essay will, for the most part, use the term to mean the private economic sector of society. This is so because the discussion will be kept within the confines of experience in the United States, and the very wording of the title suggests apposition of the state and private business. Where, as in a socialist society, all important business is conducted by the state, the idea of "roles" loses some of its meaning, although the broader concept of "business and the state" has much the same relevance as before. That business plays social and political roles often thought to be reserved to the state is not to be denied but does not alter the conclusions.

Impact of Legal Philosophy

The roles of the state vis-à-vis business are essentially political phenomena and cannot be examined without a foundation of law. "Law is frozen history," said Carl Friedrich, "but what of history? Is history conceivable without law?" [16] Certainly neither medieval nor modern history can be written or understood without careful attention to legal philosophy and institutions. This meeting of law and history is especially prevalent in the history of political thought. Holmes recognized that prevalent moral and political theories are the key to the understanding of the law. It is just as true that law is one of the crucial elements of all political theory; "in it is crystallized what men in their time consider just, and there can be no understanding of the political order without a grasp of the common coin of such values, interests, and beliefs as the idea of justice embodies at various stages of historical development." [17] Much of what we assume to be the elements of a common morality is expressed in legal terminology or prescribed through legal instrumentalities. "Law is always the prime instrument of public policy, the medium through which government makes its impact upon individual and social life." [18]

All the major themes in the philosophy of law were noted by the Greeks. One or another of them has been in the ascendancy in each branch of Western society ever since. The roles of the state have reflected these changes in prevailing views. Bentham, for example, overthrew the bland, conservative views of Blackstone and substituted an active utilitarian philosophy, which, even though not capable of close analysis or clear expression, turned the British Parliament and similar institutions in other countries into active legislative instruments, concerned with social reform, almost as much in stimulation of social needs as in response to them.[19] In the last century, we have witnessed in the Western democracies a marked change in the roles of the state with regard to business, a change in no small part owing to the replacement of one philos-

---

[16] Carl Joachim Friedrich, *The Philosophy of Law in Historical Perspective,* 2nd ed. (Chicago: University of Chicago Press, Phoenix Books, 1963), p. 233.

[17] *Ibid.,* p. 234.

[18] Merle Fainsod, Lincoln Gordon, and Joseph C. Palamountain, Jr., *Government and the American Economy* (New York: W. W. Norton & Company, Inc., 1959), p. 52.

[19] Friedmann, *Law in a Changing Society,* p. 3.

ophy of law by another. A legal philosophy that foreclosed or severely limited legislative lawmaking has become a matter of history, with only a few modern voices still espousing it. "Technical facts and a gradual change in the public philosophy thus combine to effect a drastic and organic change in the relation between lawmaking and social evolution." [20]

Let me review briefly three primary themes of legal thought. The school of natural law assumes the existence of more or less eternal verities, which may range from the tablets of law delivered to Moses at Sinai to Leonard Nelson's "ideal of human dignity." The positivists insist that there is no law except what the sovereign says it is. A third major theme is that of the historical school. Law is found in the culture, traditions, the sweep of history of a particular people. As might be expected, the law of nature began to lose influence when it came under severe attack by the rationalists, realists and skeptics. It once seemed obvious that all questions of law and of justice were relative to time, place, and changing conditions of life, and no room was left for verities. Positive law and historical law have been in the ascendancy in the Western world for generations, but a kind of natural law has always persisted and, in some ways, now appears to be reasserting itself.

Several elements have worked to restore some aspects of natural law to favor. In the first place, there has long been a powerful tendency away from positivism. This tendency was greatly enhanced as positivism was impaled upon the horns of fascist and communist totalitarianism. Second, scientific truths, based upon observations of recurrent human phenomena, have begun to replace divine revelation and abstract reason as candidates for the label of "verity." The social sciences are working out empirical generalizations based upon established matters of fact. Third, sources of "higher law" can be found in the "collective conscience of the people" (Duguit),[21] "ideal of human dignity" (Nelson),[22] a "doctrine of justice" (Friedrich),[23] and even in the existentialist "ground of being" and "authentic existence." Fourth, the emphasis among moderns has shifted away from any substantive code of eternal verities to a "science of principles," based on a fundamental resemblance of all human life and modes of existence.[24]

What is the significance of all this to the role of the state vis-à-vis

---

[20] *Ibid.,* p. 6.

[21] Leon Duguit, *Traite de droit constitutionel* (1911).

[22] Leonard Nelson, *System der Philosophischen Rechtslehre und Politik* (1924). Parts translated by Friedrich, *The Philosophy of Law in Historical Perspective,* pp. 184-88.

[23] Friedrich, *The Philosophy of Law in Historical Perspective,* Ch. XIX.

[24] *Ibid.*

business? Perhaps the important thing is that legal philosophy now tends to recognize the need for standards against which to measure positive law and supports the search for them. This recognition provides an encouraging philosophical climate, for example, for the attempts by the state to impose on business the same standards of fairness, justice, and regularity which it sees as binding upon itself. The state may go farther than these standards or not as far, but its role as mediator in the gap between reality and concept has as one of its roots the tacit acceptance of the view that standards are necessary and that they may actually be found in certain procedural ideas. Thus, to continue our example, Berle's view of the modern corporation appears to be essentially the result of narrowing the gap between organizational concepts and the reality of industrial technology; [25] the narrowing of this gap increases the discrepancies between certain basic concepts of freedom, justice and regular procedures and the reality of a society dominated by the great corporations; attempts to close this second gap are based on the idea that certain standards are necessary and are actually to be found.

Gaps that appear in autocratic states can be narrowed by direct efforts by the state to change reality or by equally direct efforts to reinterpret basic dogma. Where international revolutions of the proletariat, as described in Communist dogma, did not materialize of their own accord, efforts were made to bring them about or, at least, to make it appear that real or potential revolutions were proletarian in character. Where these efforts did not succeed, Marxist doctrines were reinterpreted or attention called to the fact that Marx established no timetables. Control by the autocratic states of almost all of the formal machinery for changing reality or for reinterpreting doctrine makes the tasks easier than they would be in a pluralist democratic society.

In the democratic states, underlying concepts are diffuse, abstract and usually not even regarded as the property or responsibility of the state. What is more, the state has no monopoly on the machinery or processes by which either the real world or the conceptual world is changed. Discrepancies appear in all segments and activities of society and are not easily related to specific or clearly defined concepts. The state's role, then, is less clearly defined, less easy to perceive, and less constant in character.

It appears that concepts of the state never themselves become quite existential, though some come much closer than others. Plato's "Republic" and More's "Utopia" are extreme examples of concepts that never

---

25 A. A. Berle, Jr., in "Foreword" to *The Corporation in Modern Society,* ed. Edward S. Mason (Cambridge: Harvard University Press, 1960), p. ix.

approached the real world; the Constitution of the United States is an example of a closer approximation. Throughout human history, men have conceived of ideal orders of one sort or another. Such conceptions are expressions essentially of an underlying morality and do not seek to be reflections of reality, but rather to alter it. Whatever their origins or their ultimate proximity to the existential world, concepts of the state play major roles in shaping reality.

THE GAP BETWEEN CONCEPT AND REALITY

A Matter of Philosophy

The human mind boggles at the complexity of the real world. It must seek a more ordered picture of reality. These pictures appear as concepts, as ideas, and as generalizations. If for no other reason than that they are ordered instead of chaotic, they can never exactly conform to reality, any more than a painting, or even a photograph, of a mountain can be a mountain. The ordered conception may not be very close to reality to start with, and it may persist long after reality has changed. There may be an unconscious, or a conscious, effort to keep the gap from narrowing, as for example where reality is considered to be intolerable or where a concept is looked upon as simply a means to some overriding end. For these and many other reasons, the gap between the real world and our conceptual world is never closed.

A dominant fact of human existence, however, is the constant need to reconcile these divergent worlds. The consequences of excessive or persistent divergence can be tragic to individuals, to societies, and to institutions. Alienation, neurosis, and psychosis are among the individual penalties for failing to reconcile. Extremist movements, both political and social, and the general decline of social effectiveness may be manifestations on a broader level. There are ways of easing the problem of reconciling reality and concept. Ignorance is not least among them. From the humblest peasant to the most learned intellectual, we are all solaced by ignorance, to a greater or lesser degree. Ignorance of reality leaves our concepts unchallenged on the field of conflict.

Most human beings are aware of examples of the gap between chaotic reality and our ordered concepts and have experienced the effects of many of them. As it has often been put, we inhabit two worlds at once and spend our lives trying to close the gap between them.[26] A maga-

---

[26] Louis J. Halle, *Men and Nations* (Princeton, N.J.: Princeton University Press, 1962).

zine story described a few years ago how the top executives of the Columbia Broadcasting System, and their architects and designers, have tried to close at least one manifestation of the gap by housing their new headquarters in a structure whose exterior, interior, furnishings, and decor are purported to fit a unitary scheme. Even the habits of the employees are sought to be molded to this "total design." [27] The desired image of the efficient, forward-looking, socially conscious corporation is made to prevail over the chaotic reality of human conduct. Or is it? One suspects that, although the gap may be slightly narrowed, it is not closed, and that the drawers of the clean, standard, freshly dusted desks contain the same chaos that existed before. The Board Chairman, it will be noted, withdrew his own office from the comprehensive plans.

Most people today are aware of the contrasts between what we conceive the "modern corporation" to be and what it really is. In a genuine sense, the corporate system in America is being subjected to the same searching questions by social scientists today that have been asked of the nation-states for generations, questions of individual responsibility and questions growing out of our conceptual habit of synthesizing individuals into the corporate "person." Individual human beings are a part of the existential world, the corporation and the state are of both worlds. At every level, the two worlds of reality and concept are in conflict. It is very difficult, therefore, to rationalize the concept of the corporation manifested by the incorporation laws with the reality of a system of giant institutions wielding economic, social, and political power.

Sometimes we are not aware of the discrepancies but only of the effects, which we often regard with mystification. If we are aware of discrepancies, we may seek to adjust our concepts to fit reality, as the physicists did when they finally accepted the fact that their concept of the "ether" did not conform to reality. Or we may, in certain circumstances, try to change the real world to match the concept. Where reality appears intolerable, we may try to change it or may retreat to a world where our concepts seem real. Man has often changed reality in order to conform to his concepts, not because reality was intolerable, but because man thought he could improve upon it. Evidence of these endeavors is all around us and increases rapidly as man masters and controls the phenomena of nature.

Efforts to alleviate the conflict between our ordered concepts and the chaos of reality may take the form of wishful thinking, where the gap is closed only in name. "Shareholders' democracy" and "people's capitalism" are probable examples. A classical example, of course, is Lenin's masterful use of names in 1903 to label his own minority group

---

[27] *Life* (April 29, 1966).

at the Second Congress of the Russian Social Democratic Party as a majority (*Bolsheviki*) and the opposing majority group as a minority (*Mensheviki*). In this fashion the reality of being in the minority was conformed to the idea that one should not seize power except as a representative of a majority.

Excessive divergence between concept and reality and failure to reconcile have far-reaching effects on human conduct and on history. Who bears the responsibility for reconciliation? While ultimate responsibility must necessarily rest with the individual, because the individual is himself a part of the real world, and because it is the inability of his mind to handle chaos that brings the ordered conceptual world into existence, every institution and organization in human society also has a role to play, though of a different kind. We turn now to the role of the state in general and then to the role of the state in regard to business.

Roles of the State in General

The Civil Rights Act of 1964 was a direct intervention by the state in the process of closing the gap between the ordered concept of the Declaration of Independence ("all men are created equal") and the grim existential reality of discrimination, brutality, and second-class citizenship for large numbers of our citizens. More than intervening in the process of closing the gap between concept and reality, the state has chosen one from among several competing concepts and is seeking to conform reality to it. The dramatic events in the arena of civil rights, shared on the part of the state by the courts, the President, and the Congress, are a manifestation of only one form of state commitment to the reconciliation of reality and concept. One should not fail to note, however, that reconciliation of this conflict in the minds of many individuals was a necessary first step to the state commitment.

Although the state may play a constructive role in resolving the conflicts of chaos and order, the state may actually increase the gap or otherwise serve in a negative role. During long periods of the Roman Empire, the emperors and the states they represented were themselves manifestations of existential chaos. This is not to say that there was no tendency at any level to reconcile the gap. The primary role of the individual remained, and other institutions, including the emerging Church, began to play enhanced roles. It would appear that Hitler, in contrast with the Roman emperors, had the concepts of a child and no knowledge of reality against which to test them.

In the Soviet Union, the state is called upon to play an even more important role in the gap between reality and concept than is the case in any democratic country of the west. Because the conceptual foundations of Communism rest on prophetic writings considered to be infallible and because these writings had, to some extent, proven to be inconsistent with reality long before the Russian Revolution, the state is now confronted with a huge gap which it must constantly bridge and rationalize in order to justify the existence of the regime itself. The revolution of the proletariat, the cornerstone of Marx's prophecies, did not materialize, even in the USSR, where there was no proletarian majority in 1917. But the Communist orthodoxy is still based upon the proletarian revolution in Russia and elsewhere and on the ultimate "withering away" of the state, a by no means easy paradox to reconcile. The deStalinization of the state and the slow shift to consumer production in the USSR are evidence of the state's role as mediator between the concept and the reality of which more and more Soviets are becoming aware.

Prophecies may tend to be self-fulfilling, however, and the record is full of the attempts of the Communists all over the world to bring them about. The Chinese Communists have aggravated the problem for the Soviet state by refusing to allow any mitigation of the concept or any relaxation of attempts to conform reality to it. The Chinese have problems of their own in this regard. Their revolution was a revolution of peasants, about whom Marx knew and said little.

The state may act to close the gap between reality and concept by intervening directly to change reality to fit the concept, as we have seen, by attempting to change the concept to fit reality more closely, by manifesting in its own conduct a changed concept, or by shifting the consideration of issues from an out-of-phase concept to another existing concept which seems to conform more closely to reality. Because the conceptual bases for conduct are more likely to be overt in the USSR than in the USA, the problems of reconciliation are intensified; there appears to be a greater reliance on changing reality and on shifting from one existing concept to another than on changing a basic concept or on manifesting such a change by conduct. In the United States, where the role of the state in this regard is less extensive, there is likely to be greater emphasis on changing concepts than in the USSR.

The very existence of the state causes it to play another sort of role in the closing of the gap. It serves as a sort of rallying point around which a concept grows and begins to shape reality. Flags, slogans, anthems, symbols, and certain beliefs center upon the state and are imitated by reality, in much the same way that we have seen athletic teams or patrols in a Boy Scout troop come to reflect the wolf, bear, Indian, or Chinese bandit that is their symbol.

Durkheim, many years ago, defined his term "anomie" as the disintegrated condition of a society that possesses no body of common values or morals that effectively govern conduct.[28] A half century later, Sebastian

---

[28] Émile Durkheim, *De la division du travail social* (1893); and *Le Suicide* (1897).

de Grazia did an elaborate and persuasive analysis of Durkheim's theme.[29] It appears that one of the causes of the decline of common values in a society is the widening gap between the concepts and the existential world. While beliefs lose the confidence of men for a variety of reasons, certainly one of those reasons is an intolerable gap between the belief and reality. The state, among other social institutions, helps to reconcile the discrepancies, to preserve the "commonness" of values and morality, and to hold off the advance of anomie.

The state has some advantages over other institutions in the role of rationalizer or reconciler in that it has a wide variety of machinery that is reasonably well designed to observe, debate, mediate, and act in this area. The Congress and the courts are sensitive to changes in public sentiment and have before them constantly the raw material by which morality and other aspects of our ordered concepts are perceived, legislated, or decreed. Civil rights legislation and decisions are good examples of the way in which the state, through its instrumentalities, helps to narrow the gap between the existential world and the conceptual one. The state also provides some of the machinery by which continuity in the conceptual order is maintained. Without the orderly procedures of the state, the adjustment of concept to reality might, itself, produce chaos.

The Role of the State vis-à-vis Business

> All persons shall be entitled to the full and equal enjoyment of the goods, services, facilities, privileges, advantages, and accommodations, of any place of *public accommodation* . . . without discrimination or segregation on the ground of race, color, religion, or national origin.
>
> Title II, Section 201(a), *Civil Rights Act, 1964*

> It shall be an unlawful employment practice for an employer—
>   (1) to fail or refuse to hire or to discharge any individual with respect to his compensation, terms, conditions, or privileges of employment, because of such individual's race, color, religion, sex, or national origin; or
>   (2) to limit, segregate, or classify his employees in any way which would deprive or tend to deprive any individual of employment opportunities or otherwise adversely affect his status as an employee, because of such individual's race, color, religion, sex, or national origin.
>
> Title VII, Section 703 (a), *Civil Rights Act, 1964*

These words support the conclusion that the state plays a major role in helping to resolve the conflicts between the material world which busi-

---

[29] de Grazia, *The Political Community.*

ness inhabits and the inherited concepts that guide its footsteps. The Civil Rights Act of 1964 manifests an effort by the state, not only to close the gap between the concept of equality expressed in the Declaration of Independence and the harsh reality of life for many in America today, but also to force into closer conformance with the real world certain inherited ideologies of business that permit intentional inequalities in trade and in employment. In order to close the more basic gap, the state seeks to adjust reality; to close the gap specifically related to business, the state adjusts the concepts. Reality is adjusted by reducing the amount of permitted discrimination; concepts of public function, private property, selection of one's own customers, and others are modified in such a way as to limit discriminations on grounds of race, color, religion, sex, or national origin.

Clearly, the state was not and is not the only factor at work in the area of race and civil rights. Powerful political, moral, religious, and social forces played important roles in the drama that conceived, drafted, debated, modified, and finally enacted this legislation, but it would be highly misleading and inaccurate to conclude that these forces alone can account for the Civil Rights Act of 1964. In the first place, the state provided the forum and the machinery by which the drama could be acted out and the end product enforced, and the forum has left its mark on the result. At least as important as the influence of the forum is the imprint left on the legislation by the particular composition of the state in 1964 and by the individuals who represented it. Sorenson's account[30] of the evolution of the bill within the Kennedy administration makes it clear that there was a marked awareness among the influential members of that administration of the role the state was playing in narrowing the gap between dream and reality, as well as awareness of the organized forces at work. John F. Kennedy said that the bill was designed to express a "sense of justice."[31]

Perhaps it can be argued that more important than any of these factors was an assassin's bullet, but again the badge of the particular state is upon the outcome. The trauma following Kennedy's death, the superior influence of Johnson in the Congress, brought about a result that might not have been possible a few months before. The gap between the two worlds of reality and concept had been visible for generations; the political and social pressures behind the bill were themselves the result of perceptions of the gap; but the reconciliation of the two worlds had been proceeding at a glacial pace for over a century. The state entered the gap, as it had many times previously, and accelerated the process. The tragic bullet only made this task easier.

---

[30] Theodore C. Sorenson, *Kennedy* (New York: Harper & Row, 1965).
[31] *Ibid.*, p. 499.

Were civil rights legislation the only evidence of the state's role in the gap between business reality and concept, we might be able to dismiss it as an isolated phenomenon. Only two sections have direct reference to business, and the more important of those sections is confined to that portion of business that offers "public accommodation." But civil rights legislation is not the only evidence. Much more important, as regards business, are other legislative, judicial, and executive activities of the state both formal and informal. Some of these will be discussed below. Before moving on, however, it will be wise to consider some of the questions revolving around the role of the state, especially those having to do with the scope and nature of the role with regard to business and how in actuality it is played.

SCOPE OF THE ROLE.   How does the role of the state with regard to business differ from its role with regard to other segments of society? Is there anything that particularly distinguishes the role with regard to business? It appears that the scope of the state's role vis-à-vis business is broader than in most other areas, for several reasons. While business is in a much better position than the state to perceive objectively the reality of day-to-day commercial details (the traditional business phrase, "if you haven't met a payroll, you don't know what you are talking about," does have some relevance), business is not in a very good position to perceive the discrepancies between concept and reality on broader and more abstract levels. (No level, obviously, is the exclusive domain of either business or state, or even of the two combined.) Some say that it is simply a matter of business being short on theory and useful philosophy, and of existing theory and philosophy running heavily to slogans.[32] Business itself is a cluster of overlapping and conflicting value systems, concepts, and ideologies, some of which deny any meaningful role for the state, but business, like other segments of society, must still depend in part on state help in defining and controlling its environment and in adjusting its conflicts between reality and concept.

While business can manifest the very essence of realism on the level of day-to-day operations, it is weak in perceiving reality on levels further removed and in reconciling what it perceives with the concepts it holds. Witness the gap between "free enterprise" and "fair trade." Such congenital inability to handle concepts and reality is not, however, universal. Walter Lippmann suggests that

> The social history of the last seventy-five years has in large measure
> been concerned with the birth pains of an industrial philosophy that

---

32 W. H. Ferry, "Forms of Irresponsibility," in *The Annals* (American Academy of Political and Social Science, September 1962), p. 68.

will really suit the machine technology and the nature of man. For
the notion that an intricate and delicately poised industrial mechanism could be operated by uneducated men snatching competitively
at profits was soon exposed as a simple-minded delusion.[33]

Business has been too busy with practical affairs to be able to devote
much time to theory or philosophy. It has, generally speaking, adhered
to economic and social slogans without genuine content, such as "growth,"
"free enterprise system," "the pressures of the market place are inexorable," or "economic progress comes only from production in the private
sector." The great corporation, our dominant business institution, is a
"callow youngster" when it comes to dealing with some of its own functions in modern society.[34] It is an expert on matters of business activity
but relatively unskilled in applying the concepts of a free political society to an economic setting. The state must and does play an important
role in filling the gaps.

The modern corporation is having a difficult time reconciling its
concepts inherited from the 19th century with the economic, scientific,
political, and social realities of the 20th. Automobile safety, until recently, was seen almost exclusively as a matter of improving the drivers,
and the safety of exotic pharmaceuticals was largely a matter of experimentation by the doctor with his patient. This was so, not because of
evil, greedy business, but basically because business had not noticed or
could not reconcile the discrepancies between their inherited 19th century concepts and slogans with the real world around them. The state,
through legislation, judicial decision, and executive order, has been trying to bring the two worlds closer together. Many of the concepts born
in the freebooting environment of the 19th century still resist alteration
or replacement by concepts more closely aligned to modern conditions.
Important social and political powers of the great corporations have not
yet been matched by social and political limitations and responsibility.
The state has had similar problems.

As a supplement to the active participation of the state in the task
of narrowing the gap between business concepts and reality, there is an
important collateral element. In business, as elsewhere in society, there
is sometimes a competitive factor involved in attempts to reconcile the
two worlds, and there may be a short run advantage to the individual,
or a lack of disadvantage, in not trying to close the gap until all or most
of his fellows do the same. It was an unusual businessman who tried to

---

[33] Walter Lippmann, *Preface to Morals* (New York: The Macmillan Company,
1931), pp. 243-44.

[34] Richard Eells and Clarence Walton, *Conceptual Foundations of Business*
(Homewood, Ill.: Richard D. Irwin, Inc., 1961), p. 311.

conduct his own business affairs so as to narrow the gap between the concepts of equality and fairness, on one hand, and the reality of discrimination on the other, however strongly his own conscience may have dictated his doing so. The competitive effects and personal dangers involved in aberrant behavior were too great to risk. Once the state had taken a clear and authoritative lead, however, as it did in the Civil Rights Act of 1964, the competitive element and personal risk were eliminated, or considerably reduced, and the individual conscience took charge. There is no other way to explain the apparent widespread compliance among businessmen, even in most parts of the South, with the terms of the Act. There is every reason to believe that the same phenomena will be observed in connection with state-prescribed policies on environmental pollution and the safety of manufactured non-food products. The role of the state has its exemplary as well as its regulatory dimensions with regard to business.

The state does not always take the lead in respect to narrowing the gap. Walton Hamilton has said that in the last century, the novel, the brilliant, and the daring innovations in statecraft itself have come, not from the state, but from business enterprise.[35] He was referring to the ways in which the modern corporation has altered its concepts, conduct, and structure in order to take into account the changed reality of technology, communication, and world politics. Even where it does not take the lead, however, the state still plays a role, in putting a stamp of legitimacy on the changes of concept or reality, by reconciling the changes with basic concepts, or by acting as a kind of whipping boy to explain changes in business practice or philosophy. As the predominant form of business organization has changed to conform to technological reality, the state has, in general, accepted it, although here there have been many inconsistencies. The Defense Department relies on the great corporations to provide its needs; educational institutions depend on the large business units for support; the Congress, the Federal Trade Commission, and the courts often condemn the great corporations for their size.

CONCEPTS INAPPROPRIATE FOR REALITY. There is a large family of discrepancies in areas directly affecting business where inherited business concepts are totally inappropriate for modern conditions, or are such as might change reality for the worse if brought to bear, or where there are no relevant or viable concepts at all. In the face of substantial evidence of improving cultural tastes in America, for example, the communication media persist in a policy based on a concept of the lowest common denominator as a measure of public taste and rationalize their

---

[35] Hamilton, *The Politics of Industry.*

own views in this connection with a statistical survey technique of so little credibility as to be ludicrous. It is assumed, apparently, that if twenty-five million people watch program "A" and sixteen million watch program "B," "B" is a failure and "A" a success; in the following season, program "B" will be replaced with another like the successful "A." While the state has made only limited forays into the resulting wasteland of bad taste, there are signs that it may do more.

In general, issues having to do with the tone, taste, and quality of society and its environment are not likely, if experience is any teacher, to be effectively reconciled by business. Prevailing concepts minimize the responsibility of business in these areas. The few gains made in the direction of improving the taste and tone of society have been made over the kicking and screaming opposition of business, with some notable exceptions. Whether it is environmental pollution, conservation, waste disposal, or television programming, the primary resistance to change has come from business, often with the captive connivance of agencies of the state.

ALIENATION ENHANCES ROLE OF STATE. "Alienation" is an ubiquitous word these days. It is used most commonly to describe the lack or failure of identity of an individual, class, or group with the rest of society. Alienation is said to cause unrest, violence, student demonstrations, and anomie. Many aspects of modern mass society are relevant to the phenomenon of alienation. The pressure of an increasingly dense population, together with the absence of practicable avenues of escape, is certainly among them, but it would seem that alienation may also be induced or encouraged by wide discrepancies between one's ordered concepts and observed reality. Excessive divergence leads the individual to seek refuge from his helplessness in the strong personality of another or in the authoritatively proclaimed "ideal" concepts of a group.

Is it possible that one of the explanations for the alleged partnership between business and the state is the result of alienation on the part of business when confronted with wide and unreconciled gaps between its traditional concepts and the existential world? Is business unconsciously seeking identity with the state in order to overcome its own feeling of helplessness in a world where its concepts are being rudely and unsympathetically handled?

There is no answer to these questions, but there are some observations that may be made. Many writers in recent years have called attention to the growing importance of the great corporations as centers of political and social as well as economic power, and have questioned the legitimacy of such power. At the same time, business as a whole, and the great corporations in particular, have become more dependent on the state than ever before. The federal government is their biggest single customer, and the only customer for many of them. A Congressional committee hearing can shake the California space industry to its heels or even jolt the complacent giants of the automobile industry. From a position of arrogant indifference to the state a generation ago, the great corporations have been moved into a position of extensive dependence. Perhaps there *is* a feeling of alienation from a reality which is very different from inherited concepts.

HISTORICAL EVIDENCE OF STATE'S ROLE. By the end of the 18th century, Adam Smith and others were beginning to bring some conceptual order out of the chaos of the economic and social revolution that was sweeping the Western world. Almost before these concepts had been enunciated, two reactions were taking place: it was being observed that these concepts were not enough to order reality even at the time they were conceived, and reality was not standing still. So it always is with man's concepts. The 18th century concepts became more and more widely separated from the existential world and had to be modified or replaced. It was to be reform or revolution. In spite of the "iron law" of wages and other prevailing concepts, the English state intervened early in the 19th century. The Morals and Health Act of 1802, the Cotton Mills Act of 1815, the Child-Labor Act in 1844, the Ten Hours Act in 1847, and the Reform Bill of 1832 all manifested a narrowing of the gap and a change of direction for history. Marx noticed it but resisted its implications.

In the United States, where industrialization came late, classical economic concepts and Jeffersonian concepts of democracy were soon in conflict with each other and with the reality of the Industrial Revolution, but efforts by the state to narrow the gaps did not appear until the end of the 19th century. In business, classical economic concepts prevailed until the 1930's and still persist in some quarters; and Jeffersonian Democracy is still an appealing concept to some intellectuals and to some members of Congress and the Federal Trade Commission. There are those who demand that reality be altered to conform to these older concepts, but it appears that reality here is irreversible, although pressures from adherents of the older views have their influence and have helped, no doubt, to shape the speed and manner in which the narrowing of the gap is brought about.

Even the self-help ethic, by which everyone is supposed to make his own destiny and by which responsibility for the poor is shifted to the poor themselves, continues to exist in a limited way, but the Great Depression so magnified reality that efforts to change the concept met with relatively little resistance. For a few years, it was still possible to say that the ethic remained unchanged and that public policies were designed simply to alleviate the suffering that the poor had brought on themselves; but the impact of a decade of depression was too much for the ethic, and it died out, except among certain elements of the political right.

Classical capitalist ideologies relied heavily upon competition to resolve the problems connected with the distribution of power in American society. By the end of the 19th century, the pressures of industrialization and the effects of unrestrained economic individualism had so altered reality that the divergence with concept was substantial. Much of the political history of the next half century was devoted to efforts to narrow the gap. At first, and to some extent still, efforts of the state were directed at trying to restore competition in order that it might perform the function that classical concepts assigned to it. The Sherman Act and Wilson's antitrust package of 1914 were manifestations of these efforts. In later years, it began to appear that neither could competition be "restored" to where it might perform its assigned function nor could competition alone perform the role even if restored to some real or alleged former condition. The depression of the 1930's was the most weighty evidence.

Sometimes for the express purpose of altering the concepts or the reality relevant to power distribution, and sometimes inadvertently the state began to use other methods of narrowing the gap and to extend the scope of its efforts beyond the economic sphere. Legislation of the 1930's helped add organized labor to the power panoply and deeply affected concepts of freedom of contract and of equal bargaining power. The state itself became a major element in the distribution of power. The giant economic organizations, which were themselves inconsistent with classical concepts, came to be accepted and even to become the legitimate spokesmen for capitalist ideologies. One strain of the concept changed in order to take into account the new reality of organized labor, of the state, and of large corporations, but another branch has tried to maintain its purity by blaming the changes in reality on the unjustified expansion and intervention of the state. Lack of effective articulation and of general application left concepts of power distribution in a somewhat suspended condition. Galbraith's theory of "countervailing power" came along later to help reconcile the gap.

The closing example of the activities of the state in the gap between ordered concepts and reality is in part an example of nominalism and in part a manifestation of the gap between inherited concepts of power distribution and government function, on one hand, and the reality of power and state responsibility, on the other. Owing to profound social change, as well as temporary social pressure, and to the search by corporate managers for grounds for their own legitimacy, business accepted without much protest the mantle of "corporate social responsibility" and "business statesmanship." Perhaps it was a mistake, but few people in business, government, or intellectual life talk today in any other terms. Business statesmen have become vigorous champions of their "corporate responsibility," except when it threatens to become institutionalized in the form of legislation or executive action. For many businessmen, the nominals do not describe reality, are not intended to, and cease to be acceptable doctrines when the state calls for real statesmanship or genuine responsibility. The state is now frequently called upon to narrow the gap between the accepted concepts and the existential world where the state is the dominant power and bears the basic responsibilities for the welfare of the public at large. Business may not be able to proclaim a concept that offers an air of legitimacy and then reject the implications of that concept when transposed to real conditions. The "real thrust of the steel-price dispute in April 1962 may well be as a turning point in the history of articulated business attitudes. Businessmen may well have discovered that the thicket of national interest and public welfare is not one they may enter without the exaction of a high cost." [36]

CONCLUSION

The purpose of this paper has been to consider the role of the state, particularly with regard to business, in the universal task of reconciling reality and concept. The role of the state is great or small, easy or difficult, voluntary or involuntary, depending upon circumstances. Among these circumstances are the prevailing concepts of the state itself, because the state is, after all, primarily a part of the conceptual world, and prevailing philosophies of law. In Western society, especially in America, law is the major instrumentality of the state; the nature, scope, and method of the state's role vary with the philosophies of law that prevail at any given time.

The state's role in narrowing the gap between the concepts of business and the real world in which business operates runs like a thread through most of the other functions the state performs vis-à-vis business. The state is a regulator of business because the concept which nominates competition as the regulator of the market economy is not entirely consistent with reality. The state has assumed responsibility for maintaining

---

[36] Henry G. Manne, "Corporate Responsibility, Business Motivation and Reality," in *The Annals* (American Academy of Political and Social Science, September 1962), p. 64.

full employment as part of its role as economic stabilizer. Classical economic theory either denied the existence of business cycles or blamed the observed cycles on state intervention or took the position that cycles are inherent in capitalism and that hills will inevitably follow the valleys if the system is left alone. None of these conformed to reality, especially not to the political reality that society would no longer tolerate cyclical extremes and widespread unemployment.

In its role as planner the state helps to close the gap between the concept of the "invisible hand" and the harsh and chaotic reality of economic life. The state dispenses largesse to small business and contracts to big business because Jeffersonian Democracy still has political power, and only big business can produce the state's military and space needs. The state is often also the conscience of business and the keeper of the common morality, because basic social concepts of fairness, justice, and equality are not approximated in the existential world.

The state does not necessarily play the most important role in rationalizing the two worlds, although, vis-à-vis business, perhaps it does now play the most important role. Each individual and group or institution in society is engaged in the same sort of activity. The importance of any particular role will vary with the circumstances. Nor does the state always, or even usually, enact its role with beneficial effects. The state may intentionally, unintentionally, or mistakenly widen the gap. In trying to bring about one result, the state may achieve another. As with individuals or other institutions, an attempt by the state to conform reality to the concepts may succeed in altering reality in unforeseen and undesirable ways. William H. Whyte said in 1963 that attempts to change the "city as it is" into the "city as it should be" may destroy the very dynamic of the city itself.[37] Attempts to conform cities to concepts of the environment in which men should live and work have had some unexpected results.

Neither the state nor its role in the gap between the two worlds is necessarily admirable, but both are observable in human society. It seems likely, however, that the power of the state and the importance of its role will increase in the years to come. Though not always admirable or beneficial, this role is becoming more and more necessary. Population, powers of destruction, speed of communication and transportation, and the pressure of human aspirations in the underdeveloped world are now rising at rates which approach the vertical. Any hopes that mankind may be harboring for the erosion of state power had best be abandoned and the effort devoted to improving our understanding of statecraft and of

---

[37] William H. Whyte, "The Anti-City," in *Man and the Modern City* (Pittsburgh: University of Pittsburgh Press, 1963), pp. 45-58.

history in all of their dimensions. Man on the American frontier could live with very little state in evidence; only a little more than a century ago, Thoreau could, not completely unrealistically, envisage a state "nowhere to be seen." All is changed. The state is an ubiquitous and necessary factor in our daily lives. For most of us, "one of our highest hills" is no longer two miles off, but many hours, and must often, even then, be shared with hordes of other human beings.

The most important issue facing Americans today is that of reconciling their inherited beliefs with the reality of the world around them. It will not be easy to accomplish. The pace is rapid, and the risks are total. Many of our most highly prized concepts are not only inconsistent with reality but are also concealing the harsh facts of the real world and causing us to adopt policies and pursue courses of action that seem destined to bring catastrophe in the long run. Because our society is dominated by private economics, the concepts of the corporate sector tend to be the concepts of society as a whole. Thus, much of what has been said here has had a general, as well as a business, application.

PART SIX

Changing
Corporate Patterns
of Response

COMMENT

One approach to understanding the prevailing conflicts between business and other social institutions is to look at the differences in their philosophies and objectives. The primary emphasis in business is to *make money* for its owners. What the business does to make that money is considered secondary. The primary emphasis in other social institutions, such as the church or the university, is to *provide a service* that is needed and considered desirable by society. Making money is not an issue at all, and how much this service should cost is considered secondary. This difference in outlook and objective is not new; the controversy dates back to the time of Aristotle. Often enough, the making of money and the providing of socially desired services are connected. As many a businessman would point out, you cannot make money without making the goods for which society has expressed a need through the marketplace. Just as often, businessmen have been accused of making money by producing and selling allegedly socially undesirable goods at unfair prices and through deceptive means. Business justifies its social role by insisting that its received rewards—profits—must be taken as an indication that society has indeed accepted its services. The dissidents cry that the rewards are unearned and unjustified in view of the unmet social needs that business should fulfill and that business must prove its social worth before it can legitimately claim the rewards it now receives.

The conflict arises not so much with regard to data or facts, but in connection with their relevance to the perceived needs and expectations of society. At the risk of oversimplification, one might suggest that business is justifying its role on the basis of the free enterprise model of economy with the concomitant assumption of individual freedom of choice exercised in the marketplace. The role of business in this case is essentially passive and is limited to responding to the demands of the market. Critics of current business practices either deny the existence of the free enterprise model or doubt its appropriateness in meeting society's needs. Consequently, they demand a new justification from business for its role in society and for the rewards it presently receives from society. This is so because the critics believe that the received model of business rationale is based on socioeconomic conditions that no longer exist. They visualize the current and future needs of society as being different from those of the past. This concern about society's future needs is much more than academic curiosity. It has to do with our individual ethics and values, institutional goals and arrangements, and distribution of social, economic, and political power. As Daniel J. Boorstin aptly points out:

> We Americans have been led to the pursuit of some self-liquidating ideals. A self-liquidating ideal is an ideal which is dissolved in the very act of fulfillment. Many of our most prominent and dominant ideals have had just that quality. . . .
>
> Perhaps we are witnessing an age of the self-liquidation of the ideal of the American democracy of things. Perhaps more and more Americans, surfeited by objects, many of which actually remove the pungency of experience, now begin to see the ideal—the ideal of everybody having the newest things—being liquidated before their very eyes. . . . When the getting of more and more begins to mean less and less, when more and more Americans begin to worry over the comparative merits of their increasingly elaborate automatic appliances performing ever more trivial functions, is it any wonder that more and more Americans become skeptical of the salvation that lies in wealth? [1]

In addition to the differences in objectives and outlook, there are certain operational considerations that further accentuate the gap and aggravate the conflict situation between business and the approaches used by other social groups in trying to solve society's problems. First, there is considerable ignorance and misunderstanding among the critics of business as to the legal and operational constraints on the ability of business to become involved in the curing of social ills without seriously impairing its basic economic function. Second, even when business has shown a willingness to respond to changing social needs, it has been beset by the lack of clear indications of what is required of it with

---

[1] Daniel J. Boorstin, "Tradition of Self-Liquidating Ideals," *Wall Street Journal* (February 18, 1970), 18. Dr. Boorstin is director of the Smithsonian's National Museum of History and Technology. The *Journal* article was excerpted from a paper presented to the House Committee on Science and Astronautics.

respect to social responsibility, the means by which standards of socially responsible behavior are to be set, and the segments of society to which business is to be accountable for its activities. Finally, business, on its part, has often failed to recognize the true nature of changing social needs, with the result that its responses to social pressures have been erroneous and its defense of "prerogatives" overzealous and misdirected.

The first article in this section deals with the types of responses business has made to demands for change by various segments of society and the reasons for the failure of those responses. The second article develops a framework within which business can learn to develop new responses and become more adaptable in meeting social changes. The third article makes an attempt at laying a foundation for measuring business performance in terms of criteria that are more closely related to society's expectations.

Space constraints, the state of the art, and the authors' own conceptual limitations preclude the presentation of all possible approaches to understanding and analyzing the problems that beset business and society. Nor can we suggest any definitive solutions. However, one thing is certain: if success is to be achieved in bringing about harmonious perceptions of the role of business by businessmen and by other social groups, a new, multifaceted approach is called for. We will have to develop improved ways of thinking about our problems. New organizational and decisionmaking structures that are more adaptable and responsive to changing social needs must be discovered. We will have to train new types of managers capable of meeting the new challenges that are likely to be faced by business. The last condition is perhaps the most important, because it is people, after all, who make organizations into social instruments and viable entities.

Can American society create the conditions that make the process of adaptation evolutionary and peaceful? Will American business rise to the new challenge and succeed in bringing its performance in line with social expectations? We believe the answer to both these questions is in the affirmative and conclude by agreeing with the optimism expressed by Boorstin when he says:

> But may not much of the peculiar greatness of our nation consist in its uncanny and versatile powers of renewal? Again and again our nation has shown an astonishing capacity for setting itself hitherto-unimagined ideals, and then proving that these ideals can be fulfilled. And then setting still others. The burden and the challenge of being an American consist in these recurrent tests of our power of renewal. Paradoxically, this is our most distinctive and most potent tradition.[2]

---

2 *Ibid.*

DO WE NEED A NEW CORPORATE RESPONSE
TO A CHANGING SOCIAL ENVIRONMENT?

Dow Votaw and S. Prakash Sethi *

> The front runners of industrial society have learned to cope superbly
> with the environment God created for them, but not with the en-
> vironment they have created for themselves.[1]

The large private corporation has come under considerable attack in
recent years on the ground that its response to a rapidly changing social
environment has been slow, inadequate and often inappropriate. This
article examines the basis for these attacks, considers them within the
broader framework of the role of the corporation in society, and pro-
poses new corporate responses to a changing social climate. The problems raised are difficult ones, both semantically and conceptually, because they lie close to matters of prevailing ideology and because most
of them are being debated in an emotional atmosphere. Any suggestion
that the great corporations are in conflict with society at large or that
they have failed to meet the challenge of change is bound to produce
reactions ranging from instant agreement to shock, chagrin, and incre-
dulity.

Because the public has come almost universally to accept the view
(first expressed in concrete form by A. A. Berle and G. C. Means in
1932 [2]) that the great corporation is one of, if not the, dominant institution in our society, more has come to be expected of the corporation,
and its functions have become more broadly perceived. Under one
banner or another, the place and role of the great corporation in society
has been the subject of discussion and disagreement since the last years
of the nineteenth century. Just as issues of "race" or "discrimination"
were, until recently, rarely debated in those unmistakable terms, however, but rather in terms of "civil rights," "law and order," "states'
rights," "socialism," "freedom," or "individualism," thus masking or
euphemizing the real issues beneath, discussions of the role of the corporation have usually been concealed behind such phrases as "antitrust,"
"social accounting," "social responsibility," "social control," "power
without property," "the new industrial state," and many others. Al-

---

* From *California Management Review,* Fall 1969, reprinted with permission.

[1] *The Economist* (June 15, 1968), 13.

[2] Adolf A. Berle and G. C. Means, *The Modern Corporation and Private Property* (New York: Macmillan, 1932).

though much useful learning has been derived from discussions of the euphemistic terminology and the collateral issues inherent therein, the real issue remains unresolved and, by some, unperceived.

The phenomenon of approaching certain basic issues through masking issues is not peculiar to matters of race and the social role of corporations but appears whenever society is unprepared to consider a basic issue directly or when some of the possible consequences of such consideration are unthinkable or unacceptable. Nuclear war and the increasing gap between the developed and the undeveloped nations are other examples of issues which are rarely confronted directly. With occasional exceptions, the masking issues are the issues discussed, and the real issues remain hidden.

REAL ISSUES STILL HIDDEN

The question of the social role of the great corporation is probably closer to the surface today than ever but has still not, itself, become the actual topic of discussion. The prevailing masking issue for the last decade has been that of "social responsibility," [3] and most parts and levels of society have become accustomed to discussing the issue in such terms. Although social responsibility is very close to the basic issue concerning the role of the corporation in society at large, remarkable skill has been shown by most parties in skirting the underlying questions. Close though it may be to the real issue, social responsibility permits discussion without great danger of a direct encounter with the basic tenets of traditional capitalist ideology, and the corporation has not been slow to accept the doctrine of responsibility, at least in name. The result has been the shifting of the area of controversy from matters of "whether or not" to matters of scope and form. Nominal acceptance is consistent with prevailing ideology, and it presents to the world a more attractive corporate image. The role of the corporation is still out of focus, but there is some increase in clarity.

When Alfred North Whitehead observed, more than a generation ago, that a "great society is a society in which its men of business think greatly of their functions," [4] he struck a responsive chord among the leaders of corporate business. An admonition to think greatly of one's functions has a strong emotional appeal and may even rouse the sounds of glory, but does leave open the questions of which "functions" and

---

[3] See good survey of literature in Clarence C. Walton, *Corporate Social Responsibilities* (Belmont, Calif.: Wadsworth Publishing, 1967).

[4] Alfred North Whitehead, *Adventures of Ideas* (New York: Macmillan, 1933), p. 124.

how one thinks "greatly." Business apparently saw in Whitehead another Luther who was giving them leave to regard their everyday activities, whatever they might be, as a "calling" rather than mere toil;
Whitehead, in other words, was not really raising the question of social
role or function at all but was simply advising men of business to think
importantly and favorably of what they were already doing. However,
it seems likely that Whitehead meant something very different by his
words: he was admonishing men of business to regard their functions
in a general social context and, thus, to think broadly and "greatly" of
them. He was advising his "men of business" to recognize the inter-
connections between their affairs and the rest of society and to be aware
of the role of business in the total social system.

There is considerable disagreement on what the broader functions
of business are and on the scope of thinking "greatly." Probably, the
range of functions and responsibilities found acceptable to one group
or another is broader today than it has ever been. The disagreement and
the broad range of views are not confined to men of business but are
found throughout society. The important differences would appear to
be between the views held in the corporation and those held in society
at large. The views which have become acceptable in society are not
always the same as those held by the men who rule our great corporations, and these differences help to account for much of the criticism to
which the corporations have been subjected in recent years. There is
skepticism on both sides as to the conviction and sincerity with which
the views of the other side are held. The wide acceptance among the
corporations of some sort of social responsibility, for example, has been
attributed to "status anxiety," [5] expediency, and the decline of corporate
legitimacy,[6] rather than to an accurate perception of a social role. The
implication is usually present in these attacks that the men of corporate
business may have been thinking, but neither greatly nor about the
right functions. It is hardly necessary to point out that the corporations
have responded in kind.

WHY THE CONTROVERSY?

REASONS FOR DIFFERING VIEWS. The reasons for these differences
of opinion and the grounds for the attacks on the corporation are
several in number.

---

[5] Paul T. Heyne, *Private Keepers of the Public Interest* (New York: McGraw-
Hill, 1968), p. 110.

[6] Earl F. Cheit, ed., *The Business Establishment* (New York: John Wiley and
Sons, 1964), chap. 5.

First, a rapidly changing social environment, the dimensions, directions and details of which are not yet entirely revealed or understood, has already had an impact on social attitudes and values and may even be producing a new view of the United States in the stream of history. The corporations have not kept pace. The steel price controversy during the Kennedy administration is an example, but attitudes toward environmental pollution, population growth, and matters affecting the taste, tone, and quality of life are probably better ones. Some observers even foretell the ascendancy of truth and beauty as dominant social values and admonish the corporate system to anticipate and adapt to these basic alterations in the environment.[7]

On numerous occasions the impacts of change appear to have come as a considerable surprise to some of the great corporations. Their responses to challenge are often borrowed inappropriately from the past. The automobile companies continued to base their safety policies on the "fool behind the wheel" idea until public indignation, federal legislation, and the courts made that view untenable. Until the Watts and Detroit riots, the prevailing corporate approach to the problems of the ghetto and race was to hire a few more black custodians and set up another platitudinous "businessmen's action committee." There have always been exceptions, and there are more now than ever, but, unfortunately, response only to crisis and too little response too late seem still to be the characteristic reactions of the men of corporate business.

Every society at all times in human history has necessarily had to operate within the constraints of certain values, concepts, and relationships prevailing in the society at the time. Some of these constraints appear to be so thoroughly accepted and so favorably regarded at any one time that they are not subject to critical evaluation or to planned change. Others are viewed as being in doubt and as the proper targets for appraisal and intentional alteration.[8] Both kinds of constraint do change, as a matter of social fact, one because we will it so and the other because no value or concept or relationship is completely static or wholly immune from the effects of changes in other aspects of society. Not long ago, it was unthinkable even to discuss the possibility of hiring unqualified or less qualified men and women because of their race, or of paying the poor a negative income tax, but such conduct is now becoming not only thinkable but actual in wide areas of our society, largely as a result of shifts taking place in other social values. Perhaps

---

[7] Berle, *The American Economic Republic* (New York: Harcourt, Brace & World, 1963, 1965), chap. 13.

[8] See an interesting discussion in Robert A. Solo, *Economic Organizations and Social Systems* (Indianapolis: Bobbs-Merrill, 1967), chap. 31.

the change could only have come about as a result of crisis; perhaps one could not have expected the great corporations to be the leaders rather than reluctant followers, but the fact is that the corporations were not the leaders, nor have they been leaders in matters of pollution or safety, where one might more reasonably have expected it, and many changes in social values and concepts have gone unperceived by the managers of corporate business. It is these discrepancies between what society accepts as being capable or worthy of change and what the great corporations accept that constitute the first reason for the conflicting views as to the role of the corporation in society.

There has been a basic alteration in our society with regard to values, concepts, and relationships affecting the corporation which are subject to doubt and rational change. It is not that the corporation's traditional economic function is sought to be supplanted by other functions, although some corporate spokesmen see it this way, but it is that a simplistic, classical view of the corporation's role is being supplemented by a social, political, and longer-range view. A few representatives of the corporate sector have accepted the newer concept, some of them without recognizing the consequences of so doing. Most have not accepted it or, perhaps, even understood it. The responsibilities of the great corporations, that is, thinking greatly of their functions, can no longer be discharged by simply providing society with goods and services at a reasonable profit. Larger and larger portions of society are coming to the view that the acute social and environmental problems of society cannot be solved unless the role of the corporation is expanded to include other than purely economic responsibilities. It has long been clear that the mindless drift of the "invisible hand" cannot be counted on to solve the problems of pollution, employment, and technology or not to aggravate issues of race, education, and population. The failure of the great corporations to see and to understand many of these important changes in social values has by now produced a credibility gap and helped to explain recent attacks on the weak corporate response to change.

A second, and closely related, reason for the discrepancies is a strong tradition in Western thought which has led us to believe that we can subdivide our society into functional elements, study each more or less in isolation from the rest, and establish criteria for the improvement of each with little, if any, reference to the remainder of the system. In a provocative little book, *Challenge to Reason*,[9] C. West Churchman recently emphasized the special need today to view and understand whole systems before seeking to improve subsystems and parts of systems and the importance of changing the traditional view. The validity of

---

[9] C. West Churchman, *Challenge to Reason* (New York: McGraw-Hill, 1968).

Churchman's ideas is nowhere more visible or more significant than in connection with the study of the great corporation and its functions in our total social system. He says that "we seem forced to conclude that anyone who actually believes in the possibility of improving systems is faced with the problem of understanding the properties of the whole system, and that he cannot concentrate his attention merely on one sector. The problem of system improvement is the problem of the 'ethics of the whole system.' " [10]

Neil Chamberlain has taken an approach very similar to Churchman's and has carried it forward into a detailed examination of the interplay between the individual firm and economic society as a whole.[11] The conclusions of the two authors, one working out of systems science and the other out of economics, are virtually identical. Churchman emphasizes the science of large systems, while Chamberlain dwells on the economic unit and its relation to society, but the thrust of both types of analysis is the same: A subsystem achieves meaning only within the context of a larger system.

The corporate subsystem is rarely so examined, however, or its improvements considered in the light of the whole system. Through most of our history, it probably would not have made much difference how the subsystem was sought to be improved, and the workings of the isolated subsystem under the rules of laissez faire may have produced the best result that could have been produced under the circumstances. Our population, in relation to available land, was small, and large "individual distances" [12] surrounded almost everyone. Changes brought about by technology were relatively slow in affecting society at large. Safety valves, cushions, and alternatives of one sort and another kept the interactions among the parts of the whole system at a minimum.

It makes a difference now, however. The mitigating factors are no longer present in the same degree. Individual distances are getting smaller day by day. Interactions among all the subsystems and parts of systems become more intimate and more immediate. The corporate decision in New York can affect the farmer in Iowa and the day laborer in Watts, not in years or months or even days, but in minutes, as a machine replaces a man, a price is changed, a product introduced or abandoned, an attitude expressed or a policy promulgated. The alternatives are fewer, the cushions thinner, the safety valves often inoperative, and our dependence on each other more nearly complete.

The environment has changed; the interactions among the parts

---

[10] *Ibid.,* p. 4.

[11] Neil W. Chamberlain, *Enterprise and Environment* (New York: McGraw-Hill, 1968).

[12] Robert Ardrey, *The Territorial Imperative* (New York: Atheneum, 1966).

of our social system have tightened; the space between man and man has decreased, but we still go about our frustrating task of trying to improve the corporate subsystem (and others) as though it were unrelated to the whole. Technology is allowed to enter the social realm screened only by the economic test of corporate profit. Society at large is still viewed essentially as a guinea pig of limitless patience and unbounded endurance. Wastes pour into lakes, streams and air. Insecticides and detergents pour into the environment without consideration for persistence, degradability, or relation to the ecology. Even the Food and Drug Administration is still under constant attack because it attempts to provide some modicum of protection against the untested or casually tested drug or chemical. All of these things grow out of the failure to understand our whole system before tinkering with or seeking to improve its parts. Furthermore, large portions of society are beginning to look at and to try to understand the whole system and, as they do, become increasingly aware of the preoccupation of the corporation with its own subsystem and its general disregard for the whole. Among the results are pressures for changes, differences of opinion as to the role of the corporation, gross incongruences between corporate and social goals, and attacks upon the corporation for its failure to respond properly to the problems that challenge the whole society.

The failure of the corporation to see its role in system-wide perspective has produced much irrational comment and behavior, some sharp inconsistencies in the views expressed in the corporate subsystem itself, and, most important, the surprise with which the new challenges have caught corporate managers. Of course, prevailing corporate ideologies make it difficult for managers to see the social system as a whole. A manager schooled in the classical doctrine that the corporation serves best when it sticks to its economic knitting who then becomes persuaded that the great corporation is the dominant institution in our society is very likely to combine the two ideas into a barrier impenetrable to notions of whole systems or their relevance. A dominant institution whose every act is necessarily best for all concerned does not have to pay much attention to the rest of the system. This, it seems to us, is one of the primary reasons why so many managers regard admonitions concerning responsibility to or role in a whole system as being attacks on the profit motive and private enterprise. They are certainly attacks on classical doctrine, insofar as it manifests the traditional Western view of subsystems and whole systems or of unqualified versions of laissez-faire economics, but it need not be regarded as an attack on the profit system or private enterprise. The admonitions seek only to call attention to the interrelations among the parts of the system, to the changing environment, and to the importance of these elements to the corporate subsystem in the long run.

An example of the effect of the failure of the corporate managers to consider the whole system is the inconsistency between the way the corporations regard the importance of flexibility and innovative skill in meeting new challenges of the market or of technology and the manner in which the corporations react to such challenges as safety, hard core unemployed, urban blight, or environmental pollution. Where the goals are, to the corporations, exclusively or primarily economic and market or production oriented, challenges are welcomed as opportunities and much social benefit and public relations mileage are obtained from the skillful application of innovative techniques and managerial talents in meeting and overcoming the challenge. When the issue of social cost or responsibility enters the picture, as with safety or pollution or hiring policies in the urban ghetto, the applicability of innovative and managerial skill seems abruptly to become, not an opportunity, but a burden. The challenge is not welcomed, but is usually consigned to the state for solution.

A large oil company, not many years ago, complained loudly and persuasively that it was not possible to solve the pollution problem involved in the discharge of waste water from its refining process without oppressively raising its costs, but a recent newspaper story revealed that, when the company finally got to work on the problem, it discovered that it could actually make a profit on the control of pollution and could discharge clean water into the streams. In fact, the treatment worked so well, said the story, "the greater the pollution potential, the greater the profit." Instead of viewing legislative standards of air pollution and safety as givens and challenges to which ingenuity and innovation might properly be applied, most of the automobile companies behaved as though they were the innocent victims of a problem which was wholly unrelated to their activities.

This paradox is hard to explain except in terms of failure to adopt a system-wide view. Opportunities are missed or even regarded as burdens when the relationship between subsystem and system is seen only in the narrow producer-consumer context. "New opportunities which a firm may encounter," says Chamberlain, "are produced by changes in its environment or changes in its role." [13] Berle puts it almost the same way: "Progress toward greater realization of the values of truth and beauty, or preferably both (not to mention others), affords scope for American industrial development to several times its present volume and intensity." [14]

Why is it that the great corporation does not appear to perceive changes in the social environment as providing opportunities or afford-

[13] Chamberlain, *Enterprise and Environment,* p. 141.
[14] Berle, *American Economic Republic,* pp. 207-8.

ing greater scope for industrial development? Because the corporate managers have not been able properly to include in the value set of the corporate subsystem the changing values of the whole system and the interplay between the two. Once the system is seen as a whole, the values of the whole can become part of the value set of the subsystem. Corporate policy and conduct will come to be affected by changing social values with respect to minority groups, the elderly, the young, the poor, the pollution of the environment, and the taste, tone, and quality of life in this society.

A third reason why the great corporations have not kept up with the changing environment, why they are under attack, and why their views of their functions are coming into conflict with the views that society takes of their role is that corporate managers are rarely philosophers. They have not, until now, been expected to be and have not very often had an occasion to be philosophers. Yet a philosophical outlook is necessary before one can understand the need for looking at whole systems, before one can detect changing social values, concepts, and relationships at an early stage of their development, before one can genuinely assume social responsibility or think "greatly" on one's functions, and before one can see one's functions in a broad context. Philosopher kings are not unknown. Philosopher scientists are almost commonplace today. Is it too much to expect the managers of the great corporations occasionally to don the philosopher's gown and to think the philosopher's thoughts?

Is it difficult to visualize the philosopher manager? Not at all. Can a philosopher manager retain the pragmatic outlook, action-oriented demeanor, and processes of reasoning which are so essential to his craft? Of course he can. He may need only a willingness to try to relate himself and his activities to society in a broader context than economics and an open-mindedness about the social and political phenomena he sees around him. Maybe, after all, what Whitehead really meant by "thinking greatly" was simply thinking "philosophically."

Nobody can expect or desire corporate leaders to supply all the ordering principles required by society, although many of the principles in current dominance had their origins in the corporate interpretations of capitalism, but one can expect some breadth of outlook and a degree of philosophical thought sufficient to orient the corporate manager to society at large. Moral challenges are not new to the corporation nor is the realization that a free society can exist only on a moral basis. When asked why they were becoming involved in finding solutions to the urban crisis, a few of the nation's corporate leaders recently gave answers substantially inconsistent with the answer expected of them. Those questioned were expected to say: "enlightened self-interest." Most of them did, or something like it, but a few explained their acts in terms of social needs and problems and the inescapable demand that something be done about them for the benefit of all.[15]

THE CORPORATION'S ROLE

ALTERNATIVE VIEWS OF FUNCTION.   Let us turn now to a brief examination of alternative views of the function or role of the corporation in society. The essential question is whether there is any function beyond the economic one. Our search is not for substitutes but for supplemental or collateral functions. There is almost universal consensus that the primary function of the great corporation is the economic one, so we need not belabor that point. Is there something more? The literature is full of answers.

The negative is argued by those who feel that the vital economic role may be weakened or destroyed if the corporation assumes responsibility outside the economic sphere and by those who fear the meddling of untrained, inexperienced, and profit-motivated businessmen in social and political matters. The affirmative view is argued on a number of different grounds ranging from the contribution which the corporation has made in creating many of the problems which face society today to the emotionally appealing "we are all in the same boat" idea. Several other arguments are based upon variations or blends of these two. In a sense, almost all of the affirmative arguments depend upon a "whole system" assumption, although it is usually unspoken.

Circulating in society today is a negative answer to the question of whether there is a corporate role or function or responsibility beyond the economic, which is based upon an ancient argument denying individual responsibility where society at large is damaged only by the aggregated action of many individuals.[16] Where, for example, the dumping of untreated waste into a river by one corporation does not kill the fish or produce stench and ugliness, while dumping of waste by several corporations does so pollute the river, it is "unjust" to expect the individual to treat his waste before discharging it. The decision on this matter, runs the argument, is a political one, and it is up to the legislature or some other political body to determine the public interest and establish appropriate sanctions. The proponents of this view, having made what appears to them to be an irrefutable point, usually stop at this stage of the argument. In doing so, they have made the same argu-

---

[15] *Fortune* (July 1968), 57-58.

[16] Heyne, *Private Keepers of the Public Interest,* chap. 8.

ment which many individual Germans made when charged with responsibility for the horrors of the Nazi era. Suppose, for one reason or another, the political body does not act or acts improperly or is slow to act or is not aware of the problem. Does the individual have a responsibility to call attention to the problem, to seek collective action among his fellows, or to urge the political body to determine the public interest and legislate?

The solution is not to conclude that there is no individual responsibility, as the advocates of this negative view usually do, but to affirm the responsibility and recognize that different circumstances may call for different ways of discharging that responsibility. It is patently incorrect today to say that the individual polluter has no responsibility. It is correct to say that he does have responsibility but that circumstances may not dictate that he can only meet that responsibility by immediately treating his waste. His response to the problem might better take the form of seeking collective action among his fellow polluters and/or pressing for politically determined standards or sanctions, or other alternatives.

The same approach should be taken whether the issue is one of pollution, or automobile design, or hiring procedures, or the attitudes of white men toward black men. Regardless of the way in which responsibility is responded to or function or role perceived, the responsibility or function or role is often there anyway. If we conclude in these special situations that there is no responsibility or that something or other is not the proper function or role of the corporation and its managers, we may be disarming the very force which could bring about the political action necessary to resolve the problem. Where no responsibility is seen, the individual may feel that he must oppose the political action aimed at solving the problem, as where a legislature seeks to impose standards of safety or pollution or hiring. If, on the other hand, responsibility is accepted and alternative courses of action recognized, the corporation and its managers may be inclined to seek or make appropriate response to the problems, whether collectively or individually caused. Is it necessarily unethical or unprofitable for corporations to exert their considerable influence and political power to encourage political determinations of public interest and standards of waste treatment, safety, or hiring that apply to all? Of course not.

Is it unethical or unprofitable for corporations to provide the means by which society can become informed with regard to social problems, to support a forum in which competing ideas can be debated, or to do as Xerox Corporation has done in sponsoring a series of television events on the role of the black American in our history. "By showing the many vital roles the Negro has played in our history—soldier, statesman, scientist, athlete, musician, author, industrialist, legislator—*Of Black America* gives us the opportunity to acquire a true perspective and perhaps a deeper understanding." [17] Might not General Motors have supported a television forum on automobile safety, instead of reacting as it did to Ralph Nader's goading? Or the lumber companies encouraged an honest public presentation of the issues involved in the proposed Redwood National Park? The list of examples could be made very long. The point is simple.

One of the reasons why corporate power is so seldom used in this direction is that corporate function, role, and responsibility are rarely seen in the necessary terms. In this most important respect, the great corporations have failed to keep up and have acted inconsistently with changing social values and concepts. One cannot say with certainty what the boundaries of corporate responsibility and function are, but it is becoming abundantly clear that those boundaries can no longer be measured by economic tests alone. The view that maximizing profits is the only way to be a responsible citizen has not been a tenable view for half a century. "If we say that all business firms pursue the generalized objective of profit, we can add that they do so in a multitude of ways, exhibiting a wide range of philosophical values, personal idiosyncrasies, and discretionary powers." [18] Large corporations are not helpless chips subject to the vagaries of overwhelming market forces, but follow certain courses and take certain directions in preference to others. "Profit," as a goal, describes only a generalized objective or stance. "Maximum profit as a basis for choosing among alternative strategies is not operational." [19]

It can no longer be argued that there is no individual responsibility where social costs and impact result only from collective action. Nor can refuge be found in the distinction between the responsibilities of corporate managers as individual citizens and their responsibilities as managers of great corporations. It is not the managers as citizens who make decisions regarding the discharge of waste, the design and safety of products, and the hiring practices of their companies; it is the managers as managers who make these decisions. Another and much more complex issue involved here is the role that the attitude of the white manager as citizen toward black men plays in the attitude of the white manager as manager. The impact of the attitude as citizen may be magnified a thousand times

---

[17] Mailed publicity regarding a series of seven weekly television programs beginning July 2, 1968.

[18] Chamberlain, *Enterprise and Environment*, p. 46.

[19] *Ibid.*, p. 55.

when carried over into attitudes and decisions made as manager of a great corporation. It is not likely that the economic test alone can resolve that dilemma.

Is what has been said here really a shocking or radical view of the responsibilities and functions of the corporation or an aberrant way of looking at how one thinks "greatly"? It does not have to be. It would seem that the long-run interests of the corporation, its managers and stockholders, depend in very large part upon the means and success with which certain critical social problems in the next decade or two are sought to be resolved. Many of our society's best minds, skills, experience and innovative techniques are reservoired in the great corporations. Many of the social problems themselves are attributable to ways in which technology and the corporation have revamped our environment. The corporations are among the major repositories of power and influence. The problems cannot and will not be solved by political bodies alone. The corporations and their racing technology are already manufacturing some of the critical problems of the future. The corporations have as great a stake in the proper solution of these problems as any person or group in society. If the challenges are not met and the problems not solved, our political, social and economic environment a few decades from now may be unthinkable in today's terms. It is not a matter of the government's doing the job if the corporation does not, although that is not an attractive prospect either; it is a matter of the sheer impossibility of the government's doing the job alone in a free society and of the destruction of the free society if the job is not done.

Is the corporation being asked to assume responsibility or to do something which it cannot be expected to do or to assume? Is the corporation being asked to take over the political role of the state? The answer to both questions is an unqualified "No."

What is being asked, as a *Fortune* editorial also asked recently,[20] is that the corporation see its function as including participation in the development of new institutional arrangements and new avenues of communication by which the major elements in society can effectively work together to reach understanding and to solve our problems. The corporation is also being asked to review its responsibilities in a broader and more nearly system-wide context than has usually been the case before and to use its influence to encourage and help political bodies determine the public interest and take appropriate action based thereon.

American corporations which establish operations abroad sometimes appear, especially in underdeveloped nations, to be more aware of, to pay more attention to, and to take more direct responsibility for

---

[20] *Fortune* (January 1968), 127-28.

the social, political, and environmental impact of their activities than they do at home. A system-wide approach seems to be becoming more common and the relevance of social costs seems to be better accepted when American businessmen operate in foreign countries than when they are considering their activities at home. Interesting and revealing results might flow from research into this question. If these casual observations are accurate, it would suggest that American corporations are not only capable of system-wide and social cost thinking but are often very successful at it.

THE PUBLIC'S VOICE

GOALS AND PUBLIC INTEREST. It is not enough that the corporation simply make itself more amenable to philosophical thoughts and regard itself as a part of a larger and more basic system. "Thinking greatly" has other dimensions, and these must be explored before we can proceed to the specific details of a new response to a changing environment. Were the corporate system a minor or inconsequential subsystem in a broad social whole, the issue of its proper response to changing conditions in the total environment would be largely a matter of its own relevance or survival. But the corporation is not an inconsequential subsystem. The issues of its conduct and of its responses to change are more than a matter of its own relevance or survival and profoundly involve the whole system. Therefore, conscious effort must be made by those who represent the corporate sector to keep corporate policy and activity in conformity with the public interest. This will often, if not usually, consist of minding strictly one's economic knitting, but, if what has been said above has any meaning at all, keeping corporate behavior in conformity with the public interest will involve more than that, and, of course, more than just the corporation.

Most important, perhaps, is the fact that most corporate decisions, at one or more stages, must be subjected to the screening effect of the public interest question. It cannot be determined whether economic criteria alone or economic criteria in combination with social and political factors are to control policy and conduct until institutional and organizational arrangements have become such that consideration of noneconomic factors can, normally, routinely, and effectively, be taken into account. Suggestions as to how these arrangements might be facilitated are discussed in Part II of this article. Our purpose at this point is not to look at the mechanism but at the concepts around which the mechanism will be constructed.

Obviously, noneconomic factors are already taken into account as a part of the process of making decisions and determining policy, but not as often, as routinely, or as timely (in the decision process) as they should be and not usually within the conscious framework of the public interest. It has been suggested that, insofar as new technology is concerned, especially where public resources are needed, the public itself should have a voice in the decision and an opportunity to ask the questions of public interest.[21] Perhaps, in some situations wide public participation is desirable, as might be the case with the hundreds of millions of public funds necessary for the development of the supersonic transport, but this method of screening is not likely to become an effective tool for general use. The examination of the public interest, in order to be effective, must penetrate the very heart of the corporation's own organizational machinery. Such questions as the following must be answered or at least considered at all stages of the corporation's activity: What are the expected benefits? How are they measured? Are they worth the costs? Have important social costs, such as pollution, nerve-shattering noise, or social displacement, been taken into account?

Precise determination of the public interest, in a definitive sense, is very difficult indeed and often impossible. But consideration of the public interest is not difficult and should be an integral part of corporate policy and decision. The exact velocity of the wind cannot always be determined from an aircraft, and such knowledge is not necessary to a satisfactory landing, but the wind, and especially its direction, must be taken into account. The public interest with regard to a new technology or a new product may be impossible to fix in detail, but the very fact that thought is given to the public interest may provide clues, insight, and a rough direction, which may, in turn, provide considerable guidance.

The meaning of "public interest" cannot be disposed of entirely by saying that it is difficult to determine precisely but relatively easy to consider. A search of the literature will reveal that the term has not often been defined but has been extensively and routinely used in a wide variety of situations, almost as though a fixed and agreed-upon definition did exist. The result has been a great deal of operational ambiguity and a certain amount of inconsistent and contradictory use. There has been little to prevent the use of the term by each of several contending parties to support diametrically opposed conclusions. Classical laissez-faire economics is as often described as being in the public interest as is the newer doctrine of social responsibility. The problem may be one of agreement on ultimate goals and disagreement on the best means for attaining those

---

21 Murray L. Weidenbaum, "A Matter for the Public to Decide?" *Bulletin of the Atomic Scientists* (June 1968), 7.

goals, or the contradiction may be the result of deliberate abuse of a necessarily somewhat ambiguous term.

"Justice" is, like public interest, a third-degree abstraction subject to considerable ambiguity, emotion, and contradictory use, but there is a spirit behind "justice" which helps to clear away some of the ambiguity. "Justice" is said to be concerned with giving to each man his due. Obviously, the questions of what is due, who decides, and how the decision is carried out are not answered by thus describing the spirit behind the term, but it does appear that we have gained some ground. The spirit behind "public interest" has been well described by Justice Frankfurter when he stated that "the public interest is a texture of multiple strands. It includes more than contemporary investors and contemporary consumers. The needs to be served are not restricted to immediacy, and social as well as economic costs must be counted." [22] These words clearly depict a balancing of factors: economic, social, political, ethical, moral, and expedient.

Spokesmen for the corporate system have been quick to seize on this approach as a way to avoid the tricky problem of defining the public interest. Many corporate managers today will describe their own function as the balancing of various interests both inside and outside the corporation, both private and public. It should be noted, however, that the result of this formulation of the public interest is to shift the open question from what is the public interest to what is a proper balance of relevant factors, a masking process we have already discussed above. Obviously, the managers want the power to determine the proper balance left to them. "Balanced" boards of directors, "public" representatives on the board, voting trust arrangements, and other organizational techniques are manifestations of the "balancing" approach to the public interest.[23] "Steward," "trustee," and "statesman" are now almost standard terminology to describe the relationship of the corporate manager to the public interest.

Inherent in this approach, however, are certain dangers. First, it often manifests a tendency to center itself around concepts of moral obligations and charitable attitudes toward those less fortunate, instead of around a direct duty or responsibility based upon interactions between a major subsystem and the whole system and upon causal connections between the corporation and many of the social problems to be alleviated. The final formulation of policy and corporate conduct, for example, may

[22] *Federal Power Commission* v. *Hope Natural Gas Co.*, 320 U.S. 591, 660 (1940).
[23] R. A. Gordon, *Business Leadership in the Large Corporation* (Washington, D.C.: Brookings Institution, 1945), pp. 346-50.

be very different where the policy is based on noncompulsive or non-obligatory charitable attitudes than what it would be if the public interest were seen in another light. Pollution, approached by the corporation on charitable or moral grounds, is not likely to be substantially reduced or prevented without the direct intervention of the state, a step which exposes the corporation to further public criticism.

A second danger, one already alluded to in another connection, is probably the result of faulty logic on the part of some corporate spokesmen and their academic philosophers. In their roles as balancers of various public and private interest factors, corporate managers, by default as well as by design, come soon to define, protect, and influence the public interest and the cultural values of our society. Because they wish the determination of the proper balance to be left wholly in their hands, the only constraints upon their actions are their own consciences. These individual consciences, taken collectively, have been integrated into what is now called the "corporate conscience," which often reveals itself in various rules of governance borrowed from the political state and including such protections against arbitrariness as "corporate due process." But there the analysis ends. There is no external standard, or even systematic internal procedure, against which the conscience can be measured. There is no way to give assurance that the public interest has been taken into account or, if taken into account, taken properly. Strangely enough, some of the people who have been quickest to accept the corporate conscience as the equivalent of true accountability in the area of social values are the same people who have complained about the concentrated economic power and the lack of accountability in its exercise. Apparently, the marketplace is not considered to be as effective a limitation as the conscience.

The "balancing" approach to public interest is largely goal oriented. The goals are that balance of factors which is best for the public interest and others more specific. Another approach is process rather than goal oriented and is based on fair or acceptable procedures rather than on goal achievement.[24] Due process again plays an important role. The contrast between the role of due process in the balancing approach to public interest and its role in the procedural approach is not unlike the contrast between substantive and procedural due process in constitutional law. Procedural due process is satisfied if a person is deprived of his life, liberty or property in a manner which society accepts as fair, but substantive due process requires that the deprivation be carried out only for reasons which society accepts. The constitution requires

---

[24] E.g., Henry S. Kariel, "The Corporation and the Public Interest," *Annals of the American Academy of the Social and Political Sciences*, CCCXLIII (1962), 39-47.

both kinds, but advocates of procedural corporate due process are apparently satisfied with adequate procedures without any particular orientation toward socially acceptable goals or reasons.

The strictly procedural approach has a certain simplistic appeal because it can with relative ease be converted into demonstrable rules and procedures, but it does not offer a solution to our basic problem: achieving better congruence of corporate goals with social ones. In a society with a static environment, procedural due process might still produce the desired congruence, because it is designed to protect and preserve the status quo. Even if society accepted different procedures, the rights protected would be the existing ones. In a rapidly changing environment, however, reasonable congruence can be obtained only if the arrangements provide for changing rights and values. Something more than good procedures is necessary.

Chamberlain assigns the ultimate responsibility for achieving balance in the whole system, and for maintaining a stable relationship among its parts, to the state.[25] Perhaps there is no other choice. The system and its subsystems will have objectives that are partly competitive and partly congruent. Conflict is inevitable. It is no longer possible to assume that the aggregated decisions of the subsystems will necessarily work in the best interest of the system as a whole. But it does not then follow that the state must make all the decisions. It does follow, as has been emphasized before, that the corporate managers must integrate the public interest ingredient into their procedures and policies at all stages and levels. The better the integration, the better the response of the corporate subsystem and the less need for state intervention.

OLD CONCEPTS OUTMODED

LEGAL AND PRACTICAL BARRIERS.   Are there any substantial legal barriers to the changes of attitude, responsibility and obligation suggested here? Do the property interests of the stockholder prevent the corporation from recognizing social claims other than for competitive economic behavior in the laissez-faire pattern or, at most, on the residuals of corporate income made accessible on the ground of charitable traditions? In the short run, perhaps, yes. In the long run, no. For a third of a century, the library shelves have been filling up with predictions, suspicions, and, finally, recognitions that traditional concepts of property were being rapidly and profoundly changed by the corporate system.[26]

---

25 Chamberlain, *Enterprise and Environment,* chap. 8.

26 See Adolf A. Berle, *Power Without Property* (New York: Harcourt, Brace, 1959).

Managers have not regarded their shareholders as "owners" for decades; [27] institutional shareholders do not behave as though they regarded
themselves as property owners; [28] perhaps, some individual investors do
still so regard themselves, but not many. A shareholder turns over his
funds to the corporate managers, the particular corporation having been
selected on the basis of past performance or future potential, knowing
that his rights are dependent almost exclusively upon the discretion of
the managers and that the only legal grounds for complaint would be
the abuse of that discretion. The boundaries of legitimate discretion
have been expanding steadily for a century. The boundaries of public
interest and the recognition of the extent and intimacy of the relationship between the great corporations and society have been doing like-
wise.

Much has changed since 1919 when the court decided that Henry
Ford had abused his discretion in failing to pay the proper dividend.[29]
The case was a hard one even at that time and even under the special
circumstances of a large and very closely held corporation completely
dominated by one man. It is inconceivable that a responsible court
would listen sympathetically today to a shareholder's argument that
Henry Ford's descendants were abusing their discretion by establishing
costly programs for training the hard-core unemployed or pouring resources and time into the New Detroit Committee.[30] Most shareholders
are probably becoming amenable to the view that the great corporations
owe major, even primary, responsibility to society at large. In some respects, stockholders may be ahead of their managers on this score. The
managers of the future are rapidly catching up: A poll of candidates for
the degree of Master of Business Administration at one of the country's
leading graduate schools of business showed that 60 percent of these
young men disagreed with the statement that "businessmen should consider stockholders' interests first, and only after that consideration may
they be interested in society's problems." [31] Interestingly enough, 43
percent of the managers attending an executive program at the same
school also disagreed.

In other words, social attitudes appear to be changing rapidly.
What is legally determined to be a reasonable exercise of discretion is

[27] See Dow Votaw, "The Politics of a Changing Corporate Society," *California
Management Review,* III:3 (1961), and "The Mythology of Corporations," *California
Management Review,* IV:3 (1962).

[28] See J. A. Livingston, *The American Stockholder* (New York: Collier Books,
1963), chap. 12.

[29] *Dodge* v. *Ford Motor Co.,* 204 Mich. 459 (1919).

[30] *Wall Street Journal* (June 14, 1968), 1.

[31] *Stanford Graduate School of Business Bulletin* (Spring 1968), 14-17.

not fixed in time and space but moves with changing values, attitudes, and concepts. The door to broader discretion has long since been opened to charitable contributions, to consumer welfare, to voluntary pollution control, and to many other exercises of managerial discretion that would have been beyond the pale not many years ago. The ascendance of social over parochial interests has long been at work in the law. The law mirrors the society in which it lives and will mirror the changes in that society as they take place. If one adopts an "image of a legal system conscious that doctrines represent and reflect policy decisions, that policy decisions require choice among competing values, and that, in making such choices, the social and institutional context is important," [32] the kind of progression which we have witnessed during the last century in the development of labor law, for example, is certainly to be anticipated and understood. Examination of substantive legal trends in such widely separated fields as contracts, torts, crimes, and the creation and operation of corporations reveals a similar progression underway in all of them—"a development of increasing concern with the public interest and of constant adaptation of the law to changes in social forms and relationships and in general social conditions." [33] One should not immediately conclude that these trends necessarily manifest a decrease in personal freedom; on the contrary, some of the changes have been brought about for the very purpose of increasing or maximizing personal freedom. Certainly, restraints and mitigations of concentrated power, of whatever sort, may be looked upon in this light.

It would be foolish to belittle the practical difficulties involved in making the changes in corporate attitude, concepts, and values discussed here. Some of the difficulties may decrease somewhat when attention is turned later to the details of the new response, but will still be present all the same. How, for example, can we expect a corporation in a competitive environment to undertake socially responsible conduct, in the broad public interest sense intended here, or to make decisions in the public interest when its competitors are not doing the same thing? Is there any way to avoid the intervention of the state or the weakening of the more responsible firms? There are some answers to these questions; a few have already been set forth. No one answer, nor any combination, is an easy way out. But the problems are real; many of them are critical; some of them affect the very existence and continuity of our society and of human life on this planet; not a few of them have been or are being caused or aggravated by the policies, technology, and conduct of the great corporations; new problems are wait-

---

32 Edwin M. Schur, *Law and Society* (New York: Random House, 1968), p. 122.
33 *Ibid.*

ing to present themselves. Within the framework of a free society, the
state cannot be relied upon to take full responsibility for all such issues
unless we are willing to accept major reductions in personal freedom.
In other words, the easy choice now is for the corporations to decline
responsibility and the duties of more broadly defined responsible conduct, at a much greater risk and cost later on. A harder choice now, but
one which seems better calculated to maintain our society in the long
run, is to seek the answers to the questions raised at the beginning of
this paragraph.

Taking the initiative in seeking cooperation on matters of pollution, as we have seen, might be a useful course of action, or calling to
the attention of the state the need for uniform standards or regulation,
or supporting techniques of public information in order both to inform
and to encourage consensus. Of course, none of these alternatives is
likely to be employed effectively if the pollution or other environmental
problem has not been foreseen at early stages of the development of a
product, process, or choice of location. Antitrust laws may also be a
hazard when seeking industry cooperation.

Perhaps a more important alternative in most situations is to avoid
the automatic assumption that responsible conduct or policy necessarily
reduces profits and the ability to compete. In many cases, of course, it
does, and escape may not be possible. On the other hand, if public interest issues are taken into consideration at the very earliest stages of
development, noncostly solutions may be found as a part of the development itself. If the assumption can be avoided that the elimination of
undesirable effects on the environment always involve costs and lower
profits, the chances are increased that just the opposite may turn out to
be the case. The problem can more readily be regarded as a challenge
to which innovative technical and administrative skills can be applied.

Issues involving cultural and social values are much more difficult
to handle than the technical ones, especially in the present state of development of social tools and methods, but there is no reason to believe
that these issues, as well as the more technical, cannot be brought under
effective control through a willingness to consider them as a part of
the normal administrative procedures.

A PARADOX

CONCLUSION.   We have asked the question whether there is a need
for a new corporate response to the changing social environment. The
question has been answered, on several different grounds, in the affirmative. The great corporations have "learned to cope superbly" with the
environment they found waiting for them, but not with the environment

they have largely created for themselves. The explanation for this paradox is found on two levels.

The corporations have failed to respond effectively or appropriately to the changing social environment, first, because they have not accurately perceived their role in society or sufficiently recognized their obligation to include the public interest and public values as parts of their own value sets and, second, because they have continued to adhere to the Western tradition of regarding subsystems relatively independently to the whole system of which they are a part, in the face of a growing body of opposing evidence. Social responsibility, whether accepted or denied, has been looked upon as a voluntary matter or as a question of charitable attitude. If no new response is forthcoming, the results will be an increasing gap between corporate goals and social ones, aggravation of existing social problems, new and unforeseen crises, increasing state intervention and, almost certainly, a decline in personal freedom.

HOW SHOULD WE DEVELOP A NEW CORPORATE RESPONSE TO A CHANGING SOCIAL ENVIRONMENT?

S. Prakash Sethi and Dow Votaw *

In Part I, we suggested that corporations have been slow to recognize certain changes in the structure and in the value system of our society and to adapt to them. This lag has been due in part to the persistence with which corporate managers have continued to look at society as a static system, to defend their actions in terms of nineteenth-century ideology rather than late twentieth-century reality, and to pursue the improvement of their subsystem without proper regard for the effects on other subsystems or on the system as a whole. We also described several approaches to a better understanding of the concept of "public interest" and to the manner in which corporations might bridge the gap between their traditional raison d'être and the new realities of social expectations for the role of the corporation in society.

_____

* From *California Management Review,* Fall 1969, where it appeared under the title of "Do We Need a New Corporate Response to a Changing Social Environment?" Part II. Reprinted with permission.

The continuing lack of recognition by the corporation of the need for a new perception of its own social role has increased the degree of incompatibility between corporate goals and values and those of society at large. It also helps to account for failures by many corporations to develop new strategies for dealing with outside pressures and with emerging interest groups and to restructure their decisionmaking machinery for greater flexibility and responsiveness to the challenges produced by unconventional and unusual changes in external environmental conditions. In Part II we discuss these failures to develop new strategies and organizational structures appropriately designed to cope with rapidly changing conditions. We also offer some hypotheses which may help to explain the causes for the failures and discuss several avenues by which solutions to the problem may be approached.

RESPONSE TO OUTSIDE PRESSURES

FAILURE OF TRADITIONAL RESPONSES. During the last decade or two, one of the most easily observed manifestations of changing social conditions has been widespread social discontent among large segments of society. This discontent has expressed itself in several different ways and has been directed at many targets, including the state, the establishment, business in general, large corporations as a group, particular industries, and even individual firms. By and large, corporations have tried to avoid or ignore matters of public discontent, whatever their source, until they have reached crisis proportions. The policy of avoidance has usually been followed regardless of whether the discontent was directed at business and corporations in general or at specific activities, industries, or firms. Corporate managements seem almost invariably, when faced with social discontent, to fall back on the time-honored and failure-prone public postures of lofty self-righteousness or studied indifference, as though by such conduct the discontent and its causes can be made to disappear. Outraged innocence has not been unheard of as a response to attacks on specific firms or industries, but it is usually accompanied by an air of noninvolvement in the fray. Until it is no longer possible to avoid direct confrontation, issues concerning racial minorities, urban decay, and desecration of the natural environment are kept on the back burner and responded to only in certain ritualized ways. When crisis blocks the avenues of escape, the resulting trauma and urgency guarantee makeshift solutions not likely to please anybody.

RESPONSES TO PRESSURES. Corporate responses to outside pressures resulting from social discontent can be grouped into three broad categories of ritualized behavior:

> Public relations responses.
> Legal responses.
> Industrial relations–bargaining responses.

These responses are used separately, seriatim, or in various combinations. For many years, their use has been marked by frequent failure. Let us take a look at each of the traditional responses and then at the apparent causes for their failure.

THE PUBLIC RELATIONS RESPONSE. A belief widely prevalent among corporate managers holds that most of the attacks made on corporations and the corporate system have their origins either in selfish, often "foreign," interests or in ignorance of the corporation and of its extensive contributions to the general welfare and to economic growth. Furthermore, so the belief develops, if the corporation is to maintain public confidence, its image must not be sullied. Direct confrontation with attackers must. be avoided, for it may result in unfavorable publicity. Corporations must avoid open engagement in politics in order not to encourage activity by political factions unsympathetic to the cause of corporate business. On the other hand, the public relations response imposes on corporations the duty to inform and educate the populace about the "American way," "enterprise democracy," and the vital role played by large corporations in providing material abundance and high standards of living. The public relations response often produces the all-too-familiar paradox of more or less specific criticisms on one hand, as of product safety, environmental pollution, or hiring policies, and vague statements as the response on the other, as suggestions of alien predispositions or ignorance on the part of the critics. The issue is usually lost in a miasma of glittering generalities.

THE LEGAL RESPONSE. Corporations frequently resort to legalistic interpretations of their rights in responding to the claims of new pressure groups. They react legalistically to most socio-ethical issues raised by conservationists, minority groups, or spokesmen for consumer interests and question the legitimacy of claims which are not susceptible to slide-rule empirical analysis. It is not uncommon for a corporation president to read at a press conference a paper prepared by the corporation's legal department and to be flanked, while he reads, by a public relations expert and legal counsel. While such procedures may reduce the dangers of litigation and protect the corporation's conventional interests, and even its image, they avoid the issue and become, in the eyes of the critics, just another form of evasive tactics. Thus, resort to the legal right of a corporation, in many cases, to pollute the atmosphere or to hire whom it pleases side-steps the real issue and assures stronger and more hostile criticisms in the future.

THE INDUSTRIAL RELATIONS–BARGAINING RESPONSE. A third form of traditional response to outside pressure is patterned on long experience in dealing with labor unions. To some extent, corporate managers appear to view these outside pressures as improper and the groups bringing them to bear as illegitimate in the corporate milieu. In the industrial relations response, however, the managers feel that these issues and adversaries are among those which cannot be avoided and with which the corporation must deal, whether it wishes to or not. Unfortunately, confrontation often takes the form of quid-pro-quo bargaining and never gets beyond that point. The bargaining process is not always carried on through the mechanism of face-to-face encounters. Public news media and civic organizations of various kinds often play intermediary roles. Hiring additional members of a minority group or establishing an employment office in the urban ghetto may be granted in return for some expectation of temporary social peace— a cool summer. In racial matters particularly, the claims, demands, concessions, counter-concessions, promised conduct, and other issues involved in the bargaining only rarely concern the basic causes of discontent and usually treat only the symptoms. It is not surprising, therefore, that an apparent bargain struck is soon followed by the reemergence of the basic problem in another form. What is surprising, however, each time a bargain is apparently reached, is the belief by the managers that they have finally solved an acute social problem and made a lasting contribution to the general welfare.

The usual corporate response to outside pressures arising from social origins has been to resort to legalistic stances or to industrial or public relations techniques. The responses have often been at odds with each other. The public relations office emphasizes public ignorance of the corporation's role and the lack of appreciation for corporate contributions to society; legal counsel recite the legal basis for private property and for the right to hire, fire, pollute, and cut down redwood trees; the bargainers agree to constraints on hiring, firing, polluting, and cutting; the underlying problems of race and corrupted environment remain unconfronted and unsolved. All three forms of response and their various combinations have met with a high incidence of failure. The evidence is discussed in detail below.

A COMMUNICATION GAP?

WHAT IS IT THAT GOES WRONG? Why, in 1968, does a corporation like Ford Motor Company announce increases in car prices owing to the high cost of governmentally imposed safety standards and then, later, in hearings before a Senate committee, admit that there was no direct connection between the cost of meeting the safety requirements and the price increases? [1] Why does a corporation like General Motors respond to criticisms by hiring a private detective to check out Ralph Nader's private life and then have to recant in a public hearing after the storm breaks? What is there about corporate responses to social pressure and about the machinery by which those responses are determined that produces this kind of result?

Similar examples of corporate insensitivity abound whether the issue happens to be civil rights, safety, pollution, or other matters of public interest. The corporations are not usually "insensitive" in the connotation of heartlessness or lack of compassion, but are often insensitive within the connotation that they fail to detect or to sense the real issues at stake or to foresee the results of their own acts.

Examples are: Eastman Kodak's inept handling of its dispute with a Rochester minority group concerning the training and hiring of hard-core unemployed; the failure of the New Detroit Committee to establish a dialogue with local poverty organizations; the attempts by International Telephone and Telegraph to pressure the news media to give favorable publicity to its proposed merger with American Broadcasting Company; and the strong opposition by the packing industry to the new meat inspection laws. Each of these situations was, in a real sense, a failure of corporate response to pressures and demands growing out of a changing environment. In each case, the response was inappropriate, inadequate, and had exactly the opposite result from that intended for it. The corporations convinced nobody and managed to raise serious doubts as to the sincerity and probity of their actions.

In 1969, many corporations are still using defensive strategies which may have been effective twenty-five years ago but which today are either irrelevant or actually harmful to corporate interests. In a changing social environment, whose harbingers are often groups which are much differently oriented than were comparable groups of a generation or so ago, a major problem for the corporation is to achieve an understanding of the new environment and of the economic and non-economic stakes, the motives and the goals of all the parties involved. The point is not that the corporation must necessarily adopt or even accede to the new values and goals; the point is that, unless the corporation and its managers see and understand the changes accurately, the risks that decisions and responses will be inappropriate and even seriously damaging to corporate interests will be greatly increased.

Use of the industrial relations–bargaining response is based on

---

[1] *Wall Street Journal* (April 1, 1968), 6.

the assumption that both parties have something to gain and to lose and that, therefore, a bargained compromise can be mutually advantageous. But, in actuality, this is not usually the situation when a minority group or a group representing the community at large faces off against a corporation or an industry. The discontented minorities and community groups usually believe that they have nothing to lose and everything to gain. Thus, when corporations—under the rules of bargain and compromise—ask these groups to yield something or pay some sort of price for incomplete and often symbolic gains, the answer is frequently a rejection of the corporations' offers. Or, more often, the noncorporate protagonists simply accept the offer or concession as something they were entitled to anyhow and respond by making new and greater demands. Typically, the corporations then express disappointment, manifest surprise, and accuse the opposing group of harassment, of making unreasonable demands, and of not entering the negotiations in the proper spirit of give and take.

CORE OF THE DILEMMA

It is in the definition of "unreasonableness" that the dilemma really lies. The corporations are seeking solutions to problems and in ways which do not upset the orthodox criteria of corporate performance or question management's prerogatives in managing corporate assets and distributing profits. To management, "reasonable" usually means "least painful" and, by implication, gradual, small, and conservative. However, social activists reject this definition. They do not accept the premise that the performance criteria of business are sacrosanct, and they question the corporation's own concept of its social role.

The social environment within which business—like all other man-made institutions—must function is continuously changing. In order to survive, business institutions must adjust their outlooks and adapt themselves to the restless nature of the social system. One can understand the necessity of assigning highest priorities to production of material things and achievement of economic goals—even at the cost of other social and human values, e.g., equitable income distribution, conservation of natural environment of the country—in a society where the masses spend their lives at or near subsistence level. However, the supremacy of such a criterion cannot be accepted in a social system where aggregate national affluence on the one hand is persistently matched by abject poverty for a sizable minority, and where the national material abundance holds no promise of the good life or opportunity for those who have been cast aside by social prejudice or technological advance. In failing to make appropriate social calculations, industry must adhere to a narrow standard of efficiency and economy which, although acceptable to stockholders, fails to convince the public at large.

It is not possible to establish standards of performance which will provide and maintain a balance between the ethical requirements of distributive justice and economic needs of productivity and growth. Corporations contend that they derive their right to produce from the right of private property or from the right of individuals to patronize industries, buy products, and pursue occupations of their own choice. However, it is misleading to equate freedoms of individuals with those of institutions for the following reasons.

> The influence on the social system is not equal.
>
> The capacity of one business enterprise to inflict damage on other enterprises, on society, and on individual human beings far outweighs the possible harmful effects of individual decisions.
>
> In the final analysis, business exists for people, and the business interests, when in conflict with those of the people at large, must therefore take the back seat.

Following in the wake of recent racial disturbances, some prominent business leaders and government officials have been bluntly outspoken in sympathizing with the unrest of the minorities and public at large and have urged the business community to be more responsive, to take bolder and more imaginative steps toward curing our social ills.[2]

---

[2] For example, George Champion, Chairman of the Board, Chase Manhattan Bank, addressing the Eleventh Annual Good Friday Breakfast for Business and Professional Men in Los Angeles on April 12, 1968, said: "Some businessmen seek endlessly for elaborate rationales to justify the social role of the corporation. Business, they say, should participate in the war on poverty because this will help build markets for the future; or because slums are siphoning off more and more business profits in the form of higher taxes; or because the alternative may be ruined cities. Isn't it time that somebody stood up and said, 'Business should participate because it's the right thing to do.' " Characterizing the business community's response to the moral problem as "ambivalent" —sometimes willing to help and sometimes evasive in finding solutions—he said that either we must bear the costs of social projects or the consequences of evading them. *New York Times* (April 13, 1968), 10.

Another example is that of George S. Squibb, former Vice President of E. R. Squibb & Sons, and now a consultant to the company which was founded by his grandfather, testifying before Senate Subcommittee on Monopoly of the Select Committee on Small Business, who said: "Exploitation of medicines used in life preserving and life saving situations by selling prices far above the cost must be avoided no matter what justification or economic temptation is felt by the manufacturer. . . . Of course, prices have declined, but the drug industry must accept social responsibility for its operations and special burdens and limitations not assumed by other industries because of its place in the scheme of medical care, now an object of public concern." *New York Times* (April 15, 1967), 24.

For example, J. Irwin Miller, Board Chairman of the Cummins Engine Co., Columbus, Indiana, warns:

> Those who rightly interpret the direction of the changes, and who respond to them, and lead response to them—such persons in history have mostly flourished. Those who remained the same, when the same was no longer fitting—they perished, thinking they were holding to the old virtues, which an irresponsible generation had abandoned. For the most part they perished because their minds had become like the body of a dinosaur, unfit for the new climate of the world. Our world is also changing, and few disagree that we are changing to a degree and at a speed that has scarcely ever been recorded. . . .
>
> We in business are clearly members on the establishment side. We possess power—power to influence, power to expand, to shape the young. But the powerful establishment in history seldom plays a role other than that of king in a child's game of King of the Hill. The only purpose the king can have is to stay on top of the hill, a purpose in which he always finally fails. . . .
>
> The American Negro knows better than any of us why the United States is not among the leading nations in eliminating infant mortality. The American Negro knows better than any of us who it is that composes most of our current unemployment figure. The American Negro knows what his relative odds are for being drafted. The American Negro knows better than any of us that the Anglo-Saxon concept of the assumption of innocence does not hold for all citizens in all parts of the country. The American Negro has seen hopeful legislation enacted by his federal government and little change in his neighborhood or opportunities. He interprets "progress" as defined by the white majority to mean it won't happen in his lifetime.[3]

It is small wonder that minority groups are no longer willing to play the game with all the cards stacked against them.

While Under Secretary of Commerce under President Johnson, Howard J. Samuels, commenting on riots in April 1968 following the assassination of Martin Luther King, Jr., stated that measures to end the economic conditions that lead to riots were going to cost $50 billion. Each year, he said, personal consumption in the nation rises by about $20 billion; half of this increase should be allocated to meeting social needs for at least the next five years. This would be a whopping reallocation of priorities. But the issue is starkly plain: "Are we going to insist on more color-TV sets and electric tooth brushes, or are we going to insist on better schools and housing, day-care centers, and health?"[4]

---

[3] Quoted by William D. Patterson, in an article titled: "J. Irwin Miller: The Revolutionary Role of Business," *Saturday Review* (Jan. 13, 1968), 62-72.

[4] *Newsweek* (April 22, 1968), 74.

The public relations response implies that there is somehow a one-way communications gap between corporations and the public. Managers believe that the contributions of business to the American way of life have not been properly understood and appreciated and, to be sure, they equate the interests of business with the interests of society, hence the heavy reliance on emphatic crusades to "educate" the public about the positive aspects of business.

As early as 1950, William H. Whyte, Jr., noted with pity the billion-dollar attempt of the two earlier decades by business to "sell business to America" and the utter failure of this campaign.

> The free enterprise campaign is psychologically unsound, it is abstract, it is defensive, and it is negative. Most important in a great many of its aspects it represents a shocking lack of faith in the American people, and in some cases downright contempt.[5]

Little thought is given to the possibility that the disagreement between the corporations and public may not be owing to lack of recognition of the contribution by business to society but may result, instead, from the failure of the great corporations to appreciate and understand their own role in society and the continuously changing nature of that role.

To date, these public relations efforts have brought business neither more respectability nor greater credibility. Yet, except for a few lonely voices, corporate leaders and industry spokesmen are still trying to sell the contributions of business and the free enterprise theme as though they were detergents. Recent evidence indicates that managers, by and large, are obsessed with the idea that business needs selling and that all will indeed be well with this country and its business if businessmen will only educate the public on the positive aspects of business. The following examples are illustrative of the point:

John H. Logan, Chairman of the Manufacturing Chemists' Association and President of the Universal Oil Products Co., recently described the situation in his industry:

> We are now selling the industry "short." . . . American public now tends to look on the chemical industry in terms of pollution rather than health, in terms of evil smells rather than fragrant aromas . . . we must equate chemicals with human welfare. Here is a $42 billion a year U.S. industry, outpacing the industrial economy for growth, performing miracles for nutrition, health and comfort of people everywhere . . . but comparatively stripped of public honor and respect.[6]

---

[5] William H. Whyte, Jr., *Is Anybody Listening?* (New York: Simon and Schuster, 1950).

[6] *San Francisco Chronicle* (April 18, 1968), 53.

Robert W. Galvin, chairman of Motorola, Inc., in a recent ad headlined "Can Business Educate Students to Its Own Goals and Values?" stated: "Business should share responsibilities for educating business-oriented students [why not others?] in business philosophies, commitments, objectives, and goals." [7]

Paradoxically, emphasis on the positive often provokes a negative reaction. If the audience is critical of corporate failures, avoidance of the issue by repeating a list of contributions tends to create further alienation. Furthermore, what the corporation views as positive achievements may sometimes appear to others as devastation of natural resources for private gain. Most important, perhaps, if the group being addressed has not shared in the corporation's contribution, citation of achievements serves only as a reminder of deprivation and exclusion.

> Even with those facts for which business can rightfully claim credit, the message represents business as essentially static and defensive. It concerns what *was* done. That we have achieved more telephones, more bathtubs, and so on per capita is a fine fact, but it is not a fact that answers the aspirations and gripes of the people business is seeking to win as friends.[8]

HOW TO BRIDGE THE GAP?

WITH WHOM SHOULD CORPORATIONS COMMUNICATE?   Another dimension of the problem of communication pertains to the questions of how and with whom to communicate. In this sense it applies equally to all three responses discussed earlier: legal, industrial relations, and public relations. The question of how is closely related to why. In a society where the minorities are unorganized it is hard to find spokesmen or organizations who know accurately what it is that the group they purportedly represent wants. Similarly, the community at large is not organized in such a manner that its interests can be clearly represented to the corporation. Failing to find established groups with spokesmen who can articulate and represent the wants of the group clearly, the corporations have generally taken one of two approaches:

> 1. They have supported and recognized spokesmen who were acceptable to corporate management, spokesmen who tended to be "moderate" and "willing to negotiate," and who appeared to appreciate the historical economic function of the corporation. However, because these people have generally been willing to accept less

---

[7] *Daily Californian* (April 18, 1968), 5. The student newspaper of the University of California, Berkeley. (Bracketed comments are ours.)

[8] Whyte, *op. cit.*, p. 14.

than would the militant groups and have delivered less than the militants promise, the people for whom they claim to speak are not long satisfied with their purported gains or with their leaders.

2. Corporations have sometimes tried to deal with the militant elements among the minority groups, not for the purpose of solving problems, but in order to reduce the risk of riots and stay the widespread publicity given to the hostile statements of radical activists. However, this somewhat crude attempt to buy peace has usually worsened the situation. The moderates among the minority groups have then accused the corporations of undercutting them, of destroying their power base, and of submitting to blackmail by the miltants. Many of the moderates are thereby converted into militants. The corporations have not even been able to buy peace. The extremists have generally regarded any association with the white establishment as dangerously infectious and one which will discredit their militant stance.[9]

Thus, both of these strategies have failed to yield any significant results. In one of its recent reports on the business community and the minorities, the *Wall Street Journal*[10] evaluated the work of the blue-ribbon New Detroit Committee (NDC) which included national Negro leaders, young ghetto militants, and Detroit's top business leaders, was linked with the National Alliance of Businessmen, and was set up at the suggestion of President Johnson and headed by Henry Ford. At the time of its establishment the Committee, because of the composition of its membership, seemed to have an excellent chance of success. However, the report in the *Wall Street Journal* came to the conclusion that the Committee had failed. It had not created confidence among the Negro population in the Detroit area nor helped give them hope for the future. Nor had it developed a dialogue between minorities and business groups in order to prevent riots and local disturbances.

The reasons for this failure can be traced, in part, to the problem of deciding "which voices to heed"[11] and to the tendency of corporate management to see new pressures in the old environmental framework and to cope with them through traditional channels. The managers expect to read reports prepared by their staff experts, to consider the several alternatives presented to them, and to select, on the basis of urgency and other means of determining priorities, the ones best suited for implementation. What management fails to realize is that discontent —be it of a minority group or of the community at large—is usually not organized enough to articulate the kind of objectives which are amenable

---

9 "Detroit Up from Ashes," *Newsweek* (January 1, 1968), 48-50.

10 *Wall Street Journal* (March 26, 1968), 16; also see *Business Week* (February 3, 1968), 120-24.

11 *Business Week* (February 3, 1968), 120.

to the traditional approach or to the assignment of priorities. For that matter, an approach based on priorities may not be feasible because the problems have been accumulating for so long that all of them have reached desperate proportions. Hence, it is not so much a question of finding spokesmen and establishing channels of authority as of understanding the basic causes and finding solutions truly related to those causes, while, at the same time, ameliorating the critical surface demands.

INTERNAL ADAPTATION

DEVELOPMENT OF NEW RESPONSES. We have seen that traditional corporate responses to outside pressures have not succeeded. Confronted with such pressures, corporations have refused to get involved, have issued bland public statements explaining their position in ritualized terms of law or public relations, or have sought to bargain in an industrial relations manner. Each of these approaches is based upon one or more of the following beliefs: that corporations should not become involved in debates with "rabble rousers"; that discontent and demands made on the corporations are caused by ignorance and misunderstanding and that "education" will remove the cause, if not counteracted by foreign ideologies; that the outside groups are adversaries against whom the corporate goals and values must always be defended; that both sides have something to lose and something to gain and that, consequently, bargaining is a means toward solution. What is not often realized by the corporate managers is that these very beliefs are a major barrier to appropriate, meaningful response and that the managers themselves are at least as much in need of education as the outside pressure groups.

The sad fact is, however, that the growing size of the corporation, the increasing complexity of its organization, the internal shift of decision-making power to the "technostructure," and many other factors have actually hardened some of its arteries and affected the intracorporate communication channels in many corporations in such a way that organizational structures, already ill-adapted to proper consideration of public interest and human factors, have been made worse. It is not surprising that corporations, generally, are insensitive to changes taking place in our social system until they reach crisis levels. One need not read very far into the house journals or other public relations efforts of the large corporations, or dig very deeply into their conduct, to find evidence to support these conclusions. Technological change and innovation are always linked to human betterment in a one-to-one relation, with no mention ever made of the personal, social or even economic costs that may be involved. Problems of racial minorities are often dispatched by increasing the number of black faces in photographs of employee groups. Having already forgotten the lesson of thalidomide, some of the great pharmaceutical companies urge their new "wonders" on the public and, at the same time, condemn and undermine the Food and Drug Administration, whose procedures are the only protection the companies have against public retribution in the event of a ghastly error.

Before one can expect much improvement in the ways corporations respond to a changing environment, there must occur a profound change in the perceptions with which corporate managers regard the role of their corporations in society at large, as was discussed in the previous article. Even though these perceptions are appropriately altered, corporate responses will not quickly or substantially improve until structural flexibility and sensitivity have been built into the organization. Once the internal machinery has been adapted to the need for prompt, accurate, and routine consideration of the public interest and timely awareness of environmental change, the decision makers can hope to minimize the problems of the future and respond appropriately to the pressures of the present. It is to these structural changes that we now turn our attention. Thereafter, consideration will be given to specific new responses to the changing social environment.

RECENT EXAMPLES

FAILURE OF INTERNAL PROCESSES.   A major factor in the failure of traditional corporate responses has been the lack of organizational structures which facilitate the recognition by corporate managers, at all levels, of changes in the social environment and which enhance the ability of the corporation to meet new, and often unconventional, challenges from the outside. Dramatic evidence of the failure of decision-making structures to respond properly to new situations is found in recent episodes involving Eastman Kodak, General Motors, and Chrysler. In each case, structural and communication deficiencies in the corporations themselves produced unpleasant results and did considerable harm to the firms involved.

During early 1966, Eastman Kodak became involved in a controversy with an organization called FIGHT, representing a segment of the black population of Rochester. FIGHT asked Kodak to hire and train 600 members of the minority groups—to be selected and referred to Kodak by FIGHT—over an eighteen-month period. Kodak management refused to accede to these demands on the grounds that:

> It could not foresee future economic conditions accurately enough to permit the company to commit itself to hiring specified numbers of people.

It could not give exclusive hiring privileges to one organization to
the exclusion of other civil rights groups.

Doing so would abrogate the rights of management and violate both
state and federal laws.

Negotiations then terminated. However, in December 1966, an assistant
vice-president of Eastman Kodak, who was asked by the top management to try to break the deadlock and re-open negotiations signed, on
behalf of Kodak, an agreement with FIGHT promising to make essentially the same concessions which FIGHT had earlier demanded and
Kodak had refused. Kodak's management immediately and publicly re-
pudiated the agreement, contending that the vice-president had no authority to bind the company by his act. This repudiation resulted in
considerable adverse national publicity for Kodak and confirmed the
suspicions of the black minority groups that the great corporations could
not be trusted.[12]

In the case of General Motors, the public relations department,
acting without the knowledge of the president, hired a private detective
to investigate Ralph Nader. Revelation of this action created such a
public uproar that the president had to make a public apology.[13]

In the case of Chrysler, one of the company's officers objected to a
scene in the video tape of a Chrysler-sponsored television program where
Petula Clark, a white female singer, touched the arm of Harry Belafonte
in an affectionate fashion. His objection was that this intimacy might
offend part of the potential audience. The demand that the scene be
changed was refused by the parties involved. Subsequent adverse publicity was so intense that Chrysler disavowed the action of its officer, let
the program stay as it was originally filmed, and eventually fired the
officer.[14]

ORIENTATION AND STRUCTURE

AGAIN, WHAT WENT WRONG? In all three cases, the officers concerned felt that they were representing the best interests of their corporations but failed to gauge the situation accurately. Each man looked
at his problem in the conventional fashion to which he was accustomed.
The basic problem seems to lie in the fact that corporate organizations
are simply not set up to deal with new or unfamiliar social situations.
They are set up to produce and distribute goods, and have rarely, until

---

[12] "The Fight That Swirls around Eastman Kodak," *Business Week* (April 29,
1967), 40.

[13] "Meet Ralph Nader, Everyman's Lobbyist and His Consumer Crusade," *Newsweek* (January 22, 1968), 65-73.

[14] "The Touch," *Newsweek* (March 18, 1968), 93.

recently, been called upon outside that area to do any more than deal with an occasional routine community problem, often easily resolvable in terms of industrial or public relations or legal posture. They are organized to make rational decisions aimed at reasonably clear-cut objectives related to efficient production of goods and services at a profit. When a new problem such as job training for hard-core unemployed, clean air or resource conservation is presented as a cost function, the system knows how to handle that aspect of it, but the social dimensions are a source of consternation and dismay. The conventional decisionmaking structure cannot be expected to cope with these problems except on an ad hoc basis and with a high risk of disastrous results.

The problems of corporate management in coping with the changing external environment can be looked at from two angles: from the angle of general management orientation and from the corporate decisionmaking structure. Corporate management tends to be problem-oriented, and this is its greatest strength as well as weakness, depending on the nature of the problem. By training and temperament, corporate management is magnificently skilled in dealing with conventional types of problems relating to its business functions.

The parameters—external environment—of these problems are well defined and are either constant or changing at a very slow rate. The only variables whose interaction needs to be interpreted, in the light of new information, are the internal variables with which the management already has the most familiarity and experience. However, the assumption of unchanging external environment is crucial to the validity of the management's evaluation of the problem, because a changing external environment will also alter the nature of the problem, thereby rendering inapplicable those solutions which might have been previously tried and found effective. Facts in themselves are innate and meaningless. The consistency of interpretation of a set of data and its analysis in terms of certain hypotheses are possible only when exogenous variables—external environment—remain unchanged. Failing this, past experience, i.e., understanding of similar facts in somewhat similar situations, is no longer valid. The problems encountered by corporate managements are a case in point. Although, on the surface, they appear similar to the problems faced by the management, e.g., jobs, training, and worker motivation, they do not lend themselves to the mode of solutions to which management is accustomed. This is so because certain other factors, like motivation, attitude toward business, belief in the equity of the social system, and congruity with the value system of the society which the management had taken for granted in earlier situations of jobs and training, are no longer valid. Furthermore, the social norms of distributive justice which were acceptable a generation ago are no longer acceptable because the changed environment—due to past action of business as well

as other social institutions and also due to different aspirations and expectations of the youth of the society—has put different interpretations
on apparently similar phenomena.

Management is not only problem-oriented, but solution-oriented.
When solutions do not fall into a priori patterns, it is frustrated and
loses heart. Management frequently deliberates for three to five years
from the time a new product or idea is tested in the laboratory until
the time this innovation is brought into the market and reaches national
distribution. Yet it expects the problems of minorities and community
problems, which are far more serious and deeply rooted, to be solved
within a short time. After reaching a decision at its top level, management often finds the man from the operational level beating on the
inner office door the next morning. "What happened? What is today's
crisis? I thought we solved that problem yesterday." When these problems do not lend themselves to quickie solutions, management gives
them up as beyond the scope and competence of the corporation and
passes them to the door of government.

The second dimension of the difficulties of the corporate management inadequately responding to today's social problems emanates from
the decision-making structure within the corporation and the nature of
decisions that corporate managements, both at the policy and operational level, are called upon to make. Even when the top management
has made a basic policy decision regarding a social issue, implementation at the operational level sometimes leaves a lot to be desired. This
is not to say that there is a lack of desire on the part of operational
personnel to implement management's decisions. The problem is more
fundamental. Decisionmaking, at a given level, is closely related to the
nature of a reward system, the availability of information, validity of
earlier experiences, and past training in analyzing that information, individual perceptual biases, the risk of failure, and the cost of uncertainty
both to the individual making the decision and his understanding of
its costs to the corporation. It is very difficult, if not impossible, by management edict alone to make people at the operational level change their
basic beliefs and operational training acquired over a long period of
time.

A NEW SET OF VARIABLES

TYPES OF MANAGEMENT DECISIONS.   Management decisions are basically of two types: routine and innovatory.[15] Routine decisions are those

---

[15] The one major exception to this generalization would be in the case of over-
seas marketing, where the decision maker is confronted with a quite different set of
external variables.

which are aimed at solving recurrent problems. The outcome of those decisions is predictable in the sense that an elaborate set of "rules" and "procedures" is devised to cope with a finite number of situations. These situations have several important characteristics: Sufficient information is available and a tested mechanism exists to collect such information; the decision maker is trained to scan the available information and determine its relevance to situations under examination; and the dimensions of the decision can be defined beforehand. Innovative decisions, on the other hand, deal with situations which are one of a kind, whose occurrence is irregular, and whose scope and effect cannot be determined or predicted beforehand.

The reward system at the operational level is based on the ability of the decision maker to scan the information for its relevance and pick the "correct" alternative from among the many that he has at his disposal. His ability is measured in terms of seeing new combinations of old situations rather than detecting and analyzing "new" situations. Even when he is called upon to make innovative decisions, e.g., introducing a totally new product, developing a new market, his primary concern is with the internal variables because the change in the nature of external variables is not likely to be radical.[16]

Decisions involving corporate contacts with minority groups and with other social pressures are basically of the innovative type and are likely to remain so for sometime to come. This is due to the fact that the causes which led to the unrest among the minorities have not been eliminated, the issues have not yet been crystallized, and the group alignment has not achieved any stability.

What happens when we force an executive who is trained to make the routine type of decision to take action in the new situation? His difficulties are great. In the first place, the information available to him is not complete, and it is not easy to determine whether the available information is relevant. The manager's past experience is of limited value because he must now deal with a new set of variables. He has only limited awareness of the actual or possible importance of the issues to himself or to his organization, and his ability to comprehend new information is limited, due to his place in the organizational hierarchy and the time available to him for learning new ways to seek and evaluate this information.

Faced with so many unknown factors, he is necessarily cautious. His perception is selective, and he tends to select only the types of information with which he is already familiar, thereby sacrificing the very information which may be crucial for the new decision. When forced to

---

[16] James G. March and Herbert A. Simon, *Organizations* (New York: John Wiley and Sons, 1958), chaps. 6 and 7.

use information of unknown prior reliability, he tries to put it into old and familiar molds or "frames of reference" which make the information usable. The effect of decisions so arrived at is not hard to visualize. Decisions, which at another time or place might have been correct ones, suddenly turn sour on the executive, take on a new dimension unforeseen by him, and have their effect transcend his limited horizon. The earlier cited examples of General Motors and Chrysler Corporation clearly bear out this point.

The problem has its emotional side as well. Consider, for illustration, the problem of hiring the hard-core unemployed. What happens to an employment interviewer who is supposed to implement a newly "liberalized" company policy? Here is a person who has been trained to select the person best qualified for a given job. All of a sudden, management says to this employment interviewer, "Forget everything that you have learned. You are going to interview some hard-core unemployed, and you are going to hire some of them." This interviewer, who for twenty years has been taught to find the person best suited for the job, is now told to hire someone solely because he is Negro, unskilled, and very likely to respond poorly to training. What are his interviewing standards now? What questions does he ask? What attributes does he seek?

If corporations are to achieve any measure of success in dealing with changing social environment, they must develop new organizational blueprints. It is to their own advantage to initiate experimentation with new procedures in corporate structure and behavior, or it will be thrust upon them by outside elements. To disregard external pressures is to provoke the kind of general public regulation for which our public institutions are ill prepared and whose side effects may be worse than the restraints for which regulation was originally intended.

INNOVATIVE DECISIONS

NEW STRUCTURES.   What measures can the corporations take to revamp their decisionmaking structure to make it more flexible and responsive to the changing social environment? There are a number of possibilities.

> 1. Corporations must recognize the innovative nature of decisions dealing with social unrest and must accept the fact that success will come slowly and irregularly. Permitting these decisions to be made within the conventional organizational framework is fraught with dangers. In a way, the minority groups have intuitively recognized the innovative nature of these decisions and have insisted on dealing only with the presidents or chairmen. But the corporations have not viewed the situation in that light. The authors have seen many operations level executives who complain that one of the rea-

sons minority groups antagonize the corporations and do not succeed in establishing good relations or making substantial gains is their lack of understanding as to how the corporations work. "They always insist on talking with the top man without realizing that the top man has other things to do" and cannot devote much time to their problem, which is secondary to the over-all job of running the business, and that in any case, the top man has to depend on his staff for information and recommendation. The minority groups, so the argument goes, can do much better by dealing with second echelon management, who will, after all, implement the program.

2. The innovative nature of the decisions requires that there must be an arrangement whereby their formulation can cut across departmental lines. The structure must provide the decision maker not only with the opportunity to develop broad and sensitive vision for scanning and collecting relevant information, but also with the opportunity to supervise implementation of his decisions through the operational departments.

3. The corporations may, in time, have to experiment with arrangements at some levels which separate officers making policy on behalf of the corporation from those making policy related primarily to the public interest. Efforts must be made to preserve the independence and authority of officers representing the public interest. There must be a genuine desire on the part of the top management to understand and respond to the public needs; otherwise these officers will be degenerated to polishing the corporate image by public relations.

4. If at all possible, decision making regarding social pressures should be divided into two parts: physical environment and social environment. The former will deal with such matters as soil conservation, air and water pollution, and other matters affecting the physical surroundings; and the latter with technological unemployment, job discrimination, consumer affairs, and social attitudes. The primary responsibility of the executives responsible for these jobs will be to consider the effects which corporate conduct will have on the community.

5. The corporations must also encourage their executives to combine the traditional qualities of good administrators, command of the tools and techniques for running a large organization, with the necessary vision to see the corporation as a social institution designed to serve the interests of the entire society.

6. Above all, nothing will succeed without a clearcut demonstration by top management of acceptance of their social responsibility. As Charles Marshall states: "We must act not because minority groups represent a market or a source of personnel that we need, not because a solution reached without our involvement could be detrimental to our form of organization, or because we cannot afford to abandon the millions of dollars' worth of physical facilities located in cities where the problem is most evident. I like to think we're big enough to abolish racial discrimination because it's an injustice that we can't stand to live with in a free society." [17]

---

[17] Charles Marshall, "Civil Rights: What Role for Business," *Saturday Review* (January 13, 1968), 54.

RECOMMENDATIONS

NEW RESPONSES.   At long last, we come to the question of new responses which we feel the corporations should make to their changing
social environment. Our concern is not with specific responses to specific
stimuli, but is instead with general patterns of response to general
changes in society and with ways of preparing the corporation for the
challenges and pressures of the future.

> The first and foremost requirement is that the corporation take a more
> positive and less self-centered view of what the "public interest" is and
> of how corporations should respond to it. In the short run, this change
> may take the form of granting some sort of due process to new special
> interests, e.g., urban minorities, consumer groups, both within and with-
> out the corporation. This will provide a framework for the development
> and crystallization of issues which are of concern to the society and will
> also suggest avenues for corporate action individually and in cooperation
> with other social institutions. Some corporations have indeed recognized
> this need for working out new arrangements and seeking new associations
> in dealing with the social problems. Two notable and successful examples
> of this process are the Bank of America, which, in cooperation with local
> civil rights organizations, has been hiring and training large numbers
> of people from minority groups, and Lockheed Corporation, which has
> set up manufacturing facilities in the Watts area of Los Angeles.[18]

> The attitude of public concern must be fostered at all levels of corporate
> structure and not be confined to top management. Policy decisions are
> likely to founder at the operational level if the intent of top management
> is not made clear and if operating level personnel cannot or will not
> identify their personal goals with those of the corporation.

> To achieve a continuing congruence of corporate and social goals, the
> corporation must, therefore, be seen from the inside and from the out-
> side in a system-wide context; corporate managers at all levels must con-
> sciously and intentionally bring public interest factors to bear on their
> policies and decisions. The reason for doing so should not be a moral
> obligation or a charitable attitude, but rather a real duty or obligation
> arising out of the causal interrelation between the corporation and the
> society at large; the public interest must be viewed at the very least as a
> balancing of many factors but not solely within the administrative dis-
> cretion of corporate managers; procedural safeguards alone must be con-
> sidered inadequate.

> Another change must come in terms of frame of mind. The corporations
> must be willing to communicate with even those groups whose values may
> not agree with the traditional values or the position of the corporation.
> The spirit should be not of antagonism, but of willingness to understand
> and discuss.

---

18 James F. Langton, "What Should the Business Response Be to the Negro
Revolution?" *Public Relations Journal* (June 1965), pp. 12-17.

Management's lack of understanding is being brought home in recent efforts by business groups to help the minorities in job training and employment. For example, the *Wall Street Journal,* reporting on the lack of success of the blue-ribbon New Detroit Committee, recently stated:

"But instead of forming a dialogue, the committee is finding itself stalled over communications—the very gap it was supposed to close. Some of its have-not spokesmen have already quit the panel, intensifying the problem. . . . In effect, New Detroit is becoming stymied because few of its establishment members have spent time roaming the slum, talking to Negroes, observing firsthand the problems of the hard-core unemployed. . . . Instead they are waiting for middlemen to give them capsule reports and analyses. This usually works in corporations, but the Negro leaders from whom they are waiting to hear may be less representative of the average Negro on the street than is generally believed." [19]

Change must also come in the area of stating the corporate position on the issues. It does not help the corporation either to keep quiet or to issue carefully drafted, legally correct, but unresponsive, position papers or public relations communiques. Both of these strategies are likely to backfire in a charged atmosphere, the former to be construed as arrogant behavior, the latter as implicit admission of guilt hiding behind the screen of legalism.

Corporations should not engage in the essentially useless tactic of attacking their "opponents" by branding them socially deviant, destructive, or anti-social. By the very nature of things, new institutions and value systems in their embryonic stages will lack central direction and goal crystallization. They may even seem destructive—at least in the short run—as they are tied together only in their opposition to an existing institution. Lacking this central purpose they are not likely initially to offer constructive alternatives or effective leadership. Neither the corporation's nor the community's interests are thereby served if the corporation mobilizes its resources to destroy new institutions before they have a chance to develop. By retaliating against these institutions when they are in their embryonic stage, the corporations cannot hope to eliminate the causes which gave rise to these institutions, but instead will prepare the ground for breeding more militant and less constructive institutions. The corporations can best help achieve social harmony and contribute to social justice by focusing on the problems that have to be dealt with and not on the spokesmen who voice them. However, with few exceptions, businessmen do not seem to appreciate the need for this change in focus.[20]

The corporate management which is accustomed to centralized policy making and a decentralized, well-oiled organization to implement policy finds it very hard to deal with new outside groups. Such a management does not know with whom to talk; it does not understand what is really expected of the corporation. It is confronted with a cacophony of voices all claiming to represent valid interests—and often making different,

---

[19] *Wall Street Journal* (March 26, 1968), 16.

[20] Langton, *op. cit.,* pp. 12-17. Also see "Target: Negro Jobs," *Newsweek* (July 1, 1968), 21-30.

exaggerated and contradictory demands which cannot be fitted into the time span prescribed. Coping with this problem requires an understanding of the process of social change and the maturing of new groups. Social ferment generates a large number of small groups. A gestation period is needed during which internal stresses may develop and be settled before strong and viable groups with effective leadership and a well-defined hierarchy of goals can emerge. During this gestation period, there will be a large number of spokesmen and self-styled leaders struggling to enlarge their power base. The system at this stage is quite fluid. The chances of success are therefore perceived by these leaders as being high. As the rewards of success appear great, when measured from the originally meager power base, it is no wonder that these "leaders" often resort to extremist and sometimes even bizarre techniques in order to achieve their immediate objectives.

The corporations cannot help in the development of either effective leadership or crystallization of group objectives by direct assistance or interference in the process. Such action would be self-defeating. If the corporations support the moderate or "reasonable" groups in an emerging movement, they sign the death warrants of those leaders by doing so. Militants immediately accuse the moderates of "Uncle Tomism" or selling out to the enemy, and the effectiveness of the moderate is lost. On the other hand, if the corporations support the militants, they will, in effect, admit that they are afraid and that militancy pays, and, therefore, encourage extremism—not only hurting the moderates, but further slowing down the slow process of positive thinking and restructuring of new groups.

What the corporations can do is to recognize that, during a "shakedown" period, internal group strife is inevitable, and that in the short run, they will face wild demands made more for the purpose of causing distrust and violence per se than for gaining beneficial results for constituents. During this period, the corporations, while keeping scrupulously apart from the internal power struggle, can help make the atmosphere more susceptible to the acquisition of power by moderate and constructive leaders. This can be done by immediate and substantive corporate action on the legitimate demands of the deprived groups and by creating an environment of trust by meeting the emerging groups more on their own terms than making the groups abide by the rules of the establishment, which they do not understand and believe to have been used as an instrument of suppression.

THE TIME IS NOW

CONCLUSIONS. It is not possible to prescribe with assurance the precise formula of conduct which will necessarily be the best corporate response to particular social challenges, changes, and pressures of the years ahead. An attempt to do so would be presumptuous and meaningless, particularly when there is no way of determining the exact form future changes in the social environment will take. In contrast, however, it is possible to analyze the failures and the successes of the past and the present and to extract from them some conclusions as to how the great corporations can improve the quality of their responses to new and unconventional pressures, whatever they may be. Corporations, however, are now being subjected to increasing pressures of an unaccustomed sort—but a sort that appears likely to prevail for many years to come. Thus, we are not entirely in the dark as to the general form of social pressure that is apt to be of immediate and continuing importance.

Some of the recommendations we have made are concrete, practical, down-to-earth, and relatively easy to achieve. Others are abstract, theoretical, and highly speculative, clearly not designed for immediate implementation. In all cases, however, our goal has been to improve the operation of the corporate system and to preserve its fundamental role in our society. We believe that the failure of the great corporations to respond promptly, accurately, and appropriately to the profound and accelerating changes taking place all around us will result in serious danger to the corporate system, to personal freedom, and to many of the goals and values of society itself. Events of the last few years tell us that the time for action is now.

CORPORATE SOCIAL AUDIT:
AN EMERGING TREND IN MEASURING
CORPORATE SOCIAL PERFORMANCE

S. Prakash Sethi *

It is relatively easy to write about the desirability or need for corporate social audit if one is considering the growing awareness of the concept among businessmen, regulatory bodies, various professional groups, and even large segments of a well-informed public. The topic is de rigueur for the keynote speakers at business association meetings. Seen in this context, it is a vaguely defined term and is often used as an euphemism to cover any and all the activities of a firm that may have something to do with society, or that some group or other may want a firm to do for society—generally meaning for that particular group. However, it is quite difficult to write about corporate social audit (1) if we are thinking about the precise definition of what the term implies or (2) how to measure a firm's performance on some of the variables so defined. It is equally difficult to determine what corporations, universities, and consulting and research organizations are doing toward making progress along these two dimensions. In fact, the gap between the litany and practice of corporate social audit is so large as to make the current rhetoric devoid of any substance and render it almost meaningless.

The great disparity that now exists between the rhetoric and practice of corporate social audit is not necessarily unique and occurs in the case of many phenomena during their development stages. In the process of evolution, a phenomenon is simultaneously affected by three sets of forces: past history or antecedents, the current contextual framework of the problem, and the anticipated future applications. These factors act as crosscurrents, pulling an idea in different directions until such time as a common understanding is reached among various elements, thereby defining the parameters of the issue and giving it a structure.

PAST HISTORY OF ANTECEDENTS

The growth of the concept of corporate social audit may be more immediately traced to the rise in popularity of yet another broadly familiar but still undefined phenomenon of the early sixties—the social respon-

* A slightly revised version of this article appeared in *Business and Society Review* (Winter 1972-73), 31-38, under the title "Getting a Handle on the Social Audit," and is reprinted here with permission.

sibility of business. The strict adherents of history and genealogy would claim that demands for businessmen and business institutions to be more responsive to the needs of the communities where they operate and to those of society at large are age-old and have appeared with regularity in periods of economic or social crises when angels were needed to bail out the societies or scapegoats upon whom to fix the blame. The fact remains that the articulation of the term and its ascendency to the top of the "issues" popularity chart got its biggest fillip from the dissatisfaction of a large number of social advocates with the whole idea of social responsibility of business as it came to be defined and practiced in the late sixties. The truncation of stages and pinpointing of dates are somewhat arbitrary, albeit forced. But the latest but by no means the last surge in the need to do something about defining the role of business in general, and large corporations in particular, in the greater scheme of things came on the heels of William Whyte's *Is Anybody Listening?* [1] This was in 1950, when he described how the billion-dollar attempt by business in the two earlier decades "to sell business to America" had turned out to be a dismal failure. At first, businessmen were loathe to concede that they ought to be doing something more and different than what they had being doing in the past in order to be socially responsible. To do so would imply that their past activities were somehow less than socially desirable and would negate their earlier claims. However, even then there were some businessmen who indeed recognized the need for more active involvement in community and national affairs, but they were primarily confined to large corporations. Business, by and large, paid only lip service to the new demands for increased social responsibility. As time passed, while some differences remained among various corporate executives and businessmen as to their motives for responding to the call for social responsibility and the extent to which business should respond, some remarkable agreements emerged:

1. Businessmen recognized that some sort of response was indeed called for, if for no other reason than to head off future demands for even greater social responsibility by the more vocal critics of business.

2. A corporation's first responsibility was to its stockholders and social needs must be met only after there were profits.

3. The nature and extent of corporate responses must be at management's discretion.

Consequently, business enthusiastically co-opted the term "social responsibility of business," and their public relations departments spewed forth press releases and statements extolling the good deeds per-

---

[1] William H. Whyte, Jr., *Is Anybody Listening?* (New York: Simon & Schuster, 1950).

formed by their corporations. "Corporate conscience" was suddenly discovered, and corporate executives became corporate statesmen who regarded their prime role as balancing the interests of their various constituents such as stockholders, employees, suppliers, consumers, and communities that were affected by their operations. The euphemism of social responsibility was successfully used to avoid discussion of the more fundamental questions: What is and what should be the role of a corporation in society? Have the economic and social needs of society so changed that they call for a reexamination of the entire process of production and distribution of economic goods and services and the right of certain people to determine this process?

Unfortunately, no substantive changes took place. Social responsibility was what every businessman chose to think it was, and he often equated it with social charity rather than with enlarged social obligation. Even where progress was made, social reformers worried about the increased power of corporate executives in influencing social values through use of their economic power in the noneconomic sphere. However, as Eisenberg effectively demonstrated, the custodianship approach has certain inherent flaws and could only succeed in making corporations more powerful and self-perpetuating without any compensating benefits to any of the recognized corporate constituencies except, perhaps, to management and, to a minor extent, to the stockholders or the public at large.[2] Nor did this approach make business any more palatable to the Americans.[3] Furthermore, the magnitude of the social problems that corporations were supposed to help solve kept increasing, with the positive contributions of business considered only marginal at best. The fact remained that underneath all the rhetoric, business still considered its primary role to be profit-making and its noneconomic functions a necessary though undesirable cost of doing business, at best, and a nuisance, at worst. Consequently, although private enterprise had been quite innovative in exploiting economic opportunities, it displayed none of its entrepreneurial skill in meeting its social challenge.[4]

The result has been an outcry by various segments of the public for stronger teeth in the concept of "social responsibility of business" by taking the discretion for determining what it is or what it should be

---

[2] Melvin A. Eisenberg, "The Legal Role of Shareholders and Management in Modern Corporate Decision-Making," *California Law Review*, Vol. 57, No. 1 (January 1969), 1-181.

[3] "America's Growing Antibusiness Mood," *Business Week* (June 17, 1972), 100-103.

[4] Dow Votaw and S. Prakash Sethi, "Do We Need a New Corporate Response to a Changing Social Environment?" Parts I and II, *California Management Review*, Vol. XII, No. 1 (Fall 1969), 1-31.

away from the businessman. It also gave rise to a legitimate concern among businessmen to delineate the problems and dimensions of their social responsibility, thus warding off or at least limiting the encroachment by outsiders on their freedom in traditional activities. Therefore, an incentive was provided to develop certain criteria for measuring the corporate performance in areas of broad social concern—"corporate social audit," which the conventional financial statements do not purport to measure.

CURRENT CONTEXTUAL FRAMEWORK

Two related trends can be identified that have led to the need for a different kind of measurement for corporate social performance. At the national level there has been a growing dissatisfaction with the gross national product (GNP) and other economic statistics as indicators of national health or quality of life. Thus, efforts are being made to develop other social indicators to provide better measures of the improvement or decline in the qualitative aspects of the living patterns of individual citizens. Examples of such indicators are crime statistics, the level of pollution, opportunities for higher learning, the availability of decent housing, individual privacy, leisure time, and equal job opportunities. Since business, in general, and large corporations in particular, are the prime sources of economic activity in this country, it follows that national concern with measuring the effect of economic activities on the overall quality of life will also be transferred to measuring the side effects of the economic activities of large corporations.

The other trend has to do with the growing range of various alleged or real social problems and the causal identification of large corporations with them. There is also the increasing realization of the economic power of the corporations and their resulting ability to attack these problems. The 200 largest manufacturing corporations increased their share of manufacturing assets from 47.1 to 60.4 percent between 1947 and 1968. Moreover, of the individual industries for which data are available, the four largest companies increased their share of the industry's output in 95 cases as compared to 75 in which they declined.[5] It is neither difficult nor unrealistic to assume that they also account for such things as a large degree of pollution, consumer complaints, and job discrimination. Those who demand an accounting of corporations' social performance argue on economic, social, and political grounds. In economic terms, it is suggested that the large concentration

---

[5] John M. Blair, *Economic Concentration: Structure, Behavior and Public Policy* (New York: Harcourt Brace Jovanovich, 1972), p. v.

of assets gives corporations substantial immunity from the price mechanism operating in a competitive market. To the extent that these corporations can plan their sales volume and administer prices, a part of their revenues is due to the monopolistic control of the market. Since it is impossible to break these economic concentrations because of economies of scale and weak antitrust laws, the next best thing is to make these corporations more socially responsible.

On social grounds, it is argued that the myth of corporate management's accountability to stockholders is no longer sustainable, even in public relations statements.[6] In any event, there is no reason why corporations should not account for their actions to those people whose lives they affect, whether or not those people are stockholders or employees of a particular corporation. External economies may be free to a corporation, but they are costs to some citizens.

On political grounds, it is suggested that although corporations may protest that they are law-abiding citizens, it is relatively painless for them to make this claim because they exert considerable influence in various legislative bodies to promote the passage of pro-business laws and to deter or weaken the passage of alleged antibusiness laws. Examples of the lobbying activities by trade associations of various industries, and the subsequent watering down or pigeonholing of various bills are not unknown. Thus, obeying laws that are not unpalatable does not call for a great deal of socially responsible behavior.

FUTURISTIC ORIENTATION

A society's expectations change continuously. These changes are affected by two sets of factors: (1) Yesterday's goals become today's given values, and any further advances may call for different cost considerations and may yield a different distribution of benefits; (2) Today's youth, who may have internalized their elders' accomplishments, may no longer wish to pursue similar goals, but may desire altogether different ones.

Both these considerations may call for a restructuring of existing social institutions to make them more responsive to changing social needs and more adaptable to fulfilling future social expectations. They may also call for the development of new social institutions on the assumption that existing ones are too rigid to be adaptable. A necessary first step in this direction will then be to find out exactly (a) what busi-

---

6 Eisenberg, *op. cit.*

ness is doing in the areas that might legitimately fall under the rubric of new social expectations, and (b) what it should be doing in this direction to make itself more socially responsible.

CORPORATE SOCIAL AUDIT DEFINED

In summary, the need for corporate social audit arose in response to the giving of more structure and meaning to the term social responsibility of business. We recognize that to make the term operational, three conditions must be fulfilled:

1. Definition—what is socially responsible behavior?
2. Measurement—how can it be measured?
3. Accountability—to whom should the corporations be responsible?

Primarily, the corporate social audit is expected to satisfy the second condition. However, in the case of definition, we are in the chicken and egg situation. It might be argued that we cannot measure what we cannot define. Conversely, the definition question will be greatly influenced by what components are measurable. The question of accountability is likely to become clearer once the affected groups are identified through satisfying conditions 1 and 2. It will be partly settled through political processes, where group pressures would bring about acceptable compromises.

At the expense of oversimplification, we might say that the social responsibility of business is not a single objective and can be defined only on a multidimensional scale. The purpose of social audit at the micro level, therefore, is to help break down all or a large part of the broad term, social responsibility of business, into identifiable components and to develop scales that can measure these components. Therefore, the objective is to assist various institutions and groups through political processes to: assign relative weights and priorities to various elements of social responsibility; fix responsibility for overseeing performance; and assist existing and emerging socioeconomic institutions, notably large corporations, to alter their *modus operandi* and goals to meet the new performance criteria thus established. The task is admittedly quite difficult and we have barely begun.

Nevertheless, the importance of the job and the challenge offered by its complexity is attracting people in industry, academic institutions, and research and consulting organizations. It is hoped that some progress will be made in clarifying the definitional issues and in devising possible approaches toward measurement.

Progress of Business toward Corporate Social Audit

A recent check by the author revealed that a handful of large corporations are currently engaged in exploring the issue. However they are quite reluctant to talk about it because they feel (1) they have nothing substantial to report in terms of progress made; (2) their investigations do not show their companies in a good light; (3) there might be a leakage of proprietary information to competitors; or (4) there is the possibility of conflict with regulatory agencies or with the justice department in its antitrust aspects. Wherever corporate "good deeds" have been reported, barring a few exceptional cases, it has been largely confined to institutional advertising and annual reports showing the company in a favorable light. Recent studies by the Council on Economic Priorities, a New York-based nonprofit research organization, show that companies in a given industry that tend to be the worst polluters also tend to be the largest advertisers of their achievements in pollution control. Mr. John J. Corson, Chairman of the Board of Fry Consultants, and a director of ARA Services, Inc., of Philadelphia, stated, in a communication to this author, "A good many companies have been reporting on their activities in such areas as conservation, pollution, minority hiring, etc. If sheer numbers were any indication, it would seem that more and more corporations were being sensitive to the possible social impact of their activities." However, Mr. Corson suggests that "this reporting of corporate social performance risks the description of an effort at self-aggrandizement and an attempt at building public relations. Few corporations yet accept the responsibility of reporting comprehensively on all of the responsibilities that society is attempting to place on the corporation."

Current Approaches to Corporate Social Audit [7]

Two broad lines of investigation are currently being pursued toward the determination and measurement of corporate social performance. One approach may be termed "Reaction to Perceived Reality" and is externally based and motivated. The second approach may be termed "Maximum Capability Utilization and Best Effort" and is internally based. As we shall see below, both approaches have certain basic philosophical differences that may lead to different alternative courses of action and outputs. Moreover, when used exclusively, they

---

[7] An excellent review of the state of the art in corporate social audit is contained in Raymond A. Bauer and Dan H. Fenn, Jr., *Corporate Social Audit* (New York: Russell Sage Foundation, 1972).

may lead to less than maximum attainable benefits to the corporation when measured in terms of public acceptance of the firm's performance, most efficient use of its physical and human resources, and retention of maximum discretion and freedom in decisionmaking without outside interference or pressure.

REACTION TO PERCEIVED REALITY

A firm may argue that there is really no criterion to determine what is socially responsible behavior and how much of it would be acceptable to the general public or to various interest groups at a given point in time. Consequently, social responsibility is whatever public expectations are, and a firm would do well to satisfy those expectations to the maximum extent possible. Thus, it is not the "real" social needs, however well defined, that are important; it is the "perceived" needs. To be effective, a firm must recognize, as clearly as possible, the public's perception. This knowledge is primarily generated through public opinion surveys, ranging from *ad hoc* polls to scientifically selected groups polled under carefully developed research designs.

The most notable example of this latter type of study is that conducted by Daniel Yankelovich, Inc.,[8] a continuing audit that studies the degree and valence of public attitudes in four major areas of business–public conflict—namely, corporate growth versus the physical environment, corporate efficiency versus consumer protection, traditional versus new rewards for work, and new versus old corporate relationships with government and society. These four broad areas are subdivided into thirty types of demands. A total of 2,700 interviews are conducted to measure these demands. Nine groups are interviewed, among them the general public (1,000), key senators and representatives (50), state government officials (50), activist organization leaders (50), and national organization leaders (50). The coverage will be updated and expanded each year as new issues arise and become pertinent. Yankelovich's approach is aimed at getting a general measure of public interest and concern on various issues dealing with business and society, leaving individual firms to decide for themselves how to develop their individual responses to these issues.

In a somewhat similar approach, General Electric has developed a research design intended to assess the "influence/effectiveness" of certain "constituencies/pressure groups" on the "major demands" made upon business corporations in the 1970s. Effectiveness is defined as the

---

[8] *Corporate Priorities: A Continuing Study of the New Demands on Business* (Stanford, Conn.: Daniel Yankelovich, Inc., n.d.).

"ability to affect: legislation, legal actions, public opinion, employee action." Thirteen groups are identified in the research design and include, among others, consumers, share owners, unions, academic critics and "moralists." The major demand areas listed are: Marketing/Financial, Production Operations, Employee Relations/Working Conditions, Governance, Communications, Community and Government Relations, Defense Production, and International Operations. These areas are further divided into ninety-six subgroups.

Another approach, also externally oriented, is to determine the perception of a company's ranking among different firms of similar size or industry on a given social issue—e.g., pollution—by either the general public or special groups whose opinions are considered important by the firm—e.g., business executives, college students, legislators, etc. The objective is to develop a standard of the public's expectations on a given issue, based on the performance of the best perceived firm, and then to strive to match that performance. One such study is currently being conducted by Daniel Starch & Staff, Inc. of Mamaroneck, New York. The company interviews 18,000 individuals and asks them to rate five large retail chains such as Montgomery Ward and Sears Roebuck on various aspects of consumer services. Two recently conducted similar studies rank fifty corporations on their "social responsiveness" by business executives and business students, respectively.[9]

The perceived reality approach has certain advantages. It helps a corporation keep its goal posture more in tune with public expectations. To the extent that public perceived reality is partly a function of what a firm does, as well as what the public believes it is doing in a certain area, a firm may maximize its short-run gains by advertising and public relations campaigns without actually improving its performance in the conflict area being measured. A continuing audit of this type can also help a firm to make marginal changes in its socially oriented programs to bring them in closer conformity to public expectations. Evolving shifts in public expectations can also be spotted so that necessary changes in a firm's long-range objectives can be made.

However, an exclusive or even primary emphasis on this approach will have certain disadvantages for the firm. A totally external orientation in goal determination does not take into account a firm's own strengths and weaknesses in attacking certain problems and may therefore result in distortion of resource allocation. It narrows down the discretion that can be exercised by management in both selecting certain projects and the time frame within which they can be efficiently executed.

---

9 "Industry Rates Itself," *Business and Society Review* (Spring 1972), 96-99; and "Corporate Ratings—from Xerox to Con Ed," *Business and Society* (July 4, 1972).

MAXIMUM CAPABILITY UTILIZATION AND
BEST EFFORT

This approach is aimed at allowing management maximum discretion in selecting those projects that will make the best use of the firm's capabilities in delivering desired and socially relevant outputs at the least cost. This approach is internally oriented, deliberately planned for the long term, and is relatively independent of current public fads. The audit may take two forms that may not necessarily be congruent.

One form of corporate social audit may be used as a *public reporting device,* wherein a corporation lists its various activities that it considers socially beneficial and that may be of interest to such groups as investors, consumers, public bodies, and the general public. In this sense, it is somewhat akin to financial statements which purportedly show the state of financial health and performance of the company. Two notable examples of this approach are typified by Linowes, and in "Social Balance Sheet and Social Income," by Abt Associates, Inc.[10] These two studies are mentioned as examples only, and no attempt is made here to evaluate their respective merits.

Public reporting will have low credibility, at least initially, since generally acceptable reporting standards will not have been developed. Moreover, a corporation is likely to report only what it considers good and to avoid mentioning what it considers bad about its operations. At its lowest denominator, such reporting, devoid of objectivity and loaded with puffery, becomes poorly disguised window-dressing. There is hardly a corporation whose glossy annual report is not replete with glowing examples of socially responsible activities. It is incredulous to think that corporate managements really believe this succeeds in communicating their social performance to people "out there."

Another form of internally generated social audit is intended for *management decisionmaking* only. Typically, it starts by taking an inventory of what is being done in the various departments and divisions. The next step relates it to certain performance criteria and identifies the areas of strengths and weaknesses and the people responsible for them. This is followed by developing new goals and setting up programs to achieve these goals. Although the process thus described is deceptively simple, its accomplishment is far more difficult and cannot be over-

---

10 David F. Linowes, "Measuring Social Programs in Business: A Social Audit Proposal for Immediate Implementation," a paper presented at the 24th Annual Meeting, American Accounting Associates, Southeast Region, Baton Rouge, La., April 28, 1972; and "Social Balance Sheet and Social Income," *Annual Report and Social Audit* (Cambridge, Mass.: Abt Associates, Inc., 1971).

emphasized. Without belaboring the point, it can be shown that an inventory of socially responsible activities will be begging the question, because the definition of what is socially responsible will differ from one person to another.

The measurement of output presents another horde of problems. To wit, it is not clear whether output should be measured in terms of dollars expended, units of output generated, or the usefulness of these outputs in some sense of the word. Again, assignment of individual responsibility for performance may be hard, as the flow of "social activities" may not be similar to those of the primary business of the firm. Finally, the firm may not want to report the data generated for internal decisionmaking for public consumption because to do so would not only make corporate decisionmaking difficult but would also make future cooperation among various management echelons highly unlikely.

OUTLINE OF A SUGGESTED FRAMEWORK FOR
DEVELOPING PROGRAMS FOR
CORPORATE SOCIAL AUDITS

A prerequisite to social audit is the creation of new procedures and changes in organization structure to enable a firm to (1) evaluate external social environment; (2) generate internal data for program development and evaluation, decisionmaking points for delegating authority, and pinpointing responsibility; and (3) select alternate courses of action for utilizing the organization's physical and manpower resources most efficiently while effectively responding to external constraints. This arrangement is not dissimilar to the organization of a firm for its primary activities—the production of goods and services for profit—where the organization is geared to respond efficiently to market conditions, profit centers are created to assign responsibility for various activities, and financial data are generated in a form that is useful for both internal control and external reporting of its financial health.

Figure 1 presents this process for internal organization adaptation in the form of a flow chart. The primary aim is to develop effective long-range goals and medium-range strategies. It is assumed that once a suitable decision structure has been developed, it should be able to respond automatically and effectively to short-run and day-to-day operational problems and tactics within the framework of long-range goals and medium-range strategies. The model recognizes four types of external constraints to which a firm must respond and adapt its behavior. These are: existing legal constraints, anticipated legal constraints, pressure from the general public and special-interest groups, and performance of other

FIGURE 1

**Process Flow for Understanding Environmental Constraints and
Development of Criteria for Measuring Corporate Social Performance**

EXTERNAL CONSTRAINTS (EC)

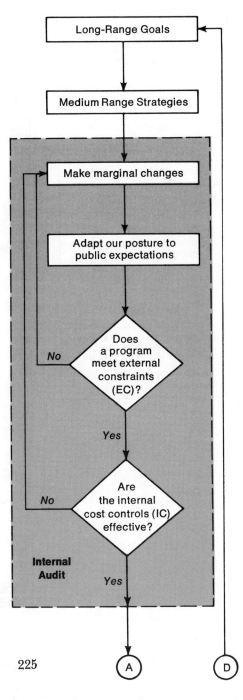

1. Existing legal constraints
2. Anticipated legal constraints.
3. Pressures from general public and special-interest groups.
4. Performance of other companies against which this company's performance is likely to be compared by various groups.

Long-Range Goals

Medium Range Strategies

Make marginal changes

Adapt our posture to public expectations

Does a program meet external constraints (EC)?

No

Yes

Are the internal cost controls (IC) effective?

No

Internal Audit

Yes

225

A

D

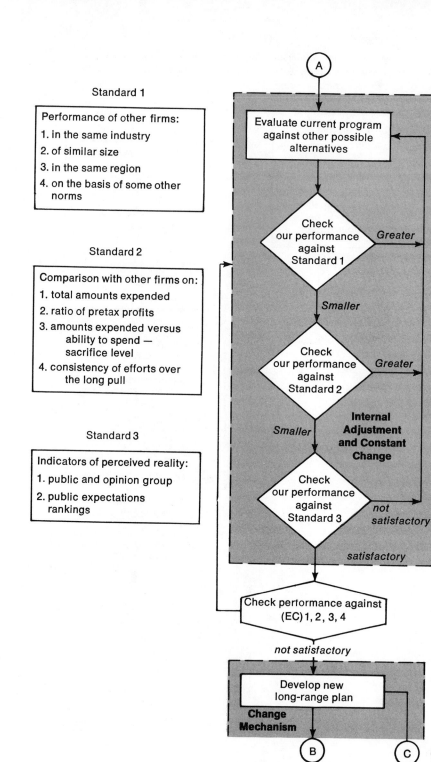

Standard 1

Performance of other firms:

1. in the same industry
2. of similar size
3. in the same region
4. on the basis of some other norms

Standard 2

Comparison with other firms on:

1. total amounts expended
2. ratio of pretax profits
3. amounts expended versus ability to spend — sacrifice level
4. consistency of efforts over the long pull

Standard 3

Indicators of perceived reality:

1. public and opinion group
2. public expectations rankings

A

D

Evaluate current program against other possible alternatives

Check our performance against Standard 1 — *Greater*

Smaller

Check our performance against Standard 2 — *Greater*

Smaller

Internal Adjustment and Constant Change

Check our performance against Standard 3 — *not satisfactory*

satisfactory

Check performance against (EC) 1, 2, 3, 4

not satisfactory

Develop new long-range plan

Change Mechanism

B

C

D

226

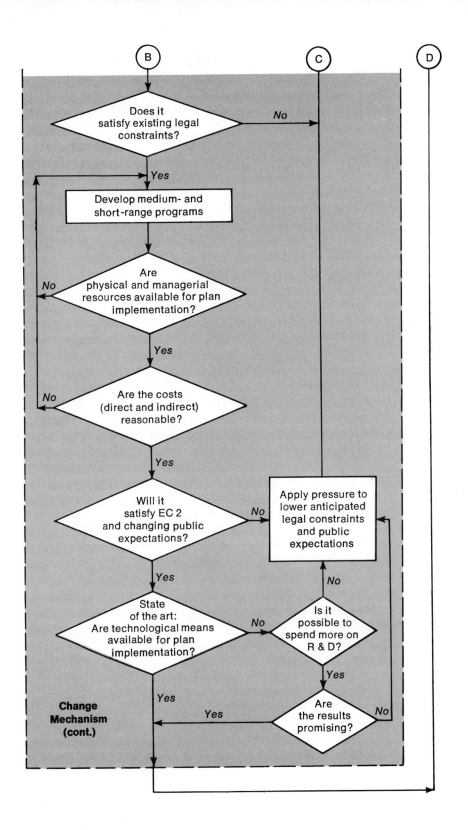

companies against which a firm is likely to be compared by various groups. Existing legal constraints are considered to be given and uncontrollable. The remaining three constraints are presumed to interact with each other with positive feedback loops where the firm's own input is likely to have some effect on the level of constraints.

Briefly, the first step in the model is to evaluate a firm's current programs via an internal audit. The next step is to compare existing programs against other alternatives and to make continuous changes in them to improve internal operational efficiency and adaptability to external constraints. This is followed by a comparison of the effectiveness of a firm's programs with those of other firms. The final step has two aspects: (1) the firm makes changes in the internal mechanism to alter its long-range goals and medium-range strategies and develops new programs to meet these goals and strategies; (2) the firm tries to exert pressure to relax those external constraints it finds either difficult or impossible to meet.

Measurement Scales

There is a tendency among technically oriented people to rush toward quantification of concepts even though the variables may be imprecisely defined and the necessary data unavailable. The objective is to somehow make the concepts operational. The assumption is that by making them operational, we somehow make them effective—they in fact measure what we want them to measure. However, this is a fallacy. The dangers of premature quantification, called by Yankelovich "the Mc-Namara Fallacy," are best described by him in the following statement:

> The first step is to measure whatever can be easily measured. This is okay as far as it goes. The second step is to disregard that which can't be easily measured or give it an arbitrary quantitative value. This is artificial and misleading. The third step is to presume what can't be measured easily really isn't important. This is blindness. The fourth step is to say that what can't be easily measured really doesn't exist. This is suicide.[11]

Conversely, people with an aversion to quantification tend to regard any such attempt as imperfect and one that is doomed to failure. However, what is suggested here is not metric scaling with all its associated properties, but an attempt at measurement that includes even

---

11 Daniel Yankelovich, "The New Odds," a paper presented at the Eleventh Annual Marketing Strategy Conference of the Sales Executives Club of New York, October 15, 1971.

nonmetric scales, where partial attempts are made at developing methods of comparison, and qualitative measurements.

The approach to development of measures for corporate social audit has to be piecemeal and stepwise, where each subsequent step is based on knowledge acquired through the preceding step. One such approach is followed by Arthur D. Little, Inc., management consultants. The firm is involved in "action research," working with some clients in pilot projects aimed at developing scales of measurement as well as the substantive concepts that should be measured. According to Dr. Daniel Gray,

> The need for a new theoretical approach to measuring corporate social problems is critical. As a first step toward the development of this theory, we must do some action research wherein we test various hypotheses and evaluate their relevance to the understanding of the underlying phenomenon. I do not believe that armchair research by itself is likely to be very productive in this field, nor is the effort to force quantification without new theory.

Efforts toward quantification must be slow and carefully designed. Given below is a brief description of the necessary steps to be followed:

1. Defining the problem in a new manner. This assumes that the problem as it is currently defined and understood cannot be solved. Therefore, a new way must be found to look at the problem.
2. Recognition of the need for a new type of data to attack the newly defined problem.
3. Search of existing data to see if they can be used in some modified form to solve the problem.
4. Break the problem into small components or into a set of hypotheses.
5. Test each hypothesis with either existing or new data.
6. Use successive hypotheses as building blocks for theory construction as well as for the generation of new data.
7. Build more comprehensive theories by combining elements of various hypotheses previously tested.
8. Refine measurement scales based on earlier tests and make them integral parts of general theory.

Promising Subjects Susceptible to Measurement

A study of available writings, discussions with various people engaged in research on corporate social audit, and the author's own research lead him to believe that the following fields of social activities involving business firms offer the greatest promise for early quantification and measurement.

—Aid to Arts and Cultural Activities.
—Aid to Higher Education and Health-Related Activities.

—Employee-Related Activities: improved benefits, equal opportunity in promotion, participation in job-enrichment programs, self-development programs, job safety, the right to dissent, and encouraging participation in political activities of their own choice.

—Community-Related Activities: local fund-raising campaigns, executive time devoted to improving the efficiency of various local governing and planning bodies, urban development, and inner city programs.

—Minority Groups: hiring; job training, development and promotion; and encouragement of minority owned enterprises through loans, technical assistance, subcontracting, and purchasing.

—Consumerism: product safety, product warranties, adequate consumer information, fair pricing policies, nondeceptive advertising, and complaint handling.

—Political Activities (external and internal): taking a position on war, apartheid, etc.; supporting public-interest legislation on such issues as gun control, stringent antipollution laws, better standards for consumer protection, and mass transit.

—Restructuring of Corporate Organization: inclusion of minority groups and other public-interest representatives on the board of directors, federal chartering of large corporations, etc.

SUMMARY AND CONCLUSIONS

The question of corporate social audit must be viewed within the broader perspective of the social responsibility of business. The former is but the means to the latter. A good program of corporate social audit should combine some elements of the perceived reality or public expectation to develop its long-range objectives and to make marginal adjustments in a company's on-going social programs. Within the constraints outlined earlier, a firm must judiciously select those projects for which its physical and manpower resources make it particularly suitable. The aim of the auditing procedure should be to develop those qualitative and quantitative criteria that:

(1) enable the firm to continuously monitor its activities to make sure that programs are developing most efficiently and are yielding the desired output;

(2) generate data to assist management in improving performance and selecting future activities in anticipation of future changes in objectives;

(3) enable management to report accurately and objectively on its activities in a manner that provides the interested public a true index of the corporation's performance and a basis for comparing it with the activities of other similarly placed corporations.

The ultimate success in corporate social audit will have been achieved when we can report a corporation's performance not merely in output terms (e.g., number of people hired), but in terms of its effectiveness and benefits to society (e.g., whether an alternative use of these resources would have provided larger social gains). We are a long way from achieving this goal and there is no guarantee we will ever get there. However, given the best intentions, the continuous societal pressure to develop this information, and an increasingly large allocation of manpower resources, the chances of significant advances during the next few years are quite good. This, in my opinion, is the best we can hope for, and I, for one, will be perfectly satisfied if it is accomplished.

Index